INTERPRETATIONS

Interpretations

ESSAYS ON TWELVE
ENGLISH POEMS

Edited by

JOHN WAIN

Second Edition

Routledge & Kegan Paul
London and Boston

First published 1955
Second impression 1962
Third impression 1965
Second edition, with new introduction, 1972
published by Routledge & Kegan Paul Ltd
Broadway House, 68-74 Carter Lane,
London EC4V 5EL
and 9 Park Street, Boston, Mass. 02108, U.S.A.
Printed in Great Britain by
Redwood Press Limited
Trowbridge, Wiltshire

ISBN 0 7100 7385 2 (c)

ISBN 0 7100 7386 0 (p)

CONTENTS

ACKNOWLEDGEMENTS

ACKNOWLEDGEMENTS are due to the Oxford University Press for permission to reprint *The Windhover* by G. M. Hopkins; to Messrs. Faber & Faber for permission to reprint *The Love Song of J. Alfred Prufrock* by T. S. Eliot; to Mrs. W. B. Yeats and to Messrs. Macmillan & Co., publishers of the Collected Poems of W. B. Yeats, for permission to reprint *Among School Children* by W. B. Yeats.

NOTE

Some of these essays appeared, under the general title 'How To Read A Poem', in *Mandrake*, and are reprinted by kind permission of the Editor, Mr. Arthur Boyars

ON THE SQUEEZING OF LEMONS

An Introduction to the
Edition of 1972 ·

I T is now seventeen years since this volume was published, and over twenty since I first had the idea of a series of essays on single poems, to appear in the magazine *Mandrake*, which I had founded in Oxford in 1945. The book now presented to the reader of the 1970s thus has its roots in the immediate post-war period. Those years, the late forties and early fifties, offer many interesting parallels with the similar post-war period of the nineteen-twenties. Both were periods in which the rising generation of men of letters shied away from anything that looked like rhetoric. During the First World War, a whole civilisation had drifted to its death on a tide of oratory, and the survivors, when at last they took up their pens, were scornful of the overblown and crenellated, preferring a style that said what it meant in a down-to-earth fashion. Many a writer whose subsequent trajectory has taken him a long way from rationalism showed, in those days, a preference for clear-cut rationality.

Moving forward to the similar period after World War Two, we find the same preference for a language of statement, though in our case the idiom to be reacted against was not so much that of politicians and journalists as of a generation of poets who chose their epithets with a view to sending up the emotional temperature of the poem rather than conveying (in our sense) 'meaning'. Criticism of the kind represented by *Interpretations* is thus linked closely with that coincidental style in poetry which became known, in retrospect, as 'the Movement'.

'The Movement', which was not of course so described by

any of the poets who actually took part in it (the title was coined by, I think, Mr. J.D. Scott in an unsigned article in *The Spectator*), was the result of this impulse away from vagueness, from the impressive-sounding language that merely gestured *towards* something instead of defining it, and towards a style that would be precise: so long, of course, as 'precise' was not defined as restrictively as it would be in a court of law. Historically, it was not so much a new style as a style which made a deliberate selection from styles previously available in English literature. There are many 'Movement' lines in Chaucer, or in the non-dramatic poems of Ben Jonson, or in the Metaphysicals. If one thinks of Housman's

> The troubles of our proud and angry dust
> Are from eternity, and shall not fail;
> Bear them we can, and if we can we must

one sees that a 'Movement' line can co-exist happily with lines of a very different *timbre*. 'Are from eternity, and shall not fail' is very much the kind of large gesture that Movement poets avoided; whereas 'Bear them we can, and if we can we must' is exactly typical of the style they were aiming at, being monosyllabic, bare, strongly rhythmical, emphatic and unadorned.

This interest in a poetry of statement, and in the question of what exactly such a poetry would entail, led to a corresponding impulse in criticism. William Empson, whose *Seven Types of Ambiguity* was reprinted in the nick of time in 1947, suddenly found his brand of Cambridge rationality much in favour: young writers at that time were capable of becoming really excited over a virtuoso demonstration of the possibilities of verbal analysis such as his discussion of Herbert's 'The Sacrifice' in *Seven Types*, chapter VII; while his poetry, to which I devoted an article in the last number of *Penguin New Writing* in 1950, also enjoyed a new phase of reputation: lines such as

> I have mislaid the torment and the fear.
> You should be praised for taking them away.
> Those that doubt drugs, let them doubt which was here

which combine a direct, main tone with a dextrous twist of ambiguity, set the tone for much of the verse of the fifties.

So much for the background of these essays. How have they worn, these twenty years? To a reader coming to them now for the first time, the most immediately striking lack will be the virtual absence of social and historical discussion. How does the language operate? is the question, rather than, What features of the social and political life of the time went to shape this poet's art and make him eager to express what we find here and not something else? Nor is there any lively interest in the poet's biography, for we were all of a generation that had been schooled to work from 'the words on the page' and refrain from specualtion about the poet's personal situation.

Our criticism, in those days, was ahistorical for the same reasons that the American 'New Criticism', which got started a few years earlier, was ahistorical, or the French *nouvelle critique* of fifteen years later. Perhaps only the largest-minded and most experienced critics of literature can concentrate fruitfully on more than one thing at a time; and we were certainly not in that class.

Speaking of large-minded and experienced critics, it is interesting to recall that T.S. Eliot found the book sufficiently interesting to devote a couple of pages to it in one of his encyclicals, the essay 'The Frontiers of Poetry' in 1956.

I have recently noticed a development, which I suspect has its origin in the classroom methods of Professor Richards, which is, in its way, a healthy reaction against the diversion of attention from the poetry to the poet. It is found in a book published not long ago, entitled *Interpretations:* a series of essays by twelve of the younger English critics, each analysing one poem of his own choice. The method is to take a well-known poem—each of the poems analysed in this book is a good one of its kind—without reference to the author or to his work, analyse it stanza by stanza and line by line, and extract, squeeze, tease, press every drop of meaning out of it that one can. It might be called the lemon-squeezer school of criticism.

After this flash of dry humour, Eliot goes on in serious vein to utter two warnings against possible disadvantages in this lemon-squeezing process. One is that such criticism might tend to spread the notion that there can be only one interpretation of a poem that is 'right', whereas the meaning of the poem 'is not to be exhausted by any explanation, for the meaning is what the poem means to different sensitive readers'. Correct. Provided that they are all *informed* readers, who have done their homework on historical and literary matters, geological faults in vocabulary, and so forth, Eliot's second warning is against any tendency to push this kind of analysis in the direction of author-psychology.

For the tendency is so general, to believe that we understand a poem when we have identified its origins and traced the process to which the poet submitted his materials, that we may easily believe the converse—that any explanation of the poem is also an account of how it was written. The analysis of 'Prufrock' to which I have referred interested *me* because it helped *me* to see the poem through the eyes of an intelligent, sensitive and diligent reader. That is not at all to say that *he* saw the poem through my eyes, or that his account has anything to do with the experiences that led up to my writing it, or with anything I experienced in the process of writing it.

There speaks the Eliot whose view of art was strictly impersonal, who laid it down that 'the more perfect the artist, the more completely separate in him will be the man who suffers and the mind which creates'. He is careful to testify that this is 'a danger into which I do not think any of the critics in the volume I have mentioned has fallen'. Correct again. We all belonged, whatever those individaul differences in temperament and outlook which have become more evident as time has hardened our characters, to the generation brought up under Eliot's authority; it was to him that we owed our conviction that the way to an understanding of poetry was not through gas or gossip, but through patience and loving attention; it was Eliot, more than anyone else, who had taught us to slow down long enough to take note of what a poem was saying, in all its dimensions of statement. I am glad he read the book and found something of interest there, for it was, among other things, a small down-payment on a very considerable debt.

JOHN WAIN

INTRODUCTION

THE provisional title of this book, during the months when it was being assembled, was *How To Read A Poem*; this could not, of course, be seriously considered as a final title—it suggests too large a claim, as if the contributors to the book either thought of themselves, or were thought of by their editor, as having 'got the answer', as saying to the reader, *This is how to do it.* Nobody, we realize, has a right to say any such thing; it is just that reading a poem is an activity at which it is possible to succeed or fail—to succeed in different ways, and to fail in different ways—and it seemed reasonable to ask a few of the younger critics to demonstrate what they meant by 'reading', and to print the results in a book. (That, by the way, is the last time the word *young*, in its simple, comparative, or superlative forms, will appear in this introduction. Nobody is trying to get the book accepted on *that* ticket.)

As the editor of this collection I am inclined to be modest about it; the essays strike me as uneven in quality, and I should be far from claiming that anyone's critical problems were going to be solved by the book. That is, of course, the hopeful thing; the contributors are so obviously aware that the writ of criticism does not run quite all the way, that there are limits to the claims a critic can make for himself. They would all, I imagine, claim to be doing no more than humbly serve the poem. (In the case of those contributors who have chosen very minor poems, they may see themselves as serving literature in general by bringing out some largely useful truth.)

This self-effacement is a new thing—new, I mean, in this generation. It results from the fact that an earlier and more strenuous generation of critics fought and won their battle. They established the right to *be* critics, to talk about a poem without going to either of the extremes; on the one hand, of merely heaping up facts *about* it, on the other, of merely describing its effect on themselves. Thanks to them, a man writing an analysis of a single poem is not thought to be acting queerly; if he comes under fire, it will be because his analysis appears wrong, not because he ought not to be doing it in the first place. It is true, of course, that there is an increasingly vocal and influential sect which calls for the purely historical investigation of literary texts; for them, 'criticism', as the rest of us understand it, not merely does not but cannot exist—all that a poem or novel can do is to illustrate the sensibility of a certain writer at a certain point in the past. But these attacks on criticism will hardly succeed in stamping it out. It is too strongly rooted in the needs of humanity; a great poem, or even a minor one, is not only a document of the past; it is a force *now*, a living thing to be reckoned with in terms of *our* responses. Some of these responses are historical, but not all of them. St. Paul's Cathedral is a document of the sensibility of a past age, but it is in use to-day. And it was not built as a document of Wren's sensibility; it was built with a purpose, and so is a poem.

A more dangerous line of argument, to my mind, is that this kind of criticism has, or appears to have, nothing really to do with the motives that make us like poetry and derive pleasure from it. Obviously there is a streak of truth in this: when a man decides that a certain poem is so important to him personally that he would like to undertake a detailed study of it, he has arrived at that conclusion before, and not as a result of, conducting the analysis. What is the deeper reaction that prompts his choice? It is, outwardly, simple to the point of crudity; it consists of catching one's breath: 'This poem is obviously going to be important to me.' How often, in such cases, are we proved wrong? How often do we have the breath-catching reaction and subsequently find that the poem loses its vitality, fades away from us, or (to use an ominously common form of words) 'will not stand up to' criticism (as if criticism were a charge of cavalry)?

Rather seldom, I think. Once we have passed that period in our lives which is, necessarily, made up of changes and readjustments, and once we have schooled ourselves to a fairly levelheaded reading of a new poem, we can tell soon enough when a poem has authority of the kind that will compel us to serve it. Something about the way the words are put together, the personal run of the rhythm, the expression, as it were, on the poem's face—this is what we learn to go by, just as we learn to size up human beings on first acquaintance. We may never become capable of saying, on first meeting, 'this person is good (or bad)', because we may never have a valid idea of what constitutes goodness or badness; but we all develop considerable *expertise* at answering the question, 'Am I going to *like* this person?'

At this point the reader will begin to think, perhaps with growing querulousness, that my idea of literary criticism is simply that it is a rationalization of an instinctive preference, and that it has nothing to do with the establishment of a demonstrable hierarchy of quality. Not at all; I am merely being honest. I do not believe that close analysis (which, for the moment, is the kind of literary criticism we are talking about) can call any qualities into being. All it can do is to demonstrate their existence and their manner of working. These qualities operated on the perceiver, the critic who is going to write his analysis, at the moment when he was just that—a perceiver, and nothing more. They acted instantaneously, like a kiss or a punch on the nose. But the reasons why a kiss or a punch on the nose has an effect are real reasons; they can be discussed; but only (to use Mr. Fraser's telling metaphor) in slow motion.

And if we do sometimes make mistakes, if a poem does have an instantaneous effect which proves not to last, or not to remain valid at the deeper levels, this kind of analysis will show it. They act as a check on one another, the swift effect and the painful slowed-down anatomization. Speaking personally again, I have found that it is the poem that takes a slightly tortuous route to the sensibility, rather than the one that knocks me down at a blow, that I am least likely to be mistaken over. Marvell's *The Garden*, for instance. How many of us felt, the first time we saw that poem, a momentary hesitation as to whether the effort to 'understand' it, to take full possession, was going to be worth it in terms of the thing possessed? I certainly did. All those jokes, all that solemn air of comic literalness, that oddly illogical construction—to come all the way from Pan and Syrinx, through the garden of Eden, to be told that bees can tell the time; such queer stuff—*can* it be important? But the poem enters, though diffidently, and makes itself part of the mind's furniture. By contrast, a poem like Mr. Empson's *The Teasers*, I am fairly sure, is a knock-down poem which does not, in the end, guard itself from inanition; the analyses have proved this, in so far as 'proof' is operative in these matters; no two people think the same about its paraphrasable content; what impresses them all, obviously, is the harshly original music, the cunning lay-out with its effective planting of powerful words—*die, dreams, flood, blood, love.* What the conflicting analyses establish, I think, about that poem is that none of us is really responding to the poem's 'argument' at all; an important element is lacking, namely, shared appreciation of what the poem communicates; and thus what criticism does here is inevitably to assign the poem to a lower category. The poem's argument is not even broadly establishable; it is not a question of disagreeing over this minor point or that, but of a complete withdrawal into the subjective. And so, obliquely, criticism has done its work, and can be said, however wryly, to have served the poem: as nothing else could have done.

And finally, to deal with the last foreseeable objection, it will be said—it *is*, frequently, said—that to take one poem at a time is an artificial procedure; and that to take the poem in isolation is more artificial still. It is necessary to set a poem, first, in its place among other poems by the same poet, and second, in its continuum of history and biography. Thus I have heard an Oxford don refuse to discuss *Tears, idle tears* when he had it before him on a cyclostyled sheet, because 'it could not be taken apart from Tennyson's feelings for Hallam, and to find out what *they* were, we should have to do some biographical enquiry'. He wanted, that is to say, the real Hallam, the real Tennyson, there at his elbow, before he would trust himself to walk along the tightrope of the poem. To this, I can only answer (without attempting to speak for anyone else) that I regard such an attitude as a fundamental, as *the* fundamental misunderstanding of the nature of literature; and I have no more breath to spare for it. The other point, about setting a poem in its social context, is just ordinary common sense; its exponents have not made some thrilling new discovery, and they have the right to cavil at the 'close' critic only if, and when, he seems in his detailed comment to be ignoring some important factor which would be brought clearly into focus by *their* kind of discussion. The effort to take a poem and say what is going on inside it, like any analytical effort, can only concern itself with one object at a time; and this is also the answer to those who say that criticism must concern itself with an author's whole output. So it should; it should analyse every line he wrote with minute attention; after which, the making of large generaliza-tions could safely be left to the *vulgarisateurs*.

It is likely, then, that the critic will be left in peace. Indeed, he may be left in too much peace; he may be ignored. The obvious objection to the competent, well-trained, decent, satis-factory criticism that any University lecturer can turn out by the ream—and does turn it out—is that it is, after all, no *use*; it does not do any good. I said something like this, once, in in-troducing an anthology of early nineteenth-century criticism; and Mr. F. W. Bateson, conscious of his duties as the Editor of *Essays In Criticism*, pointed out in reply how good modern literary criticism was in comparison with the stuff I had anthologized. This may be true, but the old criticism was at least a force; it was read, it had some effect on the taste of the time. Mr. Bateson's critics get better and better, but they are only writing for one another; none of that intelligence is flowing into the common stock—as one sees from a glance at what actually gets published, praised, taken seriously, given literary awards, and so on. The utter failure of criticism at its lower levels is one of the bitter small facts of our time, and I only wish I could, like Mr. Bateson, derive consolation from thinking how beautifully the critics higher up are doing each other's laundry, how dazzlingly white they are washing it, how lovingly hanging it out to dry.

In this situation, what we need, I should have thought, is a reasonable supply of criticism that is serious without being esoteric. If it were possible to establish the basic fact that to read a poem critically (that is to say, with discrimination that directs, without stifling, an alert sensibility and a full responsiveness) is not really an impossible ideal, something to be left to the specialist, but an activity that any sensible person can hope to train himself for, with not much more equipment than his native honesty and vitality—if we could establish *that*, we might dispel a good deal of the blankness with which the ordinary educated person, in an age of prose, looks at the poetry that comes his way. (We might also, with profit, get rid of the absurd veneration that is accorded to critics *as such*. This is, after all, only the obverse of the ignorant idea that criticism is an esoteric mystery. We have among us more than one critic who demands—and gets—a ludicrous degree of respect from his followers; the characteristic *petit-maître* of our day is not an artist but an 'evaluator' of artists; as if a critic could be, in some way, more authoritative than the art he discusses.) At the moment, it seems to be accepted as a matter of course that there is no possible means of understanding poetry; as I write, the experts are disagreeing as to whether Dylan Thomas was a good poet or not, and the 'reading public' are simply watching the battle with their heads swivelling as at a table-tennis match; it is just taken for granted that there is no hope of seeing for oneself, of checking the opinions of the experts against one's own reaction to the poems—which, after all, are accessible to anyone with a few shillings in his pocket. No, poetry is an impenetrable mystery. And not only 'modern' poetry, which is supposed to be 'obscure'. The man who complains of the obscurity of modern poetry does so, usually, because the contemporary is the only kind that lies in his path; he would find all poetry difficult, if he ever looked at it, but he does not open his weekly paper and find a few lines of Shakespeare or Dante to shake his head over. Imagine his reaction to Wordsworth's 'Lucy' poems!—recall, in fact, what *was*, as a matter of history, the reaction to them! All poetry is obscure to the closed intelligence.

And the excellence, the virtuosity, of modern literary criticism will make no headway against that closed intelligence, unless it can come down from the summit, and allow itself to be seen as an affair of simple responsiveness and common sense; of knowing something about the subject and being prepared to discuss it. That, in short, is what I had in mind in assembling this book; to get people to be less frightened of literary criticism; to show them, if possible, that they can scale even very high poems without being roped together and led by a guide.

Another point about criticism, but one that can hardly be illustrated by a book, is that it is always, at its best, an affair of give and take. I imagine most of the contributors to this book would admit to having arrived at their conclusions as a result of discussion with other people; some of them read their essays to seminars or gave them as lectures; Mr. Tomlinson has recast, in his, some material he had already used in an M.A. thesis at London University. My own case is probably typical. I did not sit down to write on the poem of my choice until I had discussed it with several friends, with my students at Reading University, with the members of the Oxford University Critical Society, and, most fruitfully of all, with my wife. A good many people strove manfully to dispel the worst of my ignorance; it was Professor D. J. Gordon, for instance, who sent me to Diogenes Laertius.

There is another side, as well, to the give and take in this book. It will perhaps be noticed that the contributors are mainly either academics—men who draw salaries from Universities—or, on the other hand, men who might be described (and might, also, repudiate the description) as members of the 'literary world' of the metropolis. This is because I happen to believe that if there is to be any progress in the current practice of literary criticism, it will probably begin to show itself on the ground where these two territories meet. Where the more literary-minded academic meets the more scholarly man of letters—that, I have felt for some years, is the probable growing-point. This book may go some way towards proving me right; or wrong.

JOHN WAIN

WILLIAM SHAKESPEARE

The Phoenix and the Turtle[1]

A. Alvarez

1. Let the bird of lowdest lay,
   On the sole *Arabian* tree,
   Herauld sad and trumpet be:
   To whose sound chaste wings obay.

2. But thou shriking harbinger,
   Foule precurrer of the fiend,
   Augour of the feuers end,
   To this troupe come thou not neere.

3. From this Session interdict
   Euery foule of tyrant wing,
   Saue the Eagle feath'red King,
   Keepe the obsequie so strict.

4. Let the Priest in Surples white,
   That defunctive Musicke can,
   Be the death-deuining Swan,
   Lest the *Requiem* lacke his right.

5. And thou treble dated Crow,
   That thy sable gender mak'st,
   With the breath thou giu'st and tak'st,
   Mongst our mourners shalt thou go.

[1] First published in Robert Chester's anthology *Loves Martyr*, 1601.

1

6. Here the Antheme doth commence,
   Love and Constancie is dead,
   Phoenix and the *Turtle* fled,
   In a mutuall flame from hence.

7. So they loued as loue in twaine,
   Had the essence but in one,
   Two distincts, Division none,
   Number there in loue was slaine.

8. Hearts remote, yet not asunder;
   Distance and no space was seene,
   Twixt this *Turtle* and his Queene;
   But in them it were a wonder.

9. So betweene them loue did shine,
   That the *Turtle* saw his right,
   Flaming in the *Phoenix* sight;
   Either was the others mine.

10. Propertie was thus appalled,
    That the selfe was not the same:
    Single Natures double name,
    Neither two nor one was called.

11. Reason in it selfe confounded,
    Saw Diuision grow together,
    To themselves yet either neither,
    Simple were so well compounded.

12. That it cried, how true a twaine,
    Seemeth this concordant one,
    Loue hath Reason, Reason none,
    If what parts, can so remaine.

13. Whereupon it made this *Threne*,
    To the *Phoenix* and the *Doue*,
    Co-supremes and starres of Loue,
    As *Chorus* to their Tragique Scene.

Threnos

14. Beautie, Truth, and Raritie,
    Grace in all simplicitie,
    Here enclosde, in cinders lie.

15. Death is now the *Phoenix* nest,
    And the *Turtles* loyall brest,
    To eternitie doth rest.

16. Leauing no posteritie,
    Twas not their infirmitie,
    It was married Chastitie.

17. Truth may seeme, but cannot be,
    Beautie bragge, but tis not she,
    Truth and Beautie buried be.

18. To this vrne let those repaire,
    That are either true or faire,
    For these dead Birds, sigh a prayer.

THE *Phoenix and Turtle* is a difficult poem, but it is knowingly so. The complications are intentional, witty and precise. They are carried off with such confidence, such buoyancy, and yet for no obvious purpose. The poem seems so self-contained that it is impregnable. Certainly, no simple approach will do on its own. Of the four ways into the poem, each is relevant, each by itself inadequate.

The usual line is to treat the poem as a wittily complicated effusion which reworks what was, even then, the well-nigh exhausted conceit of the two lovers making one flesh. This yields one level of meaning and emphasizes what is too easily overlooked: the human situation involved. Although the poem is not a direct love poem to a mistress, it is at least a description, a definition of perfect love. But approached in this way the introduction becomes a mere ornament, the six-fold repetition of the conceit a tedious exaggeration, and the Threnos (this has, alas, been suggested) a separate poem.

If this reading fails to take the poem seriously enough, to interpret it exclusively through its religious symbolism is a sin of overseriousness. No doubt the Phoenix *was* a mediaeval symbol for Christ, and the Dove might well be an unmarried lady devoted to piety and good works. But the mystical marriage

in Christ is not the only purity. The chastity of human love—
the love, say, of a Perdita and Florizel—is equally rare and as
worthy of celebration. And perhaps it is more able to assume
on its own terms and without irreverence, the poem's aimed
wit and buoyancy.

The third approach is the 'poetic'. It is best summed up by
Emerson's enigmatic statement in the preface to *Parnassus*:

I consider this piece to be a good example of the rule that there
is a poetry for bards proper, as well as a poetry for the world of
readers. This poem, if published for the first time, and without
a known author's name, would have no general reception. Only
the poets would save it.

Clearly, we are to make what we can of this. I will take it at its
face value: the poem can be read as a copy-book example of
technique; of how to take the abiding themes of love poetry—
Love, Death and the Absolutes—and give them a perfect
aesthetic order. It is a limited approach but a necessary one.

Finally, there is the approach by way of knowledge. The poem
is genuinely difficult, not because it complicates metaphysical
conceit upon conceit, nor because it presumes a hidden, a
historical depth of religious symbolism, but because we too
often fail to understand the terms it employs. It is metaphysical
in a more obviously intellectual way than most 'Metaphysical'
poetry. It states its problems precisely and consistently in the
philosophical language of the time, with a rigorous clarity
which even Donne or Herbert of Cherbury hardly attained. One
move towards understanding the poem, then, is to define some
of its terms.

In a total reading of the poem these four ways of approach
merge and clarify each other. I will start with the heavy work,
the bulldozing needed in the latter two. Once the ground is
cleared there will be room enough to assume and judge the
others.

II

My chief quarrel with symbolic interpretation is that, in
more or less covert ways, it constantly poses the question, 'What

does this poem mean?' It is a mistake of emphasis. A poem does not *mean* in any simple way. It does not stand for something else. As I. A. Richards has said, 'It is never what a poem *says* which matters, but what it is.' To criticize a poem closely is to understand and then to describe. It is an act of imaginative sympathy. On this the relevance and accuracy of the criticism rests. The elements of a poem—and its symbolic 'meaning' is one—are like traits of character; they can be isolated for convenience and clarity, but they exist only as parts of the whole.

The interdependence of the parts is particularly to the point in the *Phoenix and Turtle*. Take, for instance, the language. Shakespeare was never so obviously 'knowing' with his metaphors as Donne. On the other hand, he rarely used them as sparingly as here. Increasingly throughout the poem concrete is evaporated into abstract—'*Death* is now the Phoenix *nest*'—or even into the flatly grammatical; for instance, in one of the few ambiguities, 'mine' in stanza 9, the choice lies between a concrete metaphor and a grammatical tool. Where the language is associational it leads to the realm of speculation, not of human particularity. This rarity of diction gives the poem the generalizable quality of philosophical discourse and it strictly limits your conception of the sort of love described. It is clearly of a very different order from that of, say, Carew's *Rapture*, or even, for all its reverence, Ben Jonson's *Her Triumph*. At the same time, this bareness of language concentrates your attention on the poetic procedures themselves, and allows it little chance to be dispersed in local complexity. Puzzled, you say, 'I don't follow', not 'I don't see'.

The mechanics of the thing are important, complex and formally perfect. You are moved from an invitation to 'the bird of lowest lay' to a command to 'sigh a prayer'; from a tragic cry to a sigh of reconciled acceptance; it is the momentum of a catharsis, which unifies the actors of the three stages of the poem—the birds, the abstracts 'Love and Constancie', and the other lovers who are 'true or faire'—and makes them all part of the same coherent dramatic movement.

As the purity of the love echoes through the purified language, so the poem too, section by section, refines and withdraws itself. The structure is precise and coherent: the invocation gives the setting and announces the theme; in the antheme is the descrip-

5

tive argumentation; the bare statements of the Threnos are the climax and conclusion. The topics of the poem stretch out towards abstraction, from the 'chaste wings', through the abstract concepts of the world of Reason, to the transcendentals of the world of Love. At the same time the poem withdraws steadily into its own poetic elements. The antheme is sung by the invoked birds, themselves part of a literary tradition; the Threnos, in turn, is composed by Reason, an abstract quality within the song sung by these characters, and composed, moreover, 'As *Chorus* to their Tragique Scene'—a further distancing by theatrical metaphor. Although the N.E.D. will not allow theatrical overtones to 'Troupe' and 'Session' we are still left with a song within a song within a formal literary setting.

I have suggested that the chastity of the language at once qualifies the subject and emphasizes the poetic logic by which the work unfolds. Any unfolding, however intensely linguistic, is a series of actions, and the action of language is expressed clearest through the moods of the verbs used. In the opening section all these are imperatives. The authority of tone sets the poem in motion and creates a fitting atmosphere.

Let the bird of lowdest lay

The heavily stressed imperative and alliterating superlative give the poem a great push forward into a rhythmical buoyancy which it never loses. It is this that gives the confidence which guides the poem through the badly mapped country of speculation, and helps the sureness of its final affirmations. But the imperatives also include a number of words of command, 'obay', 'keepe', 'interdict'. Deliberately and ceremoniously a setting is being invoked. Again it is a matter of purity. The birds are summoned to a 'requiem' mass from which 'tyrants', 'the fiend' and his 'precurrer' are exorcised. They are provided with a full array of religious trappings: 'obsequie', 'Priest in Surples white', 'defunctive Musicke', 'the Requiem', 'his (the priest's or the requiem's) right' (also rite), the 'mourners'. Then there is the heraldic pomp of royalty: the 'herauld', 'trumpet' and 'feth'red King'. And above all this there is the essential purity of the birds themselves, 'chaste', 'strict', 'white', and the 'crow' who gains his place less for his mourning colour or his 'voys of care', as in Chaucer, than for his quaintly pure way of propagation, 'With the breath thou giu'st and tak'st'.[1]

But then the birds, for all the vitality of Shakespeare's writing, appear with the accumulations, the wit and familiarity, that is, of at least some two centuries of literary life. They are straight from the widely known and, to the Elizabethans, easily recognizable convention of the *Parlement of Fowles*. Scholars have accepted this for fifty years, together with the probability that Shakespeare was working directly from Chaucer.[2] Whether he was or not is beside my immediate point. The parallels are there, but their importance is negative. The conventional treatment was to follow Chaucer and let each bird come forward and say something in character.[3] Shakespeare does not make them so crudely self-explanatory. They are less symbols than literary properties. Certainly they are given considerable literary power; a power not of substance and detail but of verbal grandeur. The traditional make-believe (it has come down to us in the nursery-rhyme *Who Killed Cock Robin?*) is dignified by slow-paced and deeply serious language:

> Let the Priest in Surples white,
> That defunctive Musicke can,
> Be the death-deuining Swan,
> Lest the *Requiem* lacke his right.

Much depends on the solemnity of the language to set the tone and qualify the subject. It makes the setting, like the love of the Phoenix and Turtle, chaste, regal and holy. It helps the

[1] See Swan's *Speculum Mundi*, 1635, p. 397: 'Neither (as is thought) doth the raven conceive by conjunction of male and female, but rather by a kind of billing at the mouth, which *Plinie* mentioneth as an opinion of the common people.' Rollins' *Variorum* edition of the *Poems* gives this quotation and a full gloss to the lines.

[2] A. H. R. Fairchild in *Englische Studien*, xxxiii, 1904. He gives a history of the Renaissance use of the tradition and all the parallels from Chaucer. The Variorum, for no obvious reason, omits some of them.

[3] E.g. 'An Elegie . . . for his Astrophill', from *The Phoenix Nest*, 1593:

> The swan that was in presence heere,
> Began his funerall dirge to sing,
> Good things (quoth he) may scarce appeere,
> But passe away with speedie wing.
> This mortall life as death is tride,
> And death gives life, and so he dide.

poem to its grand manner, to make it so purposeful, detached and moving.

III

There is a difference between poetic rarity and difficulty, between the deliberate withdrawal of the invocation and the complications of the antheme. To us the birds are unfamiliar, and Shakespeare puts in details from literary and popular traditions which make them stranger yet. But this is a short-winded obscurity that takes us no further than the footnotes of a competent editor: for example, all those details about the crow. The antheme, on the other hand, presents real intellectual difficulties. It uses vocabulary which is indeed obscure, and uses it to shift and balance round metaphysical precipices with a bewildering skill.

While the invocation prepared us for their purity by literary device, the antheme insists logically on the *absolute* perfection of the lovers. In most love poems (and this includes Shakespeare's plays) actions and attitudes are judged against *implicit* moral standards. Celebration affirms them, lament and disgust deny. In this poem the lovers themselves are *explicitly* these standards:

> Love and Constancie is dead,
> *Phoenix* and the *Turtle* fled . . .;

elsewhere they are incarnations of Platonic and Christian ideals, 'Beautie, Truth and Grace'. By these terms the Christian symbolist would throw a shaft of light on to the subject, which, for all its accuracy, does not illuminate the whole bulk and humanity of the love. The theme of the poem is the transcendence of Reason by Love. The great theological paradoxes are used—often, indeed, stated in specifically theological terms —because religion *also* rests on faith. This does not necessarily limit the subject of the poem; it only qualifies it.

The very difficulty of the antheme is that it will not rest in the power of faith to transcend Reason (and this makes me suspicious of a purely Christian interpretation); it sets out poetically and logically to *prove* its case. It uses the traditional means, the paradox, accommodated to a stringent logic; for if

8

the poet is to go convincingly beyond Reason he must also include it. The simple paradox is not enough. It asserts only its
own ingenuity and gives a temporary, unqualified perception.
To prove its point, to outreason Reason, the paradox must be
rationally accurate and sustained.

Even the simplest insurance of accuracy is used: Shakespeare
develops the argument in juxtaposition with numbers, the most
precise, least misinterpretable words. 'Twaine', 'none', 'one' are
used as a set of rhymes twice in six stanzas, and two of the most
difficult lines of the poem are circumscribed in the same way:

> *Single* Natures *double* name,
> Neither *two* nor *one* was called.

(My italics.) The numbers are an assurance that the situation
can be spoken of rationally, worked out, almost, on paper—
provided, of course, you understand the basic conceit.

Much of the difficulty of the antheme lies in its accuracy.
The paradoxes are more than a literary device supporting the
weight of a questionable argumentation; they balance and
juggle technical terms from the metaphysics of Shakespeare's
time, quite regardless of the pull of philosophical gravity.[1]
Relentlessly, the constants of Reason are stated and then
destroyed in exactly the language in which the philosophers
would have upheld them. The terminology is rational, its
application flatly anti-rational.

The technical complexity stands in its own right. The
position is stated immediately, fully, accurately, and thereafter
only briefly restated in terms of the constants so briskly to be
destroyed. The whole argument moves from the lines:

> So they loued as loue in twaine,
> Had the essence but in one,

[1] After a draft of this paper had been read to an Oxford seminar, an
article appeared in E.L.H., xix, 1952, in which Mr. J. V. Cunningham
also pointed out some of the scholastic terminology in the poem. But our
paths do not cross unduly. Mr. Cunningham confines himself to the
antheme and to Thomist doctrine, whilst I try to subordinate the theology
to the human situation. Since then Professor C. S. Lewis has written
on the poem, briefly but to the point, in *English Literature in the Sixteenth
Century*, Oxford, 1954. He remarks there on the song-within-a-song
structure and the prime importance of Reason in the poem. I can only
affirm that I had delivered this paper, and made those same points, at least
two years before I read Professor Lewis's work.

It is important to keep the original punctuation: 'they', rather than 'loue', is the subject of 'had'. The poem is about these particular lovers, their embodiment, not their assumptions of ideal love. Roughly you could paraphrase it: 'They loved as though they were two separate people, or as though love resided in each of them apart; but in essence they were one.' 'So', in a minor way, is ambiguous: it has a logical force, making the stanza follow from the 'mutuall flame' of the last; at the same time it expresses the degree of their love: 'Their love was so great it had the strength of two, but their soul was one.' The important word is 'essence'. It is a metaphysical term, *essentia*, for substance or absolute being. Theologians used it to denote, as the N.E.D. says, 'that in respect of which the three persons of the Trinity were one'. More loosely, it was the soul, the 'glassy essence', joining man to God. Like Donne's *Ecstacie*, the poem turns on the grace of love, the paradox which makes the spiritual reality belie the material appearance.

But Shakespeare's objective, for the moment, is the logical results of this unity *in essentia*, and he moves towards it with a brisk rationality, stepping out in full scholastical array.

> Two distincts, Division none,

'*Definition, Division, Methodus*', says Miss Tuve, with her usual monumental authority, '. . . were cant terms; not only every budding Schoolman but every youth of parts found himself constrained to learn how to define and divide'. The point, then, for the Elizabethans was obvious and pedantic. A contemporary handbook of logic makes the paradox clearer: 'As a definition doth declare what a thing is, so a devision sheweth how many things are contained in the same'.[1] Although the definition 'loue in twaine' would show 'two distincts', the next step, 'Division', is impossible because of the common 'essence'. Yet it is logically impossible not to be able to divide when you can distinguish. The basic tools and presumptions of Reason are rendered useless. The argument is pushed forward. 'Division' is a mathematical as well as a logical process:

> Number there in loue was slaine.

The range of the logic is wide, for by 'number' Shakespeare seems to mean both a rational skill, arithmetic, and an abstract

---

[1] Thomas Wilson, *The Rule of Reason*, 1551.

concept, mathematics; for the force of the overthrow may be augmented by a mathematical dictum, 'One is no number'.[1]

The logic, in short, is teased out with more pertinacity than is usual, even in Donne. For Shakespeare argues formally and in the abstract, from a single literary trope, the paradox. Donne, on the other hand, for all his logical 'business', usually starts from an alogical hypothesis; he begins with an analogy and argues two parallel cases at once on the understanding that they are at most points convertible. Shakespeare, in this poem at least, is the more honest logician and not at all the Metaphysical poet.

Appearance, however, *is* important to his paradox, though before this can emerge, the related rational abstracts, 'Distance' and 'Space', are in turn overwhelmed by the continuing force of the logic. This done, stanza 9 reveals the source of the paradox; it is accurate description. Effortlessly and without exaggeration the paradox holds for the particular act of love the poem celebrates, the Phoenix's consuming fire. Not only is the love of God for man infinitely divisible yet always one, so too is the 'mutuall flame' in which the birds burn to their consummation. Donne, for instance, explicitly describes the rites of love in this way in his '*Epithalamion . . . on the Lady* Elizabeth, *and* Count Palatine':

> . . . as one glorious flame
> Meeting Another, growes the same,
> So meet thy Fredericke, and so
> To an unseparable union growe.
> Since separation
> Falls not on such things as are infinite,
> Nor things which are but one, can disunite . . .'

(A few stanzas later he describes the lovers as two Phoenixes.) This is why there is so much stress on visual description:

[1] This may or may not be behind Shakespeare's argument here. It is no more esoteric than the other learning he is wielding. Not many years later it had become an intellectual commonplace which even a poet as little Metaphysical as Suckling was using to underline a piece of dialectical debauchery:

> For Hymen's rites and for the marriage-bed
> You were ordain'd, and not to lie alone;
> One is no number, till that two be one.
> To keep a maidenhead but till fifteen
> Is worse than murder. . . . (*Lutea Allison*).

'shine', 'saw', 'flaming', 'sight'. Underlying all the logic is the certainty of accurate perception.

The last line works in two directions at once. It continues the description of the lovers' fire; a 'mine' is a place in which treasure is found. The lovers are their own riches, gems glinting only to each others' sight in the surrounding darkness of the ordinary world. At the same time, the sense moves forward to 'Propertie' in the next stanza: when two are one, 'yours' and 'mine' are no longer meaningful distinctions; the flat grammatical tool, like the scholastic quiddities, becomes inaccurate and useless.

So far the difficulties have been resolved, for the most part, by definition. You have only to make the words precise and, simply, the meaning follows, the direction of the poem becomes plain. Stanza 10 is more complicated. If you tug at the word 'Propertie' three skeins of abstraction emerge, instead of one. And they are all knotted, for strength, in that most intricate of terms, 'Nature'. The logic of the work embraces them all; no one seems more important than the others, for the purpose of Shakespeare's paradox is to undercut the whole world of Reason.

In its simplest sense 'Propertie' refers back to the line before: it is the power of ownership personified (it becomes 'appalled'). Concrete 'Propertie', the things you own, is appropriated under people's 'names', and so there is something legalistic in the attempts that follow to distinguish between the 'double name' of the 'single Nature' (here, perhaps, simply a person or body which might be discussed in a court of law). There is no withholding in Love; it is beyond greed and ownership.

But then 'Propertie' refers back more clearly to the earlier stanzas if taken to be one of the five Predicables of Aristotelian logic. It is the quality common to a class, what makes that class individual and separate. In Wilson's words, it is 'a naturall proneness and maner of doing, which agreeth to one kind and the same onely and that evermore'. Nature then is the principle of individuation, as in the definition in Thomas Spencer's *The Art of Logick*, 1628: 'Properties are necessary emanations from the principle of nature.' This reading makes the stanza another attack on the abstract principles of definition and distinction. Love is a shared uniqueness.

12

But 'Propertie' has still another meaning: the proper use of language, what we now call 'propriety'. Hence Mr. Ridley's paraphrase in his notes to the *New Temple Shakespeare*. He over-states the case, perhaps, but neatly: 'In Shakespearian idiom "self" and "same" are almost always identical. The phrase means, I think, that the sense of the proper use of language is outraged by the discovery that a synonym is not a synonym.' The lines, then, carry on the implications of the grammatical paradox, 'Either was the others mine'; carries them, that is, through 'Single Natures double name', where the important word is 'name', and through yet another rephrasing where the stressed rhyme-word is 'called'. Even if you do not believe Mr. Ridley that 'selfe' and 'same' were synonymous, the language difficulties are no less real, although perhaps a little more human. The point is that words, even words as precise as numbers, will not fit these lovers. Propriety is 'appalled' because what one lover calls himself is not in fact him; a 'single nature' ('essence' of stanza 7) has two distinct names. Language is a rational convention. It will not do for the mysteries of love. The quibbling with numbers only drives home the impossibility.

All this is footnoting. The critical point is a simple one. In none of these stanzas are the complications there for their own sakes. Metaphor, accurate perception, ambiguity, word-play, in short, all the associative energies of Shakespeare's verse have rarified into this abstract allusiveness, by which, as Donne often does, he feels towards the inner mystery of love. For this he builds up his own—or love's own—metaphysic. Like all valid systems, it must be proved.

With 'Reason confounded' in its own terms, the proof is well-nigh complete. In the best rhetorical fashion stanza 11 repeats the main stages of the argument. 'Division grows together', as it did in stanza 7; the lovers grow 'to themselves' (partly *towards*), hence 'Distance and no space'; 'either neither' echoes the grammatical contortions. A final antithesis rounds off the whole affair. 'Simple' and 'compound' were technical terms of alchemy, also used in theology to describe the paradoxical nature of God. Another science is stated, contradicted, resolved in mystery. The original punctuation, with commas at the end of each line, emphasizes the step by step recapitulation.

Like Sir Thomas Browne contemplating the 'involved

enigmas and riddles of the Trinity', Reason pursues itself to an *O altitudo* when confronted with the overwhelming proofs of Love:

> Loue hath Reason, Reason none,
> If what parts, can so remaine.

Note that 'If '. The rational habit dies hard, and in the end expires only before rational proof. But the paradox of pure and perfect love is at last substantiated. Reason, an abstract quality within the already withdrawn and purified setting of the Bird Parliament, having acknowledged its own worthlessness, sings the praises of the lovers.

IV

If the love Shakespeare is celebrating were merely the usual courtly Platonic passion, the perception the usual paradox of the Two-in-One, if Reason were merely transcended by Love as the poets would usually have it, then the poem deals with topics far too slight to support the weight of all that logical complication and literary device. The conclusions of the Threnos must be less commonplace to justify their difficulty. Yet at first they seem a little obvious, almost thin. It is all so detached. The poem is an artifact, something carefully made. It is also a logical construction, something clearly argued. But it is impersonal in a way Shakespeare is nowhere else. This is why it can bear, perhaps, the niggling, factual analysis I have subjected it to. There is little personal tone to violate. Its uniqueness is in its detached conviction. It handles obscurities for a purpose.

The detachment is seen in the poem's climax, the Threnos. It is largely made up of a series of powerful but bare assertions of abstract qualities. You can see it, as in the antheme, in the verbs. Again and again rhyme and rhythm force plain, dogmatic indicative statements on your attention: 'lie', 'is now', 'doth rest', 'Twas not', 'It was', 'cannot be', ''tis not', 'buried be'. Indeed, 'be'/'she'/'be' might seem to be slipshod writing without the purposeful air the Threnos exudes. The assertiveness is increased, moreover, by changing the already buoyant rhythm of the quatrains into triplets, their jauntiness exaggerated by the use of only three rhymes in fifteen lines. It begins to seem that so much vitality might be disproportionate to the abstraction and solemnity of the subject.

But I said earlier that this is a poem of proof, of articulate, aimed structure. For this reason, if for no other, the absolutes of Love are needed logically: they are the critieria by which Reason has been refuted and which Reason finally acknowledges. But the poem is *not* a celebration of Love in its generality, nor yet of Love in the dubious particularity of a myth. In homage to the Phoenix and his Turtle Shakespeare changes even the myth and the simple attributes of Love are themselves left behind. Look again at the verbs and you will see that nearly every assertion contains its own denial: 'in cinders lie', 'Death is now', 'To eternitie doth rest. Leaving no posteritie', 'cannot be', 'tis not', 'buried be'. Neither the Phoenix nor the Dove, neither 'Love' nor 'Constancie', 'Beautie' nor 'Truth' will do by themselves. They are all simplicities, all units you can name, all, in a way, aspects of that same rationality the antheme has destroyed. The perfect achievement of love is union, complex in itself, but transformed by the purity of the birds into a deeper, a stranger complexity, resolvable only in death.

Their final mystery, to which all the rest of the poem leads and which the bare statements of the Threnos bleakly assert, is the transcendence of even the simple values of Love in a last tragic paradox of purity:

It was married Chastitie.

It is the only paradox in the Threnos, the only positive value, positively and unequivocally affirmed. For the moment the myth of the Phoenix is changed to emphasize the single force of the revelation, the *raison d'être* for all the preceding theologizing. The detail, the logic, the aesthetic distancing are all necessary steps to this final inner core of purity.

From the full moment of knowledge in the 'Tragique Scene' the catastrophe follows inevitably, driven home by repetition and heavy alliteration:

> *Truth* may seeme, *but* cannot *be*,
> *Beautie* bragge, *but* tis not she,
> *Truth* and *Beautie* buried *be*.

(My italics.) But this tragedy is not final. It involves too much. The Phoenix and Turtle are more than lovers; they are all the values of Love as well. Their vitality, like their purity and their sacrifice, continues beyond them. The four approaches to the poem at last merge as the tragedy is played off against the background of Christian assurance and poetic wit. The religion is clear enough. The birds rest 'to eternitie', in a final resolution of chastity and theology. Their virtues, dignified by celebration, substantiated by logic and gaining power by the associations of their mystical paradoxes, are consummated in the act of chaste love and remain. From this energy of faith the poetic myth reasserts itself as the 'true' and 'faire' rise again from the ashes of 'Truth' and 'Beautie'. The wit keeps control. The new generation may only be the bragging semblances of the old, but they are no less true and fair for that. And the old, in whom all the transcendental qualities of Love have so passionately existed, are seen, in turn, to be only a pair of 'dead birds', not totally different from the other birds whose sighs end the poem as their laments had begun it. They are all, for all their pomp and style, a little pathetic.

What does it all add up to? A way, I think, of showing that the highest mysteries of Love demand their own metaphysic, religion and logic, and their own poetic ritual to give them at once grandeur and detachment. In the end Christianity, wit, metaphysics and poetic device are assimilated into the mystery of 'married Chastitie'; they all rest in the calm of a delicately, but logically and passionately attained sense of proportion.

Macbeth, Act I, Scene vii, Lines 1 to 28

'*Macbeth* is a statement of evil.' L. C. KNIGHTS.

Graham Martin

'STRUCTURE', nowadays, is a keyword in Shakespearean criticism. 'Analysis' by 'plot' and 'character' is out. It is 'theme' and 'organization' that describe modern critical presumptions. And one certainly cannot be without these terms and notions. To dissent, therefore, from their implications, is not to dissent from their use. If that use is to remain fruitful, it needs to be limited. Particularly, the static implication of 'structure' must be resisted. A sense of progress is a main part of a sense of drama. *Macbeth* may have more in common with *The Waste Land* than with *The Doll's House*, but it still has something in common with *The Doll's House*. This sense is very little realized in a number of well-known essays about *Macbeth*; and its absence from modern criticism of the play evidently troubles Professor Muir. He writes in his Introduction to the new Arden Edition:

> We may, indeed, call *Macbeth* the greatest of morality plays, at the same time as we are aware that Shakespeare transcends the sublime story of a human soul on the road to damnation and that he shows us also indomitable energy burning *in the forests of the night* . . . and human life . . . in all its splendours and miseries, and even in its crimes, not

                         a tale
          Told by an idiot, full of sound and fury,
          Signifying nothing. [1]

Professor Muir's anxiety would have been more fully appeased
had he also pointed out that Shakespeare particularly resists
every tendency to transcend *Macbeth*'s soul. Perhaps this is what
he means. For it is Macbeth's soul that we should be thinking
about, not 'a human soul'. *Macbeth* dramatizes the *growth* of a
certain evil man. It is true that the play supports him, and often
generalizes his significance. Certainly, all its properties and
devices subserve a total purpose, and a total effect. The purpose,
the effect is Macbeth's career. He is, at every point, the most
articulate witness, and there are many, to the dramatic structure
that contains him. The keynote of all his speech is development:
either from soliloquy to soliloquy, or within a soliloquy. The
soliloquy I have chosen here clarifies the nature of this development; and reinforces, in particular terms, this general contention: drama is a process, as well as a statement.

          If it were done, when 'tis done, then 'twer well,
          It were done quickly: If th'Assassination
          Could trammel up the Consequence, and catch
          With his surcease, Successe: that but this blow
          Might be the be all, and the end all. Heere,
          But heere, upon this Banke and Schoole of time,
          Wee'l'd jumpe the life to come.
                              But in these Cases,
          We still have judgment heere, that we but teach
          Bloody Instructions, which being taught, returne
          To plague th'Inventer, This even-handed Justice
          Commends th'Ingredience of our poyson'd Challice
          To our owne lips.
                         Hee's heere in double trust;
          First, as I am his Kinsman, and his Subject,
          Strong both against the Deed: Then, as his Host,
          Who should against his Murtherer shut the doore,
          Not beare the knife my selfe.
                              Besides, this *Duncane*
          Hath borne his Faculties so meeke; hath bin
          So cleere in his great Office, that his Vertues
          Will pleade like Angels, Trumpet-tongu'd against
          The deepe damnation of his taking-off:

[1] Kenneth Muir, *Macbeth* (The Arden Shakespeare), 1953, p. lxxiv.

And Pitty, like a naked New-borne-Babe,
Striding the blast, or Heavens Cherubin, hors'd
Upon the sightlesse Curriors of the Ayre,
Shall blow the horrid deed in every eye,
That teares shall drowne the winde.
                              I have no Spurre
To pricke the sides of my intent, but onely
Vaulting Ambition, which ore-leaps it selfe,
And falles on th'other.[1]

Macbeth's progress is punctuated by a series of soliloquies; and these have in common at least this feature: that they all reveal to the audience much more of Macbeth's situation than they do to Macbeth himself. As Wilson Knight first pointed out, what these reveal is particularly confirmed in the supporting plot: the *Macbeth* universe is created by Macbeth. The statement does not only apply to the destruction of the commonweal he brings about. The positive ethic, the very thing he has destroyed is embodied as fully in Macbeth, as he himself realizes, through his tyranny committed on the common-weal, through his own *black and deepe desires*. His soliloquies display this process of realization in him. The following analysis is an attempt to make particular a number of insidious abstractions now used of the play: Damnation, Evil, Disorder.

I have divided the speech into sections, in order to mark what have struck me as the important points of transition. As a whole, it is Macbeth's attempt to argue himself beyond his doubts and fears; he does not succeed in doing so, however; the speech is broken off by Lady Macbeth's entrance, and he says to her 'We will proceed no further in this Businesse'. As far as Macbeth is concerned, however, the speech 'means' a dispassionate appraisal of the imagined crime and of his feelings about it: that is what he is attempting. It opens, therefore, with an anxious argument, of short stabbing clauses, and heavily felt stresses:

                    that but this blow
Might be the be all, and the end all. Heere,
But heere,

The syntax unites lines 1–7. The second sentence re-states, it at first seems, the content of the first. But it also develops it.

[1] Folio text; here taken from *The New Nonesuch Shakespeare*, 1929, ed. Herbert Farjeon, pp. 503–4.

19

The point of *quickly* is more and more explored. 'If the thing could be done with sufficient expedition, "wee'l'd jumpe the life to come".' (Macbeth has already adopted the royal *we*.) All that Macbeth is anxious about is a possible revenge for the murder in this world: he confidently risks a moral and a spiritual revenge. It is 'the Consequence' here that troubles him. But the stress is anxious; and its implications are fulfilled in the concluding lines of the speech. In the meanwhile, however, 'we still have judgment heere'; and despite the larger suggestions of 'judgment', of 'even-handed Justice', and particularly of 'poyson'd Challice', the fear is chiefly for his own skin. He wants a single risk, and then a safe reward. So much for intention; the tone reveals much more. The life to come and the operations of justice present themselves to his imagination more vividly than one would expect of a man who has just claimed for himself spiritual 'securitie'. Moreover, the conditional presentation of the question implies at every point the answer *No*. 'It cannot be done quickly. The murder cannot be the be-all and the end-all. It has causes. It must have consequences. My succession will never go unchallenged. I shall run a continual risk of assassination myself. My act will bring forth its imitations, and I may be their victim. I shall in a sense be the victim of my own act.' These are not in any bald sense statements; but they seem to me justifiable implications proceeding from what is stated. They are well enough substantiated in the following acts. Macbeth prophesies truly. What he states, on the other hand, looks in another direction; and the contradiction between these is the main point. This is as hasty and as muffled in its implications as the subsequent crime itself. Dr. Johnson conjectured that line 4 should read 'With his Successe, surcease'; the 'his', he claimed, must be related to 'th'Assassination'. But the change in grammatical reference is valuable. The crime refuses to be made abstract. It insists upon its human context, slightly but definitely. Macbeth is trying to discuss it with himself as a calculation of risks and rewards, a mere 'the'; but he cannot. In the very moment of mentioning it, the crime becomes a 'his'. Professor Empson suggests: ' "His" may apply to Duncan,' ' "assassination" or "consequence".' [1] If it is allowed to do so much, it does nothing of any value.

[1] William Empson, *Seven Types of Ambiguity* (rev. edn., 1949), p. 50.

The sound similarity of 'surcease' and 'Successe' connect the crime and its result in the very instant that Macbeth tries to disjoin them. For 'Successe', the conditional *if* implies, cannot be so trammelled up: it stretches into the future, into the Consequence'. Success will bring succession to the throne; but also fulfilment of his *deepe desires*, and the consequent murder of his own humanity. These, at least, occur to us. It is mainly the possibility of opposition that occurs to him: 'if only that act of murder could include all further trouble within itself, so that I might immediately, without more effort, be and remain king.' But 'Consequence' resounds more menacingly than that; it hints of 'the consequences', the necessary flow of events leading away from that one event to balance the flow of events leading up to it; it rebuts, by implication, the *if only*. Something of this duality is lost by Muir[2] when he silently omits the comma between 'surcease' and 'Successe' given in the Folio: the pause between the words complements the similarity of sound, disjoining, joining.

An analytical intention is professed in the opening lines in order to deal with the situation conjured up. 'Conjured up', indeed, is a metaphor we might more precisely apply. The intellect, calculating in the service of the will, is bungling its work. In the process of estimating 'the Consequence', it allows the entry of elements hostile to the will's pre-decision to commit the act: these elements enter by way of 'judgment', 'Justice', 'Challice', and perhaps 'life to come'. In this way the matter of lines 1–12 is positively contradicted by the manner in which they are presented. Moreover, there is, to my mind, a distinct change of tone in the middle of line 7. The note of anxiety gives way to a judicial detachment. Macbeth's mind is more comfortable contemplating a likely and a just revenge than the chances of a successful *coup*.

> this even-handed Justice
> Commends th'Ingredience of our poyson'd Challice
> To our owne lips.

This conclusion to Section 2 answers, in a way, the uncertainties initiated in Section 1. It does so with a surprisingly calm eloquence. But it, too, has its opposite implications. The royal use

---

[2] *Macbeth*, p. 37.

'our' is mostly responsible for this unexpected serenity; but it is also responsible for a grace-note of fear. It takes us back to the earlier uses of the pronoun in lines 7–8. In the first of these Macbeth assumes the royalty of Duncan. The second is a collective use: it invites us to consider Macbeth along with the rest of sinful mankind before the judgment seat of 'even-handed Justice'; and the third shares something of this communal calm, even while it implies the personal royalty as well. Both of these uses have a right to their generalizing sense of stability. The royal 'our' has fictional right only. Within its pretension of confidence lurks the fearful Macbeth, picturing to himself the dangers of usurpation.

It remains now to stress the symmetry of these contradictions. Considering the murder: anxiety, fear, a surprising sense for these very matters that make the act heinous; all these, masquerading under the profession of a determinedly amoral intellect. Considering the punishment: sure, detached, meditative in its grasp of the necessary consequences, the undefeatable logic: Murder will out, and will be revenged; all these entertained by the mind that claims it would jump the life to come. Macbeth is a criminal with an easier, a more assured grasp of the judge's summing-up, than of the murder he expects to commit. He fairly smothers the detail of the act, fairly expands over the details of 'the Consequence'.

At line 12, what I have called 'the intellect' takes up again. There would, I imagine, be a long pause in the delivery between Sections 2 and 3; the change of manner is abrupt.

Hee's heere in double trust;

Analysis is carried out in this case on behalf of the society to which Macbeth owes allegiance. So he begins, and in the very statement of his loyalties expands 'double' to triple: kinsman, subject, host. The adjective 'strong' confers upon these positive ties a distinctly muscular quality. The hand and arm driving the knife to its destination will need a proportionately greater strength. The word 'knife' makes its first appearance in the speech at line 16. Macbeth has not used it before in the play. The audience only know of it from Lady Macbeth. As far as Macbeth is concerned it is the first reference to the murder that can be precisely visualized. It appears, moreover, not in response to the hidden decisions of the will that govern the movement of lines 1–7. It appears here, in a context of the strongest possible prohibition of the deed it implies. Macbeth has just enumerated these prohibitions. There is, too, a pro-nominal change of related interest.

> .   Then, as his Host,
> Who should against his Murtherer shut the doore,
> Not beare the knife my selfe.

The sense of a physical struggle between 'good' and 'evil', hinted in 'strong', is fully realized here. Macbeth is both 'host' and 'Murtherer'. 'Host' is qualified in the third person; so too is 'Murtherer'; but 'beare the knife', the act itself, refuses any impersonalization; it cannot but be followed by 'my selfe'. The thud of the reader's surprise, as he responds to the wrenched grammar, forces the knife home. 'Host' and 'Murtherer' come together, *after* the imaginary murder, in 'my selfe'. The act unites them. So, having confronted the full fact of his secret will, Macbeth proceeds to place it in its religious context. The moral and social obligations that tie Macbeth lead to Duncan. Macbeth has in his imagination broken those bonds. And now he considers the person and the personage whose trust he has betrayed.

We have already noted the effect of 'poyson'd Challice'. Its implications are now to be thoroughly fulfilled in lines 17–25. Duncan, dead now in Macbeth's imagination, is here mentioned by name for the first time, and fully contemplated. To define that fullness in relation to Macbeth's history, it is worth quoting from an earlier speech:

> My thought, whose Murther yet is but fantasticall,
> Shakes so my single state of Man,[1]

'Murther' refers grammatically to 'My thought'. The reference to Duncan could not be more quickly smothered. In the later speech, it could not be more fully given. For Macbeth, or for his private imaginings, Duncan only appears as a response to those considerations that make his murder a matter for damnation.

>   his Vertues
> Will pleade like Angels, Trumpet-tongu'd against
> The deepe damnation of his taking-off.

[1] Macbeth I, iii, 139–40.

The apocalyptic vision of 'Pitty' grows from a consideration of Duncan's person and office. 'His Vertues' are angelic, both in quality and strength. The word takes on almost a theological sense: Virtues, one of the angelic orders. 'Plead' too has a dual reference. The Christ-like virtue, meekness, pleads mutely by its bearing. It has resigned earthly power. It turns the other cheek to violence. The second sense, the legal process of pleading, is subsequently developed *out of* the word. 'Trumpet-tongu'd' translates 'Angels' from simile to fact. The 'judgment heere' of line 8 has become the Last Judgment conducted by Christ, the Righteous Jūdge. In this context 'plead' assumes its legal sense. Duncan's virtues, therefore, are both weak and strong; and their weakness here, gives them their strength in 'the life to come'. This strength it is, that will judge Macbeth to his 'deepe damnation'. 'His taking-off', direct statement of the completed murder, is made for the first time within this context. The duality of 'Vertues', it will be noted, 'develops' from line to line. It is impossible to come at lines 21–24 except from an acute awareness of this duality.

Professor Muir silently supplies a comma after the word 'trumpet-tongu'd'[1]: the Folio reading has none. As a consequence of the above argument, however, I find the Folio the better reading. It allows a pause, only after 'plead like Angels', and forces a continuous reading of the remainder, thus: 'Trumpet-tongu'd against/The deepe damnation'. Thus 'Vertues' is suddenly removed from its earthly situation into a heavenly one; weakness suddenly becomes supernatural strength. This is, I think, the appropriate reading. 'Trumpet-tongu'd' followed by a pause, slides over a development that should be as abrupt as possible. It is impossible to work gradually into a successful trumpet call. It is either sudden, or ludicrous.

The complex syntax of lines 21–25 is worthy of the ministrations of Professor Empson. I choose the readings that seem to me most important in emphasizing the progressive growth of the metaphor. No possible reading, and there are many, contradicts that general feature of the lines. The whole passage from 'Besides' in line 16 mounts towards the vision of 'Pitty', and the prophecy that accompanies it. The duality of 'Vertues' in the introductory passage is now openly thrust upon the

1 *Macbeth*, p. 40.

reader. Pity's features are two, and contradictory: and the syntax refuses to distinguish between them. In the introductory
passage, angelic strength *grows* out of earthly weakness. In the
culmination, the two are simultaneously presented, inextricably
inter-twined. First, the word Pity is endowed, by the line that
precedes it, with a power that its solitary appearance would
not suggest.

> The deepe damnation of his taking-off:
> And Pitty, . . .

The 'And' sums up what has gone before. Immediately, however, the natural sense of the word is particularized in the
phrase 'like a naked New-borne-Babe'. Helplessness is the first
suggestion the simile contributes, but it is not the only one.
The helplessness has a distinct human reference. It is not the
helplessness of Burns's mouse. 'New-borne' alliterates with
'naked' but it provides its own definition of 'Pitty'. Child-birth
introduces domestic and marital associations of a peculiar value
to Shakespeare, and therefore to the reader. Bearing in mind
'Challice', 'meek', 'Trumpet-tongu'd', reference to the Incarna-
tion should not surprise. That event, at any rate, illustrates the
very substantial associations aroused by the 'naked New-borne
Babe'. However these are to be discussed, they must be recognized as demanding more than a simple response.

Pity, having been likened to the 'Babe', is then described as
'striding the blast': not metaphor, but fact. There is a comma
after 'Babe' to muffle any reverberation from that comparison.
Certain difficulties arise, however, as Professor Muir's note
makes evident.

22. *blast*) Wilson comments: 'i.e. (a) of the trumpet, (b) the
tempest of horror and indignation aroused by the deed.' But I
do not understand how Pity . . . and still less how a naked new-
born babe . . . can stride the blast, i.e. the sound, of a trumpet.
But 'blast', by a hidden pun, was doubtless suggested by *'trumpet*-tongu'd' . . . and perhaps Wilson meant this.[1]

I think Wilson means exactly what he says. There is no need,
in fact there is every need not to *visualize* the imagery as Professor Muir apparently has done. His difficulty follows accord-

---

[1] Arden, *Macbeth*, p. 40.

ingly; it is an imaginary one. The 'Babe' defines the quality of 'Pitty' in the precise and yet the substantial way that we have discussed. 'Striding the blast' defines it further, discovers the God in the Child, if I may be permitted the gloss. The weakness of the 'Babe' is also the strength of the 'blast': Pity partakes of both features, principally of the second. 'Blast', moreover, while it seems mainly to look forward to the next line, and finally to 'the winde', functions also by associating with 'Trumpet-tongu'd'. That adjective, it will be recalled, first introduces us to the future strength of Duncan's present helplessness. I take this to be the function of 'the hidden pun'.

The syntax refuses to distinguish between these two attributes of 'Pitty'. The word 'or' in line 22 allows two possibilities. It initiates an alternative simile for 'Pitty', so that the main verb 'Shall blow' has only one subject. Or it connects 'Pitty' and 'Heaven's Cherubin' as a double subject for the main verb. Either, 'Pity, which can be likened to both the babe, and the Cherubins, shall blow, etc.'; or, 'Pity, or alternatively, heaven's Cherubins, shall blow, etc.' The latter seems to me the more likely, but I do not find it possible to decide. Reading the speech as a process that requires a definite, if a variable time to complete, offers, however, a persuasive solution. Before one reaches 'Shall blow', one has to read the description of 'Heaven's Cherubins'. The inner strength of 'Pitty', at once human ('babe'), and impersonal ('blast'), is finally located in a distinct heavenly Order: the intervening 'or' can thus be taken as a summation. 'Sightless', too, has a double effect: blind, impersonal, terrifying; and more slightly: blind, human, pitiful. 'Curriors' reinforces the sense of intelligent activity; 'of the Ayre' reinforces the sense of an elemental strength that is no respecter of persons. The natural phenomenon to which all these complications ultimately refer makes now a first partial appearance in the main verb 'Shall blow'. The complex noun-phrases suddenly coalesce in this simple word. 'The horrid deed', from whose implicit mention in line 16 the passage has developed, is now directly called by its most simple name. It is seen objectively. 'The deepe damnation of his taking-off' still showed the deed from Macbeth's point of view. This direct description of the murder simplifies suddenly the intricate pattern of the metaphor. The supernatural activities have this purpose alone: 'to blow the horrid deed in every eye'. The prophecy closes with a direct record of fact: wind in the eyes produces tears. And yet 'teares' also takes us back to 'Pitty': it is the human response towards an object of pity. Pity for Duncan's murder has set off a chain of powerful and supernatural movements; but these are finally directed back on to some sympathetic human being. So full of meaning is the Courier's message that it evokes a human response of even greater power than itself. The tears are tempestuous; they will 'drown' the wind; the gale is silenced by the rain it brings with it. The image has simultaneously a suggestion of the human and the elemental. The strength of 'Pitty' resides finally in its tenderness.

> I have no Spurre
> To pricke the sides of my intent,

It is scarcely surprising, after this apocalyptic condemnation, that Macbeth approaches the first direct mention of his 'intent' by way of a negative. It comes as a conclusion: 'therefore, everything dissuades me from my intent except ambition'. The word 'intent' repeats the process noted already, that direct references to the murder appear only in a context that prohibits it. The exceptional clarity of this reference is also defined by a quotation from the earlier soliloquy already cited.

> why doe I yeeld to that suggestion,
> Whose horrid Image doth unfixe my Heire,
> And make my seated Heart knock at my Ribbes.[1]

Here for the first time, Macbeth explicitly *does* yield to that suggestion; in the earlier speech he could scarcely risk entertaining it at all. Only now, following upon the supernatural context that defines its malignity, is the 'suggestion' allowed the name 'intent'. The increase of self-knowledge brings with it a mood of exhaustion. 'Ambition is very poor ground upon which to build my plans.' It is noteworthy, too, that 'Ambition' is first a spur that will encourage the presumably unwilling horse of 'intent'. It then becomes the horse (or the rider) itself likely to fall in its attempt to carry out the plan, the vault over the risks of murdering Duncan. 'Intent' is identified, therefore, with a rash 'Ambition'. Professor Muir records the suggestions

---

[1] *Macbeth* I, iii, 134–6.

of a number of a commentators puzzled by the abrupt close of the speech.[1] He himself points out that the entrance of Lady Macbeth 'interrupts the soliloquy and fills in the gap', i.e. the metrical gap. But the Folio text seems to me superior to his arrangement. The Arden Edition has

> And falls on th'other. . . .
> *Enter Lady Macbeth.*
> How now! what news!

The Folio prints

> And falles on th'other.   *Enter Lady.*
> How now! What Newes!

The entrance of a person may interrupt a soliloquy, but I do not see how it can supply a metrical unit otherwise missing. There is room here for a very suitable pause to follow 'other'. The Folio full-stop may not mean much, but it allows us to explain it, as well as to omit it; explaining it in terms of the whole speech is not difficult. Macbeth has continually avoided looking to the consequence of his crime. He can be judged to balk here, especially, since he has just been contemplating both the likelihood of its failure, and the certainty of eternal punishment even if it succeeds. Or, keeping in mind the tone of his concluding words, he could reasonably be supposed to have in mind 'And I know too well what will happen then.' The blank third stress is both the blankness of Macbeth's mind as he faces the future, and the inexpressible load of meaning in that future. This is the first sounding of the note 'Tomorrow, and tomorrow, and tomorrow.'

It will not be difficult for the reader to judge the value of these observations for himself. I believe they are as complete an account of the speech as prose substitute should provide, and as its position in the play requires. Others will feel that more or less detail makes the necessary points, or that there are other points worth making besides the one I have emphasized. The reason for that emphasis follows from a conception of the play: that it is a growth as well as a structure, a process as well as a statement, and that Macbeth is the locus of those movements. These general contentions it is now possible to elaborate

[1] Arden, *Macbeth*, p. 41.

a little, in terms of the above speech. The speech is a miniature of the play. It contains within itself Macbeth's three 'phases': the first of 'confusion', the second of 'imagination', the last of 'resignation'. Typical of the anxiously analytical Macbeth, is the soliloquy in I, iii; of the visionary Macbeth, the exchange between him and his wife on the subject of Sleep after the murder; of the resigned Macbeth, accepting the necessity of his own nature, the lament in V, v. (The most apparent verbal point is a steady decrease in his trick of grammatical distortion.) Further, the moral growth of the speech imitates that of the play. At first, deceit, darkness, fear; growing out of these a strong positive morality, whose effect is to clarify the nature of the evil muffled in the opening; the evil, thus robbed of disguise, is found to be helpless before the onslaught of the moral response it set off. The intimate involvement of 'good' and 'evil' is apparent everywhere. Macbeth provides us with the most powerful and comprehensive description of the holy king. Besides this, Duncan's own words are mere hints, those of his nobles after the murder helpful suggestions, and the discussion of kingship in IV, iii *is* a discussion. As Professor Knights insists, it is a vital part of the play's thesis. But it is also necessary to insist that intention, however thoroughly achieved, ranks in importance below demonstration. Macbeth in this speech *goes through* what Malcolm and Macduff talk about. It is always Macbeth who is the vehicle of the play's most intensely felt life; he is by that token, the play's moral sense; his deep recognition of its positive morality counts for much more than its location in other persons of the play. Macbeth is the protagonist.

Professor Muir leans confidently, both in his Introduction to the play, and in his particular notes, upon a work by Curry entitled *Shakespeare's Philosophical Patterns*. Having quoted from this work at one point, he adds this footnote:

I dissent, therefore, from Wilson Knight's opinion expressed in *The Wheel of Fire*, p. 155, that Macbeth 'contends for his own individual soul against the universal reality . . . and emerges at last victorious and fearless.' [1]

I think the following sentence from Wilson Knight's discussion does that critic better justice: 'He has won through by

[1] *Macbeth* (Arden Edn.), p. lxv.

excessive crime to an harmonious and honest relation with his surroundings.'[1] The whole passage is very valuable. I choose the above sentence to typify both its profundity and its eccentricity. It is the word 'honest' that is profound; the word 'harmonious' that is eccentric. Macbeth does not behave harmoniously when he is being armed by Seyton. Yet all his longer speeches in Act V are possessed of a serene and gloomy clarity of insight. This is a point about his career much more important than comparing it with a philosophical pattern he may incidentally illustrate. Macbeth's career is a growth. His final state of mind is an achievement quite as much as a result. That result may be damnation in a theological sense. In a human sense it is a courageous honesty. The emergence of this 'honesty' (which relates the play to *Lear*, as its absence relates *Othello* with *Antony*) is as much a theme of the play as that of Damnation, The Unnatural, or Disorder. Macbeth's deepest intentions dominate him more and more. The more they do so, the more the audience are invited to see them as delusion ('Is this a dagger that I see before me?'). Yet the more he succumbs to them, the more thoroughly does he come to accept himself, and to know himself. As Wilson Knight insists, Macbeth shares quite as much as Macduff in the clarity of the play's conclusion. 'Good' and 'evil' remain inter-involved with each other. None of this is to say, I may well add, that 'we admire Macbeth in Act V, despite his wickedness'. While we must recognize the firm moral orientation of 'good' and 'evil', we do not identify with one and contemplate the other, either openly or secretly. Macbeth's nature unfolds itself, and is unfolded for us. This enactment is entirely sufficient and self-supporting; it requires no moral props, no philosophical buttressing. Shakespeare has provided more delicate and more revealing statements than can be supplied by those particular disciplines. If, on the other hand, *Lear* strikes us as more emphatic in its sense of affirmation than *Macbeth*, that is to be expected.

[1] *The Wheel of Fire*, p. 156.

JOHN DONNE

A Nocturnall Upon S. Lucies Day, Being the Shortest Day

Richard Sleight

Tis the yeares midnight, and it is the dayes,
Lucies, who scarce seaven houres herself unmaskes,
 The Sunne is spent, and now his flasks
 Send forth light squibs, no constant rayes;
  The worlds whole sap is sunke: 5
The generall balme th'hydroptique earth hath drunk,
Whither, as to the beds-feet, life is shrunke,
Dead and enterr'd; yet all these seeme to laugh,
Compar'd with mee, who am their Epitaph.

Study me then, you who shall lovers bee   10
At the next world, that is, at the next Spring:
 For I am every dead thing,
 In whom love wrought new Alchemie.
  For his art did expresse
A quintessence even from nothingnesse,   15
From dull privations, and leane emptinesse
He ruin'd mee, and I am re-begot
Of absence, darknesse, death; things which are not.

All others, from all things, draw all that's good,
Life, soule, forme, spirit, whence they beeing have;   20
 I, by loves limbecke, am the grave
 Of all, that's nothing. Oft a flood
  Have wee two wept, and so

Drownd the whole world, us two; oft did we grow
To be two Chaosses, when we did show   25
Care to ought else; and often absences
Withdrew our soules, and made us carcasses.

But I am by her death, (which word wrongs her)
Of the first nothing, the Elixer grown;
    Were I a man, that I were one,   30
     I needs must know; I should preferre,
       If I were any beast,
Some ends, some means; Yea plants, yea stones detest,
And love; All, all some properties invest;
If I an ordinary nothing were,   35
As shadow, a light, and body must be here.

But I am None; nor will my Sunne renew.
You lovers, for whose sake, the lesser Sunne
    At this time to the Goat is runne
     To fetch new lust, and give it you,   40
       Enjoy your summer all;
Since shee enjoyes her long nights festivall,
Let mee prepare towards her, and let mee call
This houre her Vigill, and her Eve, since this
Both the yeares, and the dayes deep midnight is.   45

I

UNLESS one is naturally attuned to the complex mechanics
of Donne's metaphysical style, a first reading of the Nocturnal
produces an effect as chaotic as the experiences on which the
poet has stamped order and harmony. Images of a dying sun, of
a complicated and mysterious alchemical experiment flash and
fade into the darkness, silence and apathy pervading the poem.
The intellect is tormented by subtle thought but fails to emerge
with the clues which would give an overall pattern. This, at any
rate, was my experience. The moods and tones of a speaking
voice came across, but their relation and point escaped. It was
therefore from a mood, a sense of silence, darkness, death and
other indefinite impressions that an understanding had to start.

Tis the yeares midnight, and it is the dayes,

Midnight is a time at which curious states of mind can exist. A feeling of unreality blends with a heightened awareness of oneself and with memories of what the ordinary world is and of past experiences. The immediate distractions of noise and movement are removed and in the stillness it is possible to believe that 'things in themselves as they really are' can be seen a little more clearly than usual. The few objects that still remain present to the senses may intrude on the thoughts with the intensity of symbols, collecting an enhanced significance from the general flow of energetic and ordered mental images. If they are introduced, they can give actuality to what would otherwise be a dream. They provide a standard of comparison commonplace enough to crush or ridicule all but the most strongly based structures of the imagination. The single mention of an object close to hand—the feet of the bed—has precisely this function: it stops the abstract images of intense thought from becoming too unreal. There is after all a room and a bed: the mind that can think about 'th'hydroptique earth' can also think about the 'beds-feet', and such a mind probably has a fairly solid grasp of the actual. Possibly the speculations about a shadow requiring a body and a light (l. 36) were brought to mind by the candle in his room. All the rest of the poem is by comparison abstract, laying down patterns of destruction (the sun burning out) or of recreation by means of destruction (distillation of quintessences).

He starts the poem on the larger time-scale of the year in an unexpected way. It is as if the year pivots on this night, and as if the climax of the year is its longest night. Somehow the night summarizes and comprehends the whole year. Parallel to the year, in meaning and scale, is 'the whole world' and the 'next world', all these forming a macrocosm created and ruled by Donne's own feelings at the moment of writing. The world dies as he remembers his own disintegration: the exhaustion of each part corresponds to the lack of life he finds in himself, so that the world's death becomes the means by which he perceives and communicates his own state. For the moment he becomes the world. He identifies himself with the exhausted sun which now throws off occasional brilliances, where before both he and it sent out a steady light. By the comparison and parallel, he remembers he once possessed an effortless power similar to the sun's. His vital energy has gone, in the same way that life has sunk with the retreating sap. He is as indifferent as the earth, listless in an overwhelming desire to sleep, afflicted with the disease of indifference, underneath which is an insatiable urge towards non-existence. The immensity of sun, world and earth suddenly contracts as life shrinks to the bed's feet, and he remains the epitaph of that power. In a more literal way, he is the epitaph. There is nothing else living remaining round him at this time, existence has collapsed into himself inside the room and night. The hugeness of world and earth is a measure of their vitality, and since vitality is the primary quality he wishes to emphasize in the antithesis and comparison of the world and himself, he makes the transition between the cosmic and the human, by centring attention on the word 'life', and shrinking 'life' towards the bed's feet. There is then no ridiculous clash between the giant collapse of sun and world and the pigmy shrinkage of the human, while the primarily personal relevance of the world's death is made clear. Again, the isolation felt during the night's stillness leads logically to the conclusion that he, being the last representative of life on the earth's surface, is the epitaph of life. 'dead and enterred'.

While he successively identifies himself with the power and universality of sun, earth and world, he is also separate from them. The death–burial–epitaph sequence strengthens the contact and culminates in 'yet all these seem to laugh, Compared with me who am their Epitaph.' The culmination also asserts the complete difference of the laughing 'these' and the epitaph 'me'. The two are distinct entities, though they may be compared. Because they both share in a common quality of disintegration and even more common feelings (indifference and desire for extinction), the comparison may be extended into a metaphor. But not wholly, not absolutely. This is not a Romantic metaphor having an absolute equivalence of emotion between its two parts within the context and therefore admitting no qualifications. In fact the difficulty in commenting on Donne's poetry is due to the absence of rigidity, and the number of qualifications that have to be made, each qualification indicative of a slightly different attitude to the main theme. His treatment of the world and therefore his relation to it changes in the next verse. After seriously describing the world's dissolution and his own steeper

34

descent to an epitaph in verse one, he immediately speaks lightly of the 'next world' to be created for other lovers by next spring (verse two). Perhaps after all it does not greatly matter that the world should die,—it will be re-created. And if the cer-tainty of re-creation does not hold for himself it holds for others and for other lovers. In the first verse there is a narrowing down of the field to the poet: all the external objects are partly used as sympathetic expressions of the poet's condition. At the begin-ning of the second verse, there is an abrupt re-direction of attention on to a world which is clearly independent of the poet and opposed to his present despair. The linkage between the two worlds is Donne's ironic invitation to study him. However abrupt the change is, and it is not so complete a reversal as the words 'subjective' and 'objective' would imply, the material is held together, almost held down, by refusing it meaning independent of the poet. Nothing external, such as the future world of the lovers, is allowed to be so external that it starts questions about the importance of the poet's feelings. These feelings are the basic material of the poem and also provide the binding which holds the material together. Yet how subtly he uses them; not to suggest an enclosure, but on the contrary an expanding range of subjects, broadened by their own inter-connections. In these lines about Spring's lovers he is gently disinflating the previous account of his own experience, without detracting from its validity for him, just as much as he is poking fun at the naïvety of those other lovers who will arrive so surely with next spring. By giving his experience a background which prevents it from being unique (so many poets assume they are the only lovers who will ever exist), he increases its actuality, and stops the conceits from running away into nonsense verse. There is a grotesque foolery about inviting incipient lovers to study an epitaph, which puts love itself in a setting (Donne's setting), gives it a beginning and an end instead of letting it float unconnected in the usual platitudinous manner.

The grotesqueness is extended to love's operations on a philo-sophical-alchemical level, allied with a deeper seriousness. He plays upon the idea that he is at once everything and nothing,— he is the grave of all which is nothing (ll. 22, 23). He specu-lates on the nature of his nothingness, it is the product of absence, darkness, death (ll. 15–19). Even when they showed care to anything external they became two chaosses, but her death allows him to suffer a deeper emptiness. 'Chaos' suggests the void out of which the world was created, and the biblical association is continued in the 'first nothing' of which he becomes the elixir after she dies. The 'first nothing' (1. 29) refers to the period when they were in love and absent from each other. It also calls up via the 'nothingnesse' of l. 15, the larger scale of disintegration—sun, world, earth (verse one), which is the cosmic image of his present desolation. The double reference gives a psychological continuity to the two states, a point of comparison which illuminates both. The cosmic size of events in verse three is again redeemed from its unintelligibly vast proportions by the minuteness of the alchemical operations, the philosophical conjecture, and the personal feeling, just as it was in the first verse by 'beds feet' and 'epitaph'.

Donne goes on to say that the quintessence which love has pressed out from the nothingness of his dull privations (1. 29) has been developed—he speaks of it as 'grown' organically, so that he is the elixir of the quintessence. This leads him to speculate on his own nature. He cannot be a man since he is not aware of having any of man's attributes. He does not share the simplest properties which even beasts and stones possess (1. 33). Paradoxically it is the beasts and stones who are personified, they 'detest and love'. He is deprived of the potentiality of choice and activity (ll. 31–33), and he is not as substantial as a shadow (an 'ordinary nothing', l. 35), for the light and the body throwing the shadow are not there. In short he has neither the qualities of a man nor of anything else: his sun is extinct (1. 37). His present feelings cannot be expressed by using the feelings of any other object or person. The difference between his sun and other lovers' is clear cut in the last verse. His is at an end, theirs is beginning. The disparity has been finally established: it was touched on in the distinction between his world and their world in verses one and two. Such love is now alien to him, and with it the world to which it belongs. A communion of the dead mistress with the exhausted poet is all that is left, most suitably taking place on the year's longest night. He accepts the night as a festival which brings him closer to his departed mistress. Thus the scale of values and the method of interpretation suggested by the first line: 'Tis the

yeares midnight', is returned to at the poem's end, its meaning
clarified. What is a reversal of a normal outlook in the first line
remains so at the end, but it loses its perverseness; the apathetic
grief changes into positive acceptance.

There is a further element in the first line, which fills out this
general account of the structure. If the longest night is taken as
the year's centrepiece, then the usual associations of the 'year'
are implicitly denied. A year normally evokes some idea of the
changing seasons, of a progressive movement through spring,
summer and winter. Midnight is hardly representative of such
a cycle. The 'normal' associations so deliberately avoided when
Donne is talking directly about his present state, are attached
either to the dead or dying world, or to other lovers. The
remarkable thing is that they do reappear. He might almost have
studied modern psychologists' views on how repressed mental
contents insist on being manifested. The normal associations
are carried on 'sap' (l. 5), 'spring' (l. 11), 'grow' (l. 24),
'sun' (ll. 35, 38), and 'summer' (l. 41). Each is used only
when he is referring to what he once was or what other lovers
will be again. 'Sap' is distinguished by its absence in his present
state, 'spring' will not arrive for him, nor will his 'sun' renew.
All these words are extensions of 'year' equals life, vitality,
change and growth. The usual associations have been forced
underground and the main position is occupied by the opposite
implications of 'yeares midnight' connoting the opposite of life.
'Year' reaches out in two directions, vital and non-vital, and
their sharp differentiation parallels the more logical dissection
of the differences between his past and present self which occurs
in the explicit meditation over the 'I am the grave of all,
that's nothing' theme.

One small inconsistency occurs in l. 29:

> But I am by her death, . . .
> Of the first nothing, the Elixer grown;

'Grown' certainly conflicts at first sight with the abstract limbo
he supposes himself to be in. But there is an ironical tone: he is
saying that nothing can be less organic, less capable of life than
the fractional distillation going on with himself inside the retort,
distilling him from one degree of nothingness to a still purer
form even more devoid of life. It also echoes 'grow' of line 24:

> oft did we grow
> To be two Chaosses, when we did show
> Care to ought else;

An external, non-organic change stepped in here, to turn them into voids when they took interest in anything but each other: the ironical tone hovers over this use too. There is as well the suggestion of flexibility, that things that grow apart can grow together again: the momentum of living is sufficient to carry the movement back again. 'Grow' in line 29 does not suggest flexibility, it is more in the sense of growing to a certain stage from which there is no turning back. Once you are the 'elixer', the completeness of your existence, however barren it may be, makes it difficult if not reprehensible to turn back. The whole weight of the alchemical search establishes this growth as a one-way process. 'Grow', as does 'year', looks both ways— towards the changing developing life of his past, and ironically to the static existence of his present.

II

The poem's surface movement has now been mapped out and it is not difficult to perceive. The mistress dies, the world seems to stop with her death. Nevertheless he also knows that external life goes on, that however long St. Lucies night is, St. Lucies day must follow. Thus he hovers between viewing the fact of cessation in himself, and the fact of continuance outside himself. And the emotional power is behind the former. He is caught in the conflict of evidence: this is an experience, an actually felt problem being dealt with, not a logical conundrum being worked out with a leavening of metaphysical wit. The problem has already achieved some balance before writing begins, although not an objective impersonal balance. Therefore the interpretation cannot be limited to a description of successive feelings in the poet, because while it is true that certain feelings did follow each other originally, these feelings in the poem are joined to the structure of its total expression, they have been 'understood' by the poet and placed in an explanatory framework. For instance, the bitterness and self-mockery of the first verse culminating in the poet as epitaph is not merely bitterness and self-mockery. The means used to express that bitterness—the dissolution of all vital energy in the world—sketch the coming resolution. When Hamlet considers:

> Whether 'tis nobler in the mind to suffer
> The slings and arrows of outrageous fortune,
> Or to take arms against a sea of troubles,
> And by opposing, end them?

he is presenting himself with a real choice. But the audience can cut through the obstructive padding, and see that the way he looks at his dilemma precludes the possibility of choice. 'To take arms against a sea of troubles' is an almost impossible task. 'Arms' are ineffectual against a 'sea': the scale of the defence is out of all proportion to the engulfing power of the attack. 'And by opposing, end them' is mere wishful thinking. Which action is more noble burkes the question of which is practical. The assumption that a noble course of action is necessarily successful, illuminates the theoretical nature of Hamlet's questioning. So, in Donne. Because he has attached his feelings of despair to the symbol of temporary decline in nature, there is good reason to suppose that despair will inevitably turn into a new life, just as spring must return after winter, just as the longest night must give place to day. Shakespeare by his choice of images describes both Hamlet's overt thoughts, his conscious mind working in the full light of consciousness, and his unspoken attitude towards action which he himself is far from being clear about. Donne chooses as the symbol of disillusion emptiness and death, the things in which death is only a temporary state (year, night, world), and thus foreshadows that more obscure knowledge which insists that life goes on. There is no need to credit Donne with marvellous cleverness. Life does not go on unless somewhere underneath the state of despair there is the conviction in the 'blood' that it must continue, and that therefore a state of approximate balance will emerge. It is but accurate psychological observation. Donne is writing dramatic poetry in that he presents both present feelings, and those that will emerge, in exactly the same way that Shakespeare does.

Some of the grades of feeling attached to the changing and developing structure of metaphor can be partly translated into ordered thought. A few of them have already been mentioned:

the sun, an equivalent to masculine strength and virility, serves to evoke Donne's previous relationship and the present absence of it; the cosmic shrinkage to the 'beds feet' provides a standard of comparison, a touch of actuality, and a further description of past and present states: 'day', 'year' and 'night' each have their separate trains of associations, combining and recombining to elevate them to the level of symbols whose point of confluence is yet to be determined. The vaguely military connotations of 'spent', 'flasks', 'squibs', plus the raillery in suggesting that the sun's death is as comic and entertaining as a firework display, plus the expiration of the earth in a dropsical sleep, which is comic, disgusting, startlingly horrid, a neat introduction of knowledge and wit, and the animal complement of the sun's disintegration, plus the heavy rhymes and continuous alliteration emphasizing the situation's seriousness and parodying its gravity, add up to a changing flux of feelings, thoughts and attitudes, in which it is difficult to isolate the elements and impossible to give each a fixed position. They cannot be made simple enough to stand still under the analyst's eye, but continue to show a further facet of meaning as they come within each other's attracting range. Without going into all their logical ramifications, it can be said that their emotional intensity and hence their relative meanings fluctuate according to the reader's standpoints—the standpoints that Donne attempts to give him. The amount of fluctuation, and there is much of it, may be lodged against the poem as a defect. That Donne was trying to communicate a confused state of feelings is a partial defence. He certainly does very much more with the common equivalence of some phase of nature and love's despair. That he is extraordinarily ingenious is neither a defect nor a merit, but that every involution of his ingenuity corresponds with an actual phase of the experience described is sufficient justification of his stylistic system.

A disappointment with the structure of presentation (symbols like 'world' used to define his present misery and foreshadow his approaching tranquillity simultaneously, determine the spine of that structure), a dissatisfaction with the kind of things the style asks the reader to connect with the main topic (specimen dissatisfaction: 'what connection have quintessences and Elixers with the absence of his mistress?'), may primarily be a result of a Romantic-injected predilection for straight, hard-hitting emotions with no double aspects. In particular tragic and comic are not easily intermingled to-day, and tragedy is rarely admitted to have a comic side. It is sacrilegious to suggest that death has an objectively comic aspect as well as a subjectively tragic one, and the crime is not less if it is oneself who is dying. Death nowadays is too personal a subject, too like the end of oneself, to permit an ironical humour. The final catastrophe of 'Lear' shows the comic, cruelly comic sight if you like, of the man who is forced into death by a fate which leaves him no breathing space. Picasso uses the same device to arouse conflicting emotions in his paintings of harlequins—the clown who is laughed at on the stage is pathetic when removed from the stage. The device depends upon the fact that any event, however tragic, may also appear humorous if placed in a large enough setting, if seen in a deep enough perspective. The superimposed surroundings must be large enough to dwarf the immediate world of the sufferer and with it the power of his personal feelings to dominate the onlooker. That such humour can scarcely exist without calling down all the means of social disapproval, is a measure of the degree to which modern western society is attached to its discovery of personal feelings and thoughts and of the value it places on the immediate effects they have on people. The laughter may be called inhuman, just because the setting is so vast that personal human feelings no longer count. The condemnation is principally the result of a reluctance to define 'human' and 'inhuman'. The clown is humorous as performer, but pathetic as individual. Donne's experience is directly painful to himself, and slightly humorous when translated into cosmic terms—the larger surrounds of world, earth and sun; the *implicit* self-mockery is at first glance distasteful and the poem is therefore considered artificial.

The rebuttal of such a criticism is contained in the word 'implicit'. If a poet advertises an awareness of his misery as laughable with the same energy he applies to portraying that misery, he sacrifices the truth to the pleasure of calling attention to his cleverness and cynicism. Apathy cannot be communicated if there is also attached a request for admiration of the person because he is clever enough to feel apathetic. But Donne is ironic at his own expense without being pleased at his irony: he is implicit, not explicit. As often happens he develops the feelings within feelings, the experience seen from inside and outside, one stage further than expected. He goes on to insist in the second verse that he is clever and he smiles at his own arrogance. Future lovers are to take lessons from him. He patronizes them when he takes their arrival for granted, as if everything is already known about them, and they arouse no further interest. But the tone of the lines shows he is also mocking at his own arrogance. In addition he is half serious when he equates 'next world' and 'next spring'. He places these lovers on the same level of interest as he himself was when in love. This effect is obtained by continuing the 'world' metaphor of the first verse: the world which died there was his previous vitality and love, and its resurrection will be not for him but for other lovers.

Donne is able to keep on getting outside the subjective limits of his feelings. He can therefore describe the past with the verisimilitude of an observer, while maintaining its essential inner connection with the present. What he is now, does not distort what he was, nor does it prevent him from re-creating the past as it actually occurred. The same ability is seen in his purely descriptive verse: he writes about a storm with the exactness he applies to anatomizing love. The two abilities of writing metaphysical poetry and of vividly visualizing an event are two sides of the one talent.

His method of using metaphor and the literal sense of the metaphorical objects to aid each other and of using a metaphor which illustrates a local point while it also prefigures and strengthens the poem's overall structure, is employed as has been said to go beyond subjective impressions, to develop through the refinement of his reactions a precise and three-dimensional account of his subject. More and more complicated and exact attitudes to the subject are established until from any one attitude any other may be reached. The method implies the unity of the material. Instead of a series of points round which the poet gathers appropriate detail to achieve a cumulative effect, there is one point to which everything else is related. It may be called the 'experience'. The experience is seen and treated as a unity however disparate its constituents. The whole takes pre-eminence over the parts. For instance the time sequence of the actual events becomes subsidiary to the structure which makes those events into a unity. Since it is the unity which above all gives significance to the events, it is not surprising that it should dictate their inter-relations and alter their time sequence.

Everything is done to make time branch out from the moment of writing. The non-sequitur of the first verse is a result of this. If it is the year's midnight at one instant, the sun cannot be shining at the same time. The punctuation might be revised, but it is preferable to regard the contradiction as an attempt to make all the important slices of time subservient to and under the control of the short period during which the poet is writing. 'The sun is spent' could refer in general to the shortened days of winter, but 'and now his flasks' etc., rules that possibility out. Instead the deficiency is well hidden by the sequence 'year', 'day', one line of description (l. 2), and 'sun', which stops the mind spotting a contradiction.

Looking once more at those future lovers, it is seen that they are sandwiched between an invitation to study the poet's condition and explanation of why his love-forlorn person will be so interesting to them. True, there is also mention of the 'next world' and 'next spring' which might be thought to break the present moment's domination; on the contrary they keep the attention inside the moment, because their direction towards it has already been outlined in the first verse. Equally what has happened in the past does not stand by itself; it enters only because it reflects directly on the present. The several statements: 'I am every dead thing', 'I am the grave of all', 'I am the elixir of the first nothing', 'I am not an ordinary nothing', sum up the effect of her death on him. Although they may have roughly corresponded to successive states in himself, they now appear as facets of the one thing: himself at this moment. They have been robbed of temporal separation in order to become simultaneous descriptions. One of the easiest methods of binding events more closely together other than just by their relevance to a central topic, is to make them appear to occur at the same time. Indeed the literal equivalent of the 'radial time' technique is the choice of a clearly defined instant as the beginning and ending of the poem. The poet is, by this means, one up on the experience before he starts writing.

He has achieved one measure of control, imposed order and unity by limiting the discreteness of his subject in time. It is only when he has made the moment secure enough to resist being split up into time intervals, that he explicitly introduces her death (l. 28), because her death brings in a clearly defined period of time whch threatens the central dominance of the present. Paradoxically it is not until then that the simultaneity of the various equivalences is recognized, that for instance

> I am every dead thing,
> In whom love wrought new Alchemie

refers to a period after her death, not to the beginning of the affair.

The material is never allowed to escape from its unity into water-tight compartments of time. The love of the past is not to be considered as a whole in itself. It is hedged about with sign-posts to all the other elements of the experience. In fact some of the descriptive terms are the same:

> Oft a flood
> Have wee two wept, and so
> Drownd the whole world, us two;

Remove 'world', a term already loaded with various connotations, and 'flood' loses its point: the lines just boast their copious weeping. And if 'world' had not had its significances previously attached, the description of their weeping would degenerate into a trite and somewhat exaggerated metaphor.

It is interesting to trace the positive gains of this method. He is able to dispense with a motive: they do not weep about anything, neither for joy nor grief: the motive is irrelevant, the fact alone counts. To present the reader with a fact, assumes that he can understand it in relation to something else, and so the framework of understanding is provided by the terms of the description. 'World', of course, refers back to the two opposing questions it poses in verse one: whether life has stopped completely or whether it is temporarily suspended and will again issue in new life. These qualities do not mix directly with the equivalence of 'us two' and 'world' here, but they contribute a sense of depth to the word; something important and complicated is being mentioned. 'World' draws together some present characteristics of Donne's present desolation and his past happiness.

In verse one his own emptiness coincides with an absence of energy in the world. Whether the absence is temporary or permanent is a question hovering in the background. In verse three Donne and his mistress are the whole world. The two uses of the word obviously refer it to different objects, but by using the same word, the possibility of a relation between the objects is suggested. Thus 'world' is the term which is to reveal something about his present situation and something of his previous condition. In both cases the word's normal use contributes an impression of largeness—'there's more to this than my personal feelings'—but there is a very marked distinction between the two functions of this large cosmic element. He has no vital energy in the first verse, he is a piece of writing on a tombstone commemorating the power, energy and harmony of sun, world and earth. Being empty of feeling, indifferent to everything, he drags in these outer elements to illustrate his apathy. In verse three, however, he sees no outer elements; the only world which is, is created by themselves and provides a sufficient universe for them to live in. Nature's disorganization and collapse is not of his own making, but is conveniently there for him to project his feelings on to. When he was in love there was no order of nature beyond that which they created for themselves. The breakdown of their personally created world allows him to perceive an external organization. When she was alive the world started with themselves, when she died the identification split into its components: Donne and the 'world' became separate entities. I think this subtle presentation of the difference between the two states disposes of the opinion that the poem is an elaborate but fundamentally artificial piece of mourning over a deceased patroness. If it had been written under these circumstances he might have drawn the distinction between the mental conditions resulting from grief and love, but he would not have united them in such an integral way by using the same word to comprehend both. Two parts of the same metaphor describe his love and its absence.

In the last paragraph the objects which the word refers to in its two uses have been supposed similar and because of this the one word unifies present and past conditions much more closely than could have been done otherwise. But the only likeness mentioned is a common quality of 'largeness'—a vague attribute which springs more from the word's common usage than its contexts in the poem. Most readers would probably agree that the word has some such unifying effect as has been described; the reasons for the effect are not so easy to find. I think the effect must repose either in common properties or in a common substance, and as there seems to be no trace of the latter the former must be responsible.

Such a search might have been playing with words: the only argument against the accusation was the impression of a more deep-seated structure than appeared on the poem's surface.

The world in both metaphors is acted upon by external forces: nature or the lovers. The second metaphor, dissociated from its application, has many possible associations. The 'flood' recalls the biblical inundation (the Old Testament is also behind the succeeding 'chaosses' and elsewhere in the 'first nothing'). The common factor of the associations is annihilation followed by a new construction. Although the destruction is absolute ('drowned the whole world') there is never any doubt that a full harmony will be restored; the destruction is intimately part of the creation. In the context, on a personal level the lovers oscillate between the extremes of nothingness and unity, between the absence of individuality and distinctness because they are drowned, and their presence united in one whole, because they are mutually and fully recognized. The poles have no intermediate stages, and so the final unity is complete, undisturbed by extraneous or local qualifications. The same effect of absolute polarity is gained from the movements into and out of 'chaosses' and 'carcasses'. The lovers are the agents and the objects of the processes: everything is comprehended in their being. The Old Testament associations also contribute the idea of purification, of a more intimate union (wicked removed by drowning).

The metaphor in verse one is a close parallel: a dying world may herald another spring, a long night does precede the day: destruction may be followed by new life. The similarity is a major and striking link. The underlying shape of the poem begins to form.

Lovers are somewhat akin to 'primitives': they share a sense of communion with their environment, so that they do not need to distinguish between themselves and it; an outworn term is 'participation mystique' and it fits very well here. Whether this environment is 'objective' or whether it is conjured out of the unconscious does not much matter. The lovers in this poem provide their own environment: themselves; anything outside it does not exist in its own right, since it breaks the bond between them. 'Chaosses' and 'carcasses' do not feel, see, or think, at the best they are in a state of becoming. The corollary is that external objects must become parts of the private environment, must be understood on those terms, if they are to be included at all. For instance the change of the seasons either harmonizes with the private world or is discounted as alien and hostile. It is for the lovers to choose or reject. Those who are guided by the position of sun among constellations, waiting expectantly for it to reach the Goat, are a dull sort, controlled in their love-making by external forces. The real lover notices that the constellations have organized themselves well enough to provide a suitable conjunction for the occasion, or he may go further and see their movements as part of the pattern of his own love.

When separation finally and irreversibly occurs, Donne becomes a chaos in his own right, a void single and alone. No longer able to look for a renewed relation, his mind begins to register the external world. A fresh 'participation mystique' is established. He perceives the begetters of his own apathy, 'absence, darkness and death', under the image of the collapse of day into night. He brilliantly selected a faulty metaphor, for the night does not remain eternal. It must become day. Therein lies the metaphorical presentation of his own predicament. How can he ever move forward into the day? Light and new life cannot figure despair, even if the coming day only unmasks herself for seven hours.

Out of this first metaphor, he provides the material for a further description of his feelings, and for the coming resolution (in the context this is literally the new day). At first the night is made to seem permanent, making an apparent eternity of his grief. This is done by constructing his poem round the centre of the darkest night, so that its gloom and prodigious length seem to go on for ever; and by placing himself inside it—

the epitaph of all dead and dying objects. The graveyard is an apt image: although there is a certainty of resurrection, epitaphs stay put, there is no second life for them: and so he condenses his own death for as long as is required, that is, until the movement towards re-creation makes the continuation of the death untrue and therefore irrelevant. The equivalence of poet and epitaph might be read as an attempt to throw off the logic of the night-day metaphor. A stage in the cycle of night and day is selected and perpetuated, because it best represents the poet's feelings. But it is unsatisfactory to believe that grief, however severe, is eternal except in Romantic poetry. The pretence is a deliberate refusal to admit what is well known, and what is well known under the literal terms of the metaphor is that day follows night. Donne is very adroit in the way he puts this piece of detail across: the presentation reflects the sequence of his reactions after her death. The natural first reaction is a dogged adherence to his overpowering feelings of grief. Yet he manages to suggest that the first reaction is temporary without going any further into it. In fact he uses the same elements that portrayed his grief to image the new life that takes its place. The metaphors are worked out so that they describe, interpret and anticipate. In this respect, they bring together three levels of time: the time immediately after her death, the succeeding reflections and the reintegration. The reflections themselves describe the intervening journey in relation to the initial dissolution and the final rapprochement.

The Old Testament echoes of 'flood' have been mentioned earlier; they reinforce the destruction-creation theme, common to Donne's love when his mistress was alive and when she is dead. Purification is suggested: selective drowning removes the bad from the good. Purification and refinement are what he is subjected to during the intermediate stage on the way from grief to reconciliation. On the surface the refinement appears to have no purpose, and its only effect is to intensify his grief. The poem now splits up into three parts which can, when put together again, reconstruct the whole experience. There is destruction-creation and less noticeably purification when they are both alive; a complete destruction of this self-created world on her death, which may either stagnate into permanence or receive and produce a new alignment; a final integration of the broken pieces. The poem's success hinges on the ambiguity of its middle section. To accept the apathy as permanent is to be encased in one's own grief and would give an unsatisfactory and incomplete ending; to pretend that a reconciliation was easy would be equally untrue to the facts; therefore the ambiguity must be continued. Reintegration or relapse must appear equally possible almost to the end. The chance of either happening would be prevented, if one was definitely chosen. Equal power has to be given to factors which might result in either. Of course the reader knows by looking at the last lines, and the poet knew by experience, the actual outcome, and the balance is therefore slightly in favour of reintegration. How subtly this is done, without either falsifying the possibilities or disturbing the convincingness of the ending, I hope to show in a moment. It is Donne's master-stroke: the tying-up of all loose ends, at the same time not departing from the letter of his experience: exact description and interpretation become one.

The poem has been fully explained with the help of Paracelsus. But Donne was not so naïve as to believe in alchemy, and not believing, he could not base his poem directly on that particular philosophy. Jung has made a convincing case for alchemy as the guise under which the process of individuation was described in western Europe; certainly something of a mysterious and sacred atmosphere must have surrounded the practice of alchemy, even when it was avowedly scientific. Jung's hypothesis provides a deeper reason for Donne's choice here; something like individuation takes place. However, this essay is only concerned to show how intimately the alchemical image is linked with the rest of the subject matter, and if it had not been so linked, the symbolical meaning and power of alchemy would have been insufficient to pull the poem together.

Alchemy was an attempt to reduce the world to its primary substance, to discover and isolate the true nature of material and spiritual being. Love comes along and alters all that:

> Love wrought new alchemy

what was before incapable of success is now to be achieved. The wildest dreams are to come true; who would have expected the fifth essence, the basic material of the universe to be present in 'nothingness', who but love could isolate it? Donne is tilting at

49

the alchemists and at himself taking himself too seriously. The occurrence of 'grow' has been previously noticed. It is one of a group (sap, spring, etc.) which are never applied to his present state. The use in line 29 which contradicts this generalization may be explained as ironical. It was, however, this example which first suggested to me the underlying plan of the poem. 'Growth' necessarily means a more than mechanical change, it implies development in a living organism away from an immature stage. But it is clear that love creates a deeper and deeper despair, refining a tenuous material into something less substantial. To change from the 'first nothing' to its 'elixir' is a further step towards non-existence, and can scarcely be called growth. The word links the beginning of the poem where the poet's despair is described in terms of arrested natural order and change, and the period of harmony when she was alive. Its use here points the difference between what appears to be the nature of an experience to the subject—an affair of sudden alterations—and the much more continuous change which goes on unnoticed. The superficial transition in the poem is from the depths of despair to some degree of tranquillity. The intermediate stage is not noticed, although it occurs simultaneously with the deepening of the unhappiness. But this stage is indicated by 'grown', both in itself, and in its relations in the poem which widen its range of significance. The two complementary sides to the experience,—the deepening of despair outbalancing the groping towards tranquillity, are exactly parallel to the metaphor of the first verse. The temporary death of the sun leads to the following day, just as the poet's increasing unhappiness precedes its own resolution.

The poem succeeds best where it is most obscure, that is in the sudden movement from a process of destruction culminating in transcendental non-existence, to a period of renewed being. There appears to be no transition. That there should be none is a skilful presentation of what a person's reactions may be: he can feel transported from grief to joy, from one state to an opposed state without a noticeable break, and with scarcely any reason apparent to him. Yet he assumes that there is a connecting link, that there are reasons for the replacement, and perhaps on reflection he is able to propose some causes. Both elements are needed for an experience to appear credible to an observer, and further for him to share that experience. He must see destruction and tranquillity with something of the force of their impact on the subject, he must also be able to relate them intelligibly: they should not be haphazard. Further, any relation deduced must spring from their own nature. I mean the explanation cannot be a cliché: 'he became happy because all human grief will terminate in joy'. That is insufficient. The explanation must be able to secure thinking assent, as well as agreement through habit. The reader is to perceive that this is how the poet felt, and he must somehow absorb with the poet's description the reasons why the poet's experience changed so abruptly. This can be done by putting description of the two phases of the experience in the same metaphors as its analysis and interpretation.

Donne does exactly this. He preserves psychological realism by playing up the distinctness of the long destructive phase and the succeeding reconciliation: 'this is how it appeared to me at the time'. But the terms of his description of destruction anticipate the re-creation. Night is always followed by day, even the longest night of the year must be followed by the day; winter presages spring. Each of these things has the two qualities: present annihilation, future life. The division is objectified further: alchemy is a more specific example of failure in a search or of continuous and apparently permanent annihilation, and the division is developed in a very complex way. Alchemy aims at an act of creation more ambitious than most others: the deprivations and sufferings (when the metaphor is applied to the suffering lover) are therefore more thoroughgoing. The result of an alchemical experiment is a foregone conclusion: failure (they never find the philosopher's stone). The prospect of certain defeat seems to cut off the possibility of reconciliation more firmly than the description of the dying sun. The potentiality for life of the alchemical experiment seems practically nil. This potentiality is split off and appears hardly perceptible in 'grow' of

> the first nothing, the Elixer grown

Reduction from one stage of annihilation to the next is also growth. At the same time, within the conditions of an alchemical experiment, the goal, the unattainable has been

51

obtained: the Elixir has been produced; but the Elixir of in-substantiality seems useless. This is not the place for a neat metaphysical paradox: wit perhaps, or dry humour, but what principally happens is a new juxtaposition of creation and destruction on which the poles are as far apart as possible: the Elixir and nothingness. The echoes of 'nothing' save the meta-phor from declining into cleverness; that from which the world came, which was a temporary chaos felt individually by the lovers, is not negligible.

Here it would be easy to say that the poet supposes himself to achieve some spiritual communion with his dead mistress, and that the mystic intensity of their souls' interanimation balances (if it is not explained by) the longer account of his death to the world. But this appears to be fitting a ready-made interpretation on to the poem, whereas that interpretation actually evolves itself and doesn't need to be a superimposed hypothesis. Every human attribute has been stripped from the poet; everything that is positive, even the capability of casting a shadow, has been removed: the poet approaches a state of non-being. On the other side of the dividing line is Lucy. Thus Donne's utter emptiness is a void of different quality from the particular examples chosen to illustrate it. Each of the latter was a temporary stage towards a further positive creation: the day, spring or whatever it was. But the tranquillity that settles on the last four lines is not pregnant with a new upheaval: 'nor will my Sun renew'. It is a balance which no mischievously vital dialectic will overturn. Slight adjustments such as dying in the normal human sense may be indicated in

> Let mee prepare towards her

but no major disturbance is wanted to make the harmony com-plete. Lucy the mistress and St. Lucy are combined, because the midnight of the saint's day is furthest removed from all im-mediate aspects of life. The poet travels through a series of destruction–creation units, whereby he approaches a negative existence, ending where destruction and creation are not two opposed and complementary events succeeding one another in time, but where destruction becomes a mode of creation. The time-lag, in itself suggestive of the poet's withdrawal from ordinary dimensions of living, has been removed, because the destruction of each human quality, of the will, the power of choice, brings him nearer to communion with her. Thus what might appear to be a spiritual paradox, 'destruction and creation are to be regarded as two halves of the same event' (or some such statement), is worked out in careful detail and logically developed.

The antithetical principles at work in the poem, which are responsible for its movement, cease to operate in the final lines of the poem. The absolute balance attained in the last line between year, day, midnight, makes it impossible to write any more. Once these elements, so liable to explode into warring ideas and produce the movements of life, have been subdued, then nothing remains alive. The basis has fallen out of the poem, the final reconciliation of opposing principles has been achieved.

Donne's conclusion is not so far from life as it at first seems to be. 'Eve' and 'vigil' re-establish the passage of time, and locate the poem as springing from a mood in time; 'enjoys' is deliberately applied to Lucy and her festival and the 'other lovers' eagerly awaiting the sun's passage to the Goat. He does not definitely commit himself to the harmony of death nor the dialectic of living.

III

There remains Donne's style. Critics often say that the direct almost conversational tone compensates for the roughness, with the implication that a man as passionate as Donne can get away with unpolished verse where less furious poets would be mundane. This is no excuse. The style is appallingly rough, and grates on the ear. The proliferation of hisses in the first four lines—nineteen of them—shows a poet who is determined to disregard the sensitivity of his audience. Assonances are crowded alongside incessant alliteration, the rhythm jerks along, the heavy rimes drag the mind away from the sense of the lines, and tricks of syntax are irritatingly repeated. There is no need to write like this to be direct, nor have such deplorable mannerisms any connection with colloquial speech.

'All others, from all things, draw all that good.' By the third 'all' the ear has wearied of the sound, and the meaning has been more than established. However that is not enough; the word crops up in the same verse:

> am the grave
> Of all, that's nothing.

in the next verse:

> All, all some properties invest;

and in the last verse:

> Enjoy your summer all;

where annoyingly enough it is made a rime-word, so that the ear gets quite accustomed to the sound. By which time, the reader notices it in verse one:

> Yet all these seeme to laugh,

Directly Donne's mind seizes a word, he seems to require to hear it over and over again. Renew, you, new, you, he sounds in the final verse; and in the last two stanzas: her, her, were, were, prefer, were, were (here), her, her, her, her. Allowing for changes of pronunciation, there are a multitude of repetitions.

> and often absences
> Withdrew our souls, and made us carcasses.

The rime falls on the unaccented syllables, which tends to prolong the sounds of both words; as they are prolonged so each second syllable is more clearly articulated, the difference in pronunciation becomes more marked. The rhythm also helps to lengthen them. Thus the two factors which are supposed to produce at least a semblance of order in verse, have an opposite result. This result satisfactorily accounts for the reader's irritation with the style. Adding to his irritation is the blatantly obvious hissing of too many s's. Donne is not writing smooth verse, nor attempting to: an explanation can be found.

Each word in this last example is wrenched away from its usual sound pattern by the rime, and has to be pronounced with more deliberate articulation than is normal. The words receive more attention, and because they contain the principal meaning of the lines, such attention reinforces the sense of the passage. The separation in sound also contributes to the impression of disorganization following on the cleavage between soul and body. The external force used to rime these words is parallel to the external force (whatever it is) which parts the lovers. The former, while designed to cause cohesion, produces disunion, and the latter produces disunion directly. Because the rime has these two aspects of unity and disunity stemming from the same cause a conflict arises, which helps to make the strain of the lover's absence a physically real thing.

In a general way the unvoiced s's convey the emptiness and purposelessness of separation. The s's are first associated with the 'absences' of 'souls' so that their recurrence in 'carcasses' primarily recalls this. Thus the gaps left by the souls' withdrawal are represented by the hissings in 'carcasses'. An absolute vacuum is not left: the heavy vowel sounds of 'carcasses' are the auditory equivalents of the physical bodies deprived of their animating force: they still exist, although they have no principle of action. At no point does the sound interfere with the meaning, it is integral to the purpose, being neither a decorative trimming nor an innocuous addition. Donne describes the effect of absence, the emptiness of bodies without souls, and he does not omit the continuing solid existence of those bodies condemned to passivity and senselessness until they have been reanimated by the soul's presence. 'Else' and 'chaosses', and possibly 'chao-' with 'care' and 'aught' have a similar function in the previous two lines. Showing 'care to ought else' makes them two 'chaosses'; the sounds translate the meaning: showing interest in other things physically resulted in two 'chaosses'.

Verse 1 has three consecutive accented rimes: sunk-drunk-shrunk. If each is given a full emphasis monotony results, but the rhythm varies the weight placed on each. The pause after 'sunk' fixes the rime word in the mind, where it remains to chime, but not to obtrusively shout, its agreement with 'drunk' and 'shrunk'. The rime scheme itself is utilized to silhouette the meaning's movement. The three lines contain a descent increasing in momentum from the world, to life buried in the earth. They embrace and unite the magnitudes of cosmic and human things. The images change more quickly and the steps between them grow larger. The reader is again distracted from the rimes' insistence, by the balance set up between the halting, rushing rhythm, and the lines' meaning which is the negation of energy.

Alliteration of 's' is especially prominent:

Lucies who scarce seven hours herself unmaskes

nine s's, four in the next line and so on. In this line the day's tremulous weakness is expressed by the repetition of 's', in combination with 'k' and/or long vowels. In the next two lines, the same alliteration is associated with the expiring sun but mostly with shorter vowels, explosives and dentals which take the place of liquids and continuants. The similarity of the two occurrences is seen in the shared rime 'flasks' and 'masks'. They are also dissimilar. Instead of the day trembling into and out of existence, the sun is dying in convulsive bursts of light and cracks of explosion, a longer and greater struggle. So what appears to be an excessive alliteration of 's', now splits into two types of alliteration, joined respectively to the day and the sun—

who scarce seven hours herself unmaskes

is associated with a different range of sounds and of meaning from

The sun is spent, and now his flasks
Send forth light squibs, no constant rays;

The alliteration ties the two processes together: a rapidly diminishing day, and an exhausted Sun, they are two aspects of lessening energy in the world, yet the alliteration does not seem overdone, because it also represents both aspects as essentially distinguishable things.

The images are also separate. It is difficult to relate by any sort of imaginative effort, the more and more infrequent explosions of the sun, to the retiring self-effacement of the day. The sun erupts violently, the day maintains a constant weakness. The sun is masculine, he 'sends forth' light squibs, while the day is feminine, she 'unmasks' herself. I have already suggested a temporary identification of Donne with the sun's power, and therefore Lucy with his mistress, and there is a further way of looking at this identification. The moment of midnight, that is when Donne composes his Nocturnal, belongs to day and year. The day is specifically stated to be Lucy, and the year is her complementary unit on the larger time-scale. The year's significance is expanded in the image of the sun dying. They are both united in the possession of the moment of midnight, because they are both in a state of weakness and exhaustion, and they are united only in this moment. Under the terms of my identification, Donne and his mistress can feel themselves most united at this instant, in the possession of a common quality symbolized by midnight. It is not necessary to insist on the interpretation outright; it should be treated as an implication, present but not intended to be fully and consciously realized.

> Tis the yeares midnight, and it is the dayes

The union is temporary, the rhythmic units within the halves split by the caesura are different in pattern. They move in opposite directions, 'day's' is drawn on to 'Lucies', and only then does its sense seem completed: when it is involved with the actual existence of a particular day. However perfunctory the day is, it is sufficient that it exists. The 'unmasking' seems an action complete in itself, more expressive of being than all the energetic splutterings of the sun. But the year is general, diffuse, energetic without a purpose, it bursts upon the reader with an assertive determination and abruptly ceases.

Not until the end do the year and day achieve harmony and cease to pull in opposite directions. The intervening lines reduce the divergences by regarding the past love, the intervening misery, and the present state, as parts of the one experience. Once the unity has replaced the sharpness of each part of the experience, as the dominant feature, then that unity leads directly to its full completion, to the restoration of a perfectly balanced union. The threads that seemed to lead in so many different directions in the body of the poem have linked up:

> since this
> Both the yeares and the dayes deep midnight is.

'Year' and 'day', masculine and feminine, are given equivalent status, the rhythm no longer divides into incompatible parts split by an impassable caesura. Donne does not claim sentimentally, mystically or in any other easy and incomprehensible way, that he has secured absolute harmony. The possibility of it was hovering in the background at the beginning, but now that he has fitted the pieces together and established his own identity by recognizing his nothingness, he says:

Let me prepare towards her, and let me call
This hour her vigil and her eve.

It is not a perfect union, it is a preparation, a vigil and an eve, but
not a consummation. Neither the yearning for the impossible,
nor the contemplation of the improbable, but the meditation
resolving in the acceptance of what is.

ANDREW MARVELL

An Horatian Ode upon Cromwel's Return from Ireland

L. D. Lerner

The forward Youth that would appear
Must now forsake his *Muses* dear,
   Nor in the Shadows sing
   His Numbers languishing.
'Tis time to leave the Books in dust,   5
And oyl th'unused Armours rust,
   Removing from the Wall
   The Corslet of the Hall.
So restless *Cromwel* could not cease
In the inglorious Arts of Peace,   10
   But through adventrous War
   Urged his active Star.
And, like the three fork'd Lightning, first
Breaking the Clouds where it was nurst,
   Did thorough his own Side   15
   His fiery way divide.
For 'tis all one to Courage high
The Emulous or Enemy;
   And with such to inclose
   Is more then to oppose.   20
Then burning through the Air he went,
And Pallaces and Temples rent:
   And *Caesars* head at last
   Did through his Laurels blast.

'Tis madness to resist or blame   25
The force of angry Heavens flame:
  And, if we would speak true,
  Much to the Man is due.
Who, from his private Gardens, where
He liv'd reserved and austere,   30
  As if his highest plot
  To plant the Bergamot,

Could by industrious valour climbe
To ruine the great Work of Time,
  And cast the Kingdome old   35
  Into another Mold.
Though Justice against Fate complain,
And plead the antient Rights in vain:
  But those dò hold or break
  As Men are strong or weak.   40

Nature that hateth emptiness,
Allows of penetration less:
  And therefore must make room
  Where greater Spirits come.
What Field of all the Civil Wars,   45
Where his were not the deepest Scars?
  And *Hampton* shows what part
  He had of wiser Art.

Where, twining subtile fears with hope,
He wove a Net of such a scope,   50
  That *Charles* himself might chase
  To *Caresbrooks* narrow case.
That thence the *Royal Actor* born
The *Tragick Scaffold* might adorn:
  While round the armed Bands   55
  Did clap their bloody hands.

He nothing common did or mean
Upon that memorable Scene:
  But with his keener Eye
  The Axes edge did try: 60
Nor call'd the *Gods* with vulgar spight
To vindicate his helpless Right,
  But bow'd his comely Head,
  Down as upon a Bed.

This was that memorable Hour   65
Which first assur'd the forced Pow'r.

So when they did design
  The *Capitols* first Line,
A bleeding Head where they begun,
Did fright the Architects to run;   70
    And yet in that the *State*
    Foresaw it's happy Fate.

And now the Irish are asham'd
To see themselves in one Year tam'd:
    So much one Man can do,   75
    That does both act and know.

They can affirm his Praises best,
And have, though overcome, confest
    How good he is, how just,
    And fit for highest Trust: 80

Nor yet grown stiffer with Command,
But still in the *Republick's* hand:
    How fit he is to sway
    That can so well obey.

He to the *Commons Feet* presents   85
A *Kingdome*, for his first years rents:
    And, what he may, forbears
    His Fame to make it theirs:

And has his Sword and Spoyls ungirt,
To lay them at the *Publick's* skirt.   90
    So when the Falcon high
    Falls heavy from the Sky,

She, having kill'd, no more does search,
But on the next green Bow to pearch;
    Where, when he first does lure,   95
    The Falckner has her sure.

What may not then our *Isle* presume
While Victory his Crest does plume!
    What may not others fear
    If thus he crown each Year!   100

A *Caesar* he ere long to *Gaul*,
To *Italy* an *Hannibal*,
    And to all States not free
    Shall *Clymacterick* be.

The Pict no shelter now shall find   105
Within his party-colour'd Mind;
    But from this Valour sad
    Shrink underneath the Plad:

Happy if in the tufted brake
The *English Hunter* him mistake;   110
  Nor lay his Hounds in near
  The *Caledonian* Deer.
But thou the Wars and Fortunes Son
March indefatigably on:
  And for the last effect   115
  Still keep thy Sword erect;
Besides the force it has to fright
The Spirits of the shady Night,
  The same *Arts* that did *gain*
  A *Pow'r* must it *maintain*.   120

T HE trouble with Marxists who write on literature is that though their principles may be fertile and illuminating they are not, usually, very good critics. Not only do they tend to draw crudely direct links between economics and poetry, they may miss just those poems which give support to their theories. Thus one would have thought that Marvell's *Horatian Ode* would long since have been claimed by the Marxists as an expression of the social consciousness of the time; for though it is much else as well, it is certainly that. The intention of the ode is clearly to express an attitude towards Cromwell: a subtle and balanced attitude, in which the balancing forces correspond to balancing social forces in the poet's environment; and this correspondence is lightly but firmly insisted upon. Marvell however is not merely a Marxist, and the correspondence is also with natural, and possibly also with divine forces.

One must begin by establishing just what the attitude to Cromwell is. There is disagreement here among critics: enough to testify to the subtlety of the poem, if not to the astuteness of its readers. The question (sometimes asked) whether Marvell admired Cromwell, may be dismissed. Of course he did, and the poem is not a veiled attack (its omission from the 1681 edition confirms that). It seems justifiable to go outside the poem to biographical evidence for a moment, and point to Marvell's political services to the Protectorate. But few modern readers are prepared to treat it as unqualified praise: in what way is

Cromwell admired, and for what qualities? Marvell seems to me to consider him a force disruptive of nature, which is nonetheless natural: or (if you prefer) disruptive of society but nonetheless the product of inevitable social forces. This he deplores but accepts, and the very completeness of the acceptance becomes a kind of admiration. This attitude is communicated largely by the similes which at the same time state the correspondences with natural and social situations.

> And, like the three fork'd Lightning, first
> Breaking the Clouds where it was nurst,
>   Did thorough his own Side
>   His fiery way divide.

The lightning is a force against nature, but still a natural force: its destruction of the clouds where it was nurst is allowed for by nature, is not in fact destruction at all but a necessary preliminary to its real work, in this case further destruction. So the formation of the New Model did not in fact really damage the Parliamentary side, it was the best way to destroy the royalists. Marvell is not by this simile saying that Cromwell only seems destructive; destructive he is, but in a more accepted way than seemed at first. I cannot decide whether 'Side' is a pun in this verse. With Marvell it is usually safe to assume a pun when in doubt, but I cannot see the relevance of suggesting that it was by damaging himself that Cromwell progressed, a thought that is nowhere else hinted at.

The next image presents Cromwell as God's instrument:

> Then burning through the Air he went,
> And Pallaces and Temples rent:
>   And *Caesars* head at last
>   Did through his Laurels blast.

The lightning image was suspended for the comment of the fifth verse; now it is resumed, but differently. Lightning is no longer a merely natural force: it is the evidence of God's special intervention which the Puritan visionaries of the time constantly discovered, and constantly cast into light imagery:

Receiving . . . some quickenings of a divine principle within me, I presently arose and (as it were) shook off my night-dresses, and appeared to myself, like the sun, dawning out its

refulgent splendour, from behind the dark canopies of the earth.
(Jo. Salmon: *Heights in Depths and Depths in Heights*, 1651.)

The point is made more explicitly, and without reserve, in *A Poem upon the Death of O.C.*

> Those Strokes he said will pierce through all below
> Where those that strike from Heaven fetch their Blow.
>
> (ll. 183–4)

This contrast is typical of the difference between the two poems. The *Ode* is of course subtler: the first line of the verse reveals that there has been a change: there is a new rhythmic strength, the long emphatic second syllable ('burning') starts the line on the loud pedal (it is one of the few really sonorous lines in the poem). The lightning has become a portent. The next line hovers: this could be natural or divine, this rending of temples. The next couplet is decisive: the associations of '*Caesar*' (cunningly buttressed by the innocent-looking 'at last') announce that something special is coming, and the fourth line brings the miracle—laurel is normally a protective against lightning.

This very deliberate and meditative poem has by now thrown off its calm; and by contrast with the rest the climax of the next couplet is almost hysterical: gone is the Horatian mode, we have the utter conviction of the inspired Puritan. Marvell has never ceased to speak in his own person, and in a sense the enthusiasm is genuine, and his; but a retreat is necessary, and it is made with a masterly change of tone:

> And, if we would speak true,
> Much to the man is due.

This is on the one hand a transition like that in the second part of *East Coker*:

> That was a way of putting it—not very satisfactory:
> A periphrastic study in a worn-out poetical fashion,
> Leaving one still with the intolerable wrestle
> With words and meanings.

We have had enough heroics: do they really represent what we think? But Marvell here is not only speaking about his way of writing poetry, for the preceding verse was not merely a heightened moment of the poem, it was a slipping into Cromwell's own inspired Puritan self-exaltation. This is true on either of the possible readings of lines 25–6—'tis madness for us to resist Cromwell, or 'tis madness for Cromwell to resist his destiny: the latter, less obvious, may receive a shadow of corroboration from lines 15–16 of the *Death of O.C.*

> And he whom Nature all for Peace had made,
> But angry Heaven unto War had sway'd.

Out of this attitude Marvell has to extricate himself, without retracting what he has said. This is done chiefly by the withering, quietly-said 'true': withering because a Puritan is saying of Puritan inspiration 'that was a way of putting it, not very satisfactory'.

Natural, divine, then social: the third account of Cromwell must convey an attitude towards a social force. His movement from private to public life draws attention to this; it also helps the style to gather itself once more for the renewed climax of the ninth verse:

> Could by industrious Valour climbe
> To ruine the great Work of Time,
> And cast the Kingdome old
> Into another Mold.

The splendour of that second line is almost sheer impudence: the assurance with which Marvell has made 'ruine' into a term of praise. Its romantic associations (no doubt much weaker then) are caught up by the reverberant 'great Work of Time' until the core of meaning is overlaid. The line is a huge *tour de force*, for Cromwell's achievement is a *tour de force*, though permanent as well. Here the poem becomes most Marxist. The previous state of society has thrown up a force that disrupts, not gradually, but suddenly; verse 11 is a sort of statement of the dialectic. The contrast 'ancient Rights/greater Spirits' is satisfactorily Marxist; so is the recognition that justice rests on power. All that is missing is the recognition of an ultimately economic source of the apparently military power.

However, though Cromwell is the antithesis and the poem is about the acceptance of the new synthesis, it is fuller than a

Marxist (or perhaps more accurately Hegelian) statement, for the social is only one way of seeing Cromwell, who is also a natural and (with reservations) a divine phenomenon.

Here then is the attitude that is the main theme of the poem. It is substantiated and clarified by the linguistic subtlety, and by the two episodes of Charles and the forward youth; and is finally restated in the last two verses.

The exact point of the forward youth is bound up with the logical relation between the first two verses and the third, i.e. the meaning of 'so' in line 9. For 'so' cannot mean 'therefore' unless we stretch the 'now' of line 2 to impossible lengths. According to Hugh MacDonald, 'this may refer to more than one period'; but this is surely impossible, not only because that is not the meaning of 'now', but also because the whole poem is concerned with the present state of affairs: all the verbs either refer to how this came about, or else are in the present tense (cf. lines 28, 73, 114, &c.). But if 'now' means 'now'—i.e. the moment of writing the poem—it refers to the consequence of Cromwell's rise, and the first two verses are saying 'Now that Cromwell has arrived we live in a revolutionary era.' What then of 'so'? It cannot mean 'therefore' because the third verse states the cause, not the result. The O.E.D. does not give 'because' among the possible meanings of 'so'. Does it mean 'similarly'? It does, but we must be careful. Cromwell is not an example of the 'forward Youth': he has not forsaken his Muses dear to put on the corslet, he left gardening, not poetry. The third verse is not an example, but a parallel; the point of likeness is the forsaking: Cromwell began it, and now it has become general. And writing poetry is, for the youth, a natural occupation (surely he has a touch of Marvell himself about him: 'if I am to get on in the world I shouldn't be wasting my time writing this poem.'). We live in a revolution, then, which has upset the proper way of living: hence Cromwell who began it was 'restless *Cromwell*': he did not follow but 'urged' his star. This opening statement gives the full force to lines 27–8: we have seen all the damage he did; however, it was necessary, and in conceding its necessity the poem moves through acceptance to admiration. For it is not altogether a static poem—Cromwell figures better and better as it proceeds, until the recapitulation of the last two verses.

If this view of the poem's attitude to Cromwell is correct—
that he is a revolutionary but necessary force, destroying the
order of things but ultimately produced by that order—then
the function of Charles is clear: he represents what is being
destroyed. The attitude towards this must be the opposite: we
like it, but realize it must go. I don't think Marvell's judgment
has been sufficiently praised here, that he represents this passing
order by means of the aesthetic: an even finer decision than
the further one (if indeed they were separate and not simultaneous) to select drama from the fields of aesthetic activity.
For the aesthetic, in contrast to the practical which Cromwell
represents, is self-sufficient: the value of Charles's scene on the
scaffold lies in the enacting of that scene itself, not in any consequences that need to be enforced by Charles; so it is a value
not diminished by the fact that Charles is being executed (or,
more generally, that this order is now finished). Nor is aesthetic
value multiplied by counting: there is a sense in which one fine
scene is as valuable as a dozen, so that the value is not diminished
by the fact that Charles won't be around to perform again. By
presenting the passing order as a sort of performance, Marvell is
asserting that it means a lot to him but he is prepared to see it
eliminated: its value, being aesthetic, will not be damaged.

The choice of the dramatic among the modes of the aesthetic
has a twofold value. It enables Marvell to suggest that the full
flowering of the old order came as a result of its destruction:
that Charles rose to the occasion, a phrase surely more applicable
to the actor than to any other artist. Further, it points the nature
of Cromwell, and what he represents: his sincerity. Sincerity is
on the whole an ugly quality—seldom graceful, often discon-
certing. Its value in a man of action lies not in the intrinsic
value of being sincere, but in what he is likely, in consequence,
to do. The grace of Charles's behaviour is put on: the justification for this is the behaviour itself, and its possible consequences
(now prevented by his execution) might be worse than the un-
attractive violence of Cromwell, which does produce a kingdom
for his first year's rents. Perhaps one should add a third appro-
priateness in making Charles an actor, the obvious one that it
reminds us of the Puritan opposition to the stage, and thus of
the anti-aesthetic nature of the Cromwell force.

Charles and the forward youth, then, have this much in

common: both show that this necessary but insensitive revolution means forsaking the Muses dear.

The details of the actor-comparison have been frequently remarked and praised, and make it perhaps the finest passage in the poem:

> That thence the *Royal Actor* born
> The *Tragick Scaffold* might adorn:
> While round the armed Bands
> Did clap their bloody hands.
> *He* nothing common did or mean
>
> Upon that memorable Scene:
> But with his keener Eye
> The Axes edge did try:
> Nor call'd the *Gods* with vulgar spight
> To vindicate his helpless Right,
> But bow'd his comely Head,
> Down as upon a Bed.

The rhythmic command is perfect, culminating in the suggestion of perfect acquiescence in the last line; one may notice how the open vowels in 'the Axes edge did try', enforcing slight pauses before their words, suggest the cool deliberateness, the lack of hurry, of Charles himself. 'Born' in the first line reminds us of the contrast with Cromwell urging his active star; the only adjective attached to Charles, apart from the label '*Royal*', is aesthetic—his 'comely' head. The references to the stage are frequent but never overemphasized: there is the satisfying pun of '*Scaffold*'; the tragic mockery of an audience in the 'clapping' of the armed bands (not a verbal pun, but a play upon their motive); and the 'memorable Scene'—this last probably not a pun either, since the word Scene would appear never to be used in the seventeenth century without a conscious reference to the stage. I cannot better Empson's comment on the next two lines, that they 'seem to be remembering the Latin *acies*, 'eyesight' and 'sharp edge'! 'Vulgar' has partly an aesthetic but chiefly a social meaning; and is reinforced by the suggestion that the 'armed bands' are like the groundlings, the dregs of an audience (a neat comment, this, on their Puritanism).

The next couplet, commenting, is double-edged:

> This was that memorable Hour
> Which first assur'd the forced Pow'r.

One can hardly take it as perfectly straightforward: yet the sarcastic reading, with heavy emphasis on 'this' and ironic stress
on 'assur'd', may not be quite right either. It is as if Marvell
has been sarcastic, and then set himself to save the situation
with his subsequent simile. And the fact that the situation is not
quite saved, that we remember that Rome did, in the end, fall;
that no doubt is deliberate too.

Here we have already moved to the next point: the enforcing
of the poem's attitude by its linguistic subtleties. We may distinguish between a double-edged and a poised remark (I cannot
think of less clumsy terms): the former offers two alternative
readings, the latter conveys a dual attitude at the same time, in
which the praise would not be possible without the disparage-
ment, and vice versa. Lines 65–66 are not quite a double-edged
remark, because the one edge is soon dismissed as not meant, the
other is later seen to be qualified. A better example is line 87:

> And, what he may, forbears
> His Fame to make it theirs:

which can either mean 'Cromwell is so great that his modesty
cannot hide his deserts' or 'Cromwell is so arrogant that he
cannot really succeed in being modest', and where the two
meanings are surely alternatives. Or the very qualification which
alters the couplet about the 'memorable Hour' is itself two-
edged:

> And yet in that the *State*
> Foresaw its happy Fate.

You can take 'happy' as meant, or as ironical, but not both at
the same time.

A remark of Leontes illustrates this two-edged quality very
well:

> What you can make her do,
> I am content to look on: what to speak
> I am content to hear: for 'tis as easy
> To make her speak as move.
> (*The Winter's Tale*, iii, 92)

This can be read as pooh-poohing the idea that the statue can
move, or as a quietly happy revelation that he had begun to
suspect the truth.

Examples of the poised remark are these:

> So restless *Cromwell* could not cease.

I have already sketched in what seems to me the point of 'restless': there is a kind of itch about Cromwell that we are asked to admire; but the admiration is only a modification of our distress at his destructiveness, so that there is no question of our choosing between two shades of 'restless'.

> Then burning through the Air he went
> And Pallaces and Temples rent.

The touch of triumph lingering round 'rent' is not detachable from the deploring.

> The forward Youth that would appear
> Must now forsake his *Muses* dear.

Is 'forward' praise or blame? The point is that it is both, and that they are a single compound attitude. The word (like 'restless') has been chosen not because you can turn it upside down if you like (as was the case with 'happy'), but because it holds in itself a possibility of being attached to different value judgments. The ambiguity, that is, was potential in the word, and is not simply the result of looking at it differently.

> Nature that hateth emptiness,
> Allows of penetration less:
>   And therefore must make room
>   Where greater Spirits come.

This seems to be two-edged. The natural complexity of 'must' is so great that it seems impossible to think of it as conveying a single attitude. Cromwell is illustrating a property of nature; he is also putting nature in her place. These seem, though both attachable to the normal use of 'must', completely separate meanings; but they are unified in the poem's assertion that this sort of forcing is itself part of the nature of things.

> They can affirm his Praises best,
> And have, *though overcome*, confest
>   How good he is, how just,
>   And fit for highest Trust.

This is a genuinely doubtful case. 'His virtues are so clear that even those overcome confess'—or is the 'though' ironical: 'Yes, they confessed it all right: they had to'? Stated this way it seems a two-edged remark: yet one might suggest that this is an ambiguity inherent in the idea of confessing though overcome.

It seems reasonable to suggest that a poised remark is better for the poem's purposes, since Marvell is not hovering between two ways of looking at Cromwell: his greatness is unthinkable without the damage he does. The poem is about a revolution.

One is tempted to add that a poised remark is always more valuable poetically than a two-edged, but this would not do for those (perhaps not very common) poems which state praise meant as praise, but add a hint that the poet is himself not quite convinced, a hint which only appears when the poem is turned round to catch the light a different way. *Henry V* may be a case. But normally the more integrated attitude conveyed by the balanced remark seems more valuable poetically.

I cannot fit either of these methods of ambiguity into one of Mr. Empson's seven types. This may be because he classified according to the greatness of the contrast between the two elements of an ambiguity, rather than the manner in which they are held together in the poet's mind. From the descriptions of the seven types in the table of contents, one would say that both methods are of the fourth type—where 'the alternative meanings combine to make clear a complicated state of mind in the author', and indeed this could serve as a definition of all poetically valuable ambiguity (one could maintain this: that the first is not, strictly, ambiguity, the second and third are merely trivial except insofar as they partake of the fourth, and the last three are subdivisions of it). However, actual examples of the two-edged and the poised ambiguity are scattered all through the book: it seems such a poise as we are considering when 'this particular pair is one so normal in ordinary life, the situation itself is so "strong", that the various meanings are felt as a coherent unit' (of Herbert: p. 130) or where 'the doubt as to the merits of brooding . . . is a "mood", or enshrines the poet's permanent attitude to the word' (of Yeats: p. 191); the two-edged ambiguity is more or less defined in Empson's saying of lines in Donne's *Apparition* that 'the alternative versions seem particularly hard to unite into a single vocal effect' (p. 147).

71

The truth is surely that Empson's classification will not and ought not to coincide with those used in an essay on 'How to Read a Poem'. Such an essay is, to adopt his own distinction, appreciative in aim, and answers the question 'How should we read this poem properly?' Empson is primarily an analytic critic, and answers the question 'What are we doing when we read the poem properly?' Hence the frequently noted uselessness of Empson's most brilliant analyses when we are *evaluating* poetry. Pure analysis I should regard as a digression in an essay such as this one.

We may return to the poem with a discussion of the ending, especially the brilliant last verse:

> But thou the Wars and Fortunes Son
> March indefatigably on:
> And for the last effect
> Still keep thy Sword erect;
> Besides the force it has to fright
> The Spirits of the shady Night,
> The same *Arts* that did *gain*
> A *Pow'r* must it *maintain*.

'The Wars and Fortunes Son' states what we have seen to be one half of the poem's meaning: Cromwell is the product of disruptive forces. This leads us to the matter of the sword. Who are these spirits of the shady night? Surely so carefully constructed a poem is not ending on a reference to something not previously mentioned. I cannot convince myself of any of the easy solutions, such as that they are the Royalists, or the Picts, or the Irish. Yet no one can feel the lines to be a blemish. I can only suggest that Cromwell might be expected to have bad dreams: the source of his authority is such that there are powers to be appeased, and though this has not been mentioned we have been shown Cromwell in such a way that we can now realize it had to be so. Yet this I am aware will not quite do. If this is conscience, why 'shady' night? He cannot have painted Cromwell so black that he has his values all reversed. Furthermore, this is Cromwell as a public figure, not his private dreams. Yet I retain my confidence that the lines are 'right'.

The last couplet is beautifully double-edged: if the power is that of England, or Puritanism, or the bourgeoisie, it is saying

'You helped us, and we still need your help'. If it is Cromwell's, then it is saying: 'You got it this way, and you can't expect to keep it by any nobler way.' Yet this couplet, with the weight of the poem pressing upon it, is perhaps joining these alternatives into a single, poised, complex assertion, neither appeal nor taunt but acceptance: that in fact is the nature of forced power. Not we like or we dislike you, but we've got you now.

I conclude on a tentative speculation. Why a Horatian Ode? It is common to speak of Marvell as a transitional poet, looking back to Renaissance and Metaphysical, forward to the Augustans. This is indicated by his leaving literature for politics, lyric for satire, more complicated measures for couplets. Marvell's later poems on Cromwell, though not without subtlety, are more direct in statement, more like the work of the Member for Hull, and, of course, written in couplets. They are more unequivocal, too, in their praise of Cromwell. And *On the Death of O.C.* carries all this further than *The First Anniversary*. Here are some typical lines:

> I saw him dead, a leaden slumber lies,
> And mortal sleep over those wakefull eyes:
> Those gentle Rays under the lids were fled,
> Which through his looks that piercing sweetnesse shed.
>
> (ll. 247–250)

The polish is now wholly of the surface (and even that not very thorough, for the clumsiness of 'those . . . those . . . that' would have been removed by a good Augustan). The effects are simpler, no delicate balance, but a crude antithesis: 'mortal: wakefull'.

Now it may be that the very choosing to write an Horatian Ode (form is never arbitrarily chosen by a Renaissance poet) means that Marvell has placed himself on the conservative side. The poem is not going to be restless, not plume its crest with Victory. It even begins with a short discussion of the present state of the Arts: 'tis time to leave the very things Marvell is sitting down to do. Few readers are disturbed by the thought that, logically, this should be followed by an apology for writing, but isn't. One must therefore read it as defiance, perfectly concealed by the Ode's elegance. And in the scene of Charles on the scaffold, the poem is behaving like the Royal Actor; Marvell's keen eye hesitates over the puns and nuances; the language nothing common does or mean. In this assumption that to assess the brave new world one has to use an insight that is part of the old, Marvell adds, not satirically but with complete grace, an extra dimension to his view of Cromwell that by the later, state poems has gone.

Elegy to the Memory of an Unfortunate Lady

Christopher Gillie

What beck'ning ghost, along the moonlight shade
Invites my step, and points to yonder glade?
'Tis she!—but why that bleeding bosom gor'd,
Why dimly gleams the visionary sword?
Oh ever beauteous, ever friendly! tell,   5
Is it, in heav'n, a crime to love too well?
To bear too tender, or too firm a heart,
To act a Lover's or a Roman's part?
Is there no bright reversion in the sky,
For those who greatly think, or bravely die?   10
    Why bade ye else, ye Pow'rs! her soul aspire
Above the vulgar flight of low desire?
Ambition first sprung from your blest abodes;
The glorious fault of Angels and of Gods:
Thence to their Images on earth it flows,   15
And in the breasts of Kings and Heroes glows!
Most souls, 'tis true, but peep out once an age,
Dull sullen pris'ners in the body's cage:
Dim lights of life that burn a length of years,
Useless, unseen, as lamps in sepulchres;   20
Like Eastern Kings a lazy state they keep,
And close confin'd to their own palace sleep.
    From these perhaps (ere nature bade her die)
Fate snatch'd her early to the pitying sky.

As into air the purer spirits flow, 25
And sep'rate from their kindred dregs below;
So flew the soul to its congenial place,
Nor left one virtue to redeem her Race.
    But thou, false guardian of a charge too good,
Thou, mean deserter of thy brother's blood! 30
See on these ruby lips the trembling breath,
These cheeks, now fading at the blast of death:
Cold is that breast which warm'd the world before,
And those love-darting eyes must roll no more.
Thus, if eternal justice rules the ball, 35
Thus shall your wives, and thus your children fall:
On all the line a sudden vengeance waits,
And frequent herses shall besiege your gates.
There passengers shall stand, and pointing say,
(While the long fun'rals blacken all the way) 40
Lo these were they, whose souls the Furies steel'd,
And curs'd with hearts unknowing how to yield.
Thus unlamented pass the proud away,
The gaze of fools, and pageant of a day!
So perish all, whose breast ne'er learn'd to glow 45
For others' good, or melt at others' woe.
    What can atone (oh ever injur'd shade!)
Thy fate unpity'd, and thy rites unpaid?
No friend's complaint, no kind domestic tear
Pleas'd thy pale ghost, or grac'd thy mournful bier; 50
By foreign hands thy dying eyes were clos'd,
By foreign hands thy decent limbs compos'd,
By foreign hands thy humble grave adorn'd,
By strangers honour'd, and by strangers mourn'd!
What tho' no friends in sable weeds appear, 55
Grieve for an hour, perhaps, then mourn a year,
And bear about the mockery of woe
To midnight dances, and the publick show?
What tho' no weeping Loves thy ashes grace,
Nor polish'd marble emulate thy face? 60
What tho' no sacred earth allow thee room,
Nor hallow'd dirge be mutter'd o'er thy tomb?
Yet shall thy grave with rising flow'rs be drest,
And the green turf lie lightly on thy breast:
There shall the morn her earliest tears bestow, 65
There the first roses of the year shall blow;

While Angels with their silver wings o'ershade
The ground, now sacred by thy reliques made.
  So peaceful rests, without a stone, a name,
What once had beauty, titles, wealth, and fame.   70
How lov'd, how honour'd once, avails thee not,
To whom related, or by whom begot;
A heap of dust alone remains of thee;
'Tis all thou art, and all the proud shall be!
  Poets themselves must fall, like those they sung;   75
Deaf the prais'd ear, and mute the tuneful tongue.
Ev'n he, whose soul now melts in mournful lays,
Shall shortly want the gen'rous tear he pays;
Then from his closing eyes thy form shall part,
And the last pang shall tear thee from his heart,   80
Life's idle business at one gasp be o'er,
The Muse forgot, and thou belov'd no more!

I ONCE thought that Pope's Elegy was an easy poem. The brilliance of certain passages and the deceptive fluency of others combined—perhaps not for me alone—to produce this impression. It was only after attentive reading that I came to feel, first, that there were obstacles to the appreciation of the poem as a whole, and then that considered as a whole it was a great deal more interesting than I had originally supposed.

There are some superficial difficulties of diction and tone which may alienate a modern taste: what has been called the histrionic opening, and the formal treatment of an emotional theme throughout. Most readers will make allowances for these, though they may not be the right allowances. They may, for instance, be prepared to shrug the histrionics off, without ever considering whether such an introduction is necessarily undesirable in itself; or they may allow for what they think to be the requirements of the taste of the period, without asking themselves whether the diction is really in this sense dated, or whether, by its intrinsic virtue, it survives comparison with the diction of other periods. These are important questions but I think they can wait; there are greater difficulties which lie deeper.

The first of these concerns the poet's ethical attitude to the tragedy. The Lady has committed suicide for love, and he demands:

> Is it, in heav'n, a crime to love too well?

The position of the phrase 'in heav'n' in the sentence implies, 'as it is, of course, on earth'. And then, 'too well' causes one to ask 'too well for what?' For worldly prudence, no doubt; at all events to love in such a way that the consequences are disastrous; or worse, to attach such value to the loving that any consequences whatever are to be faced for its sake. But then comes this passage:

> Why bade ye else, ye Pow'rs! her soul aspire
> Above the vulgar flight of low desire?
> Ambition first sprung from your blest abodes;
> The glorious fault of Angels and of Gods:
> Thence to their images on earth it flows,
> And in the breasts of Kings and Heroes glows!

Is the demand in the first couplet merely rhetorical? If 'love' is concerned, then presumably the powers require the soul to aspire to the love of God, but that the Lady killed herself for this is not in question. The fact remains that she has risen far above 'the vulgar flight of low desire', and that it is the superior quality of her nature that has been responsible for the tragedy— a double tragedy according to this view, since it concerns both her life in the world and her after-life.

Next, 'Ambition first sprung . . .' surely recalls the downfall of Satan, and more particularly the Satan of 'Paradise Lost'. Satan was the origin of all evil, but he was also Lucifer, the most splendid of the Angels. Ambition, in fact, is a fault, but a glorious fault, found in the most splendid, if not the most saintly, of the human race.

And since we are on the subject of ambition, we may pass to a couplet occurring later in the poem, summarizing the Lady's end on this earth:

> A heap of dust alone remains of thee;
> 'Tis all thou art, and all the proud shall be!

Pride is usually associated with ambition, but here it is dissociated from it. We have seen that it is the Lady who has been convicted of the 'glorious fault'; that is to say, she has had the

presumption to carry her passion far beyond the socially pre-
scribed limits of it; but it is her enemies, her family and in particular her uncle whose inhumanity drove her to suicide, who are
here comprehended under the epithet 'proud'. We remember
that her ambition was not of the kind that pursues worldly
greatness, but on the contrary seems to have demanded defiance
of it. But still it is clear that Pope is using the word 'ambition'
in by no means the conventional sense; we are faced with
paradox.

The resolution to the paradox is to be found in these couplets
from different parts of the poem:

> Thence to their images on earth it [ambition] flows
> And in the breast of kings and heroes glows.

> So perish all, whose breast ne'er learned to glow
> For others' good, or melt at others' woe.

We have just seen how Pope sets in contrast two words
usually felt to be akin; in these couplets, by the repetition of
'glows' in connection with 'breasts' (and he is still attacking
the 'proud'), we see him associating two emotions rarely
thought easily compatible—ambition and compassion. The
bosom of the truly living human being glows, as though ignited
by an object transcending itself. It matters little, where the
quality of human life is concerned, whether we describe such
responsiveness as ambition or as compassion or by some other
word; the objects responded to are different, and so the responses
are different, but it is the responsiveness that matters.

We can see now how the Lady is contrasted with her relatives.
They, too, no doubt, were ambitious, but they were ambitious
only in the vulgar sense of the word. They wanted greatness;
they sought to avert degradation: but the greatness they
cherished was such that either no sacrifice or else a sacrifice
infinitely too great was demanded for its attainment; love itself
must give way to the externals of rank. She, on the other hand,
is ready to sacrifice life itself, but only because life itself is
already consumed by love. We are all of us guilty, seems to be
the conclusion, but in what very different senses are we guilty,
and how extremely reckless it is to cast a stone.

The theme of the poem, then, may be said to be moral

heroism at war with moral meanness. Its most celebrated lines are indeed explicit on this:

> Most souls, 'tis true, but peep out once an age,
> Dull sullen pris'ners in the body's cage:
> Dim lights of life that burn a length of years,
> Useless, unseen, as lamps in sepulchres;
> Like Eastern Kings a lazy state they keep,
> And close confin'd to their own palace sleep.

This is one of the passages that 'tells' unforgettably. Following as it does immediately on the description of ambition springing from heaven into the breasts of kings and heroes, its effectiveness is increased once we have worked out just what Pope means by ambition—how it is the most conspicuous manifestation of that responsiveness without which human nature is scarcely alive. But ambition is not the only word whose meaning is explored in the poem; death, beginning with this passage, is another. After all, the two facts that we are given about the Lady are that she loved, and that she took her own life.

Most souls are like lights in sepulchres: that is to say, even in life they are spiritually dead. But they are also like kings keeping a 'lazy state', and this simile has ambivalent force. It reminds us that the soul is kingly, but also that the significance of kingship depends on its mediation between the divine and the political spheres; a king who merely keeps his state is in a deep sense a most contemptible figure, for he takes upon himself the fruits of the prestige while abdicating the authority for it. He becomes a symbol, not of the continuity of the temporal and the divine, but of the opposite—of the material grossness and the spiritual meanness of man. In another way the simile prepares the reader for the lady's proud relations; they regard themselves as kings, but apart from their state—their visible social importance—what is there about them that justifies their pride? In the next passage they are alluded to as 'dregs'; when the Lady departed from them, she took all the virtues of the race with her:

> Nor left one virtue to redeem her race.

One remembers that 'virtue' has as its first meaning the sense of power, a positive force, and hence, derivatively, a force of character for good.

They, and more particularly her uncle, 'false guardian of a charge too good', drive her to suicide, and the poet invokes a curse upon them:

> On all the line a sudden vengeance waits,
> And frequent herses shall besiege your gates.

or shall, that is, 'if eternal justice rules the ball'. The fate would be just, not merely as vengeance for the Lady in particular, nor even because the spiritual death they embody ought poetically to become manifest in actual death, but because the spiritually dead are, in general, death-breeders; they destroy by their mere existence all that is most fruitfully alive:

> Cold is that breast that warmed the world before,
> And those love-darting eyes shall roll no more.

The breast that had glowed with passion had warmed all the world accessible to its rays, but the proud were inaccessible to them. Being inaccessible to love, they are also inaccessible to the tragedy of death. They might, it is true, have feigned response to it in terms of conventional 'state'; they might have worn mourning, erected pretentious but insipid monuments, ordained prayers to be 'muttered' by perfunctory priests:

> What tho' no friends in sable weeds appear,
> Grieve for an hour, perhaps, then mourn a year,
> And bear about the mockery of woe
> To midnight dances, and the publick show?
> What tho' no weeping Loves thy ashes grace,
> Nor polish'd marble emulate thy face?
> What tho' no sacred earth allow thee room,
> Nor hallow'd dirge be mutter'd oe'r thy tomb?

Heartless as it would all be, even so much is denied her. But what does it all matter, since a genuinely creative spirit breeds life even in death, just as the spiritually moribund breed death even in life:

> Yet shall thy grave with rising flow'rs be drest,
> And the green turf lie lightly on thy breast:
> There shall the morn her earliest tears bestow,
> There the first roses of the year shall blow;
> While Angels with their sacred wings o'ershade
> The ground, now sacred by thy reliques made.

There is a buoyancy about this death that contrasts greatly with the oppressiveness of the life that is no more than a light in a sepulchre. It may, indeed, be retorted that even so the lines are mere sentimental ornament, expressing wishful thinking; the body of the lady will in fact fertilize the ground, but not otherwise than any other body. And in fact, returning to earth as it were, Pope seems to hint as much himself, in the couplet already quoted:

> A heap of dust alone remains of thee;
> 'Tis all thou art, and all the proud shall be!

But in spite of this, the fact remains that the passage is not sentimental ornament. Its real significance is manifested in the poem's conclusion, where the poet shows how the Lady's life and death are, for poetry, directly creative.

> Poets themselves must fall, like those they sung;
> Deaf the prais'd ear, and mute the tuneful tongue.
> Ev'n he, whose soul now melts in mournful lays,
> Shall shortly want the gen'rous tear he pays;
> Then from his closing eyes thy form shall part,
> And the last pang shall tear thee from his heart,
> Life's idle business at one gasp be o'er,
> The Muse forgot, and thou belov'd no more!

It may be of biographical interest, but it is not of critical importance to establish the Lady's historical identity. Pope seems to have been intentionally obscure about it, perhaps regarding it as a convenient red-herring suitable for pursuit by those unable or unwilling to catch up with the poem itself. For other readers, she is given a poetic identity in these concluding lines. The tragedy of the Lady is that she responded to life with a passion which those responsible for her were not willing to understand. To them, people like her were among life's nuisances; she may not even have been a major one. To the poet, on the contrary, such a nature is both the material of his art, and the best part of his audience, for poetry both issues and concludes in passionate response. When the poet himself dies, it is his kinship with such natures that is the last tie to be loosed. 'The Muse forgot'—the Lady is not far from being identified with the Muse herself; she is at all events something like a martyr for all that poetry owes its existence to. 'Life's idle business at one gasp be o'er': the poet can expect no better fate than equivalent neglect at the hands of such a public. That he, too, has to face such a martyrdom is implicit right at the beginning:

> What beck'ning ghost, along the moonlight shade
> Invites my step, and points to yonder glade?
> 'Tis she!—but why that bleeding bosom gor'd
> Why dimly gleams the visionary sword?

In fact, it may be objected, Pope had no occasion to complain of his public; but that is not the point. He is concerned to align himself with the Lady on the side of Life; on the other side are the pride, stupidity, and heartlessness of a society that sets up its conventions as ultimate criteria.

The poem is not concerned with a private grief. The tragedy is indeed a particular one, but the fact that it could occur calls the values of all Society in question, and it is Society that Pope is addressing. The very assurance of tone that he uses shows that even if, like Dr. Johnson, Society rejects his accusation, he can rely on it to give attention. Society in Pope's day did not merely tolerate, but respected the office of Poet, in a way that is nowadays hard even to imagine. In return the poet, however critical he might be, respected Society, and addressed it in a form that he knew to be acceptable to it. Nowadays, we expect poets to speak in personal accents, and perhaps hardly realize how very marginal in relation to Society such a demand condemns them to be. In Pope, we have to realize, although the object may often be generalized in a way that suggests lack of original vision, yet the thought, in which the object is merely a detail, is highly particular. This may become clearer if we reconsider the following passage:

> Yet shall thy grave with rising flow'rs be drest,
> And the green turf lie lightly on thy breast:
> There shall the morn her earliest tears bestow,
> There the first roses of the year shall blow:
> While Angels with their sacred wings o'ershade
> The ground, now sacred by thy reliques made.

I have already described this passage as 'buoyant', but another reader might prefer to say 'platitudinous'. 'Rising' is, after all, insipid for flowers, and so many roses have blown in poetry that now we scarcely notice them. 'Tears' is again excessively obvious for dew, and the suggestion that the morn is grieving hardly redeems the cliché. Finally, the angels with their silver wings may seem hardly less a tombstone property than the 'weeping loves' referred to satirically a few lines earlier. Such easy censure, however, only misinterprets the poet's intention. It is not to Pope's purpose that the flowers, the dew, the roses and the angels shall be seen; this would in fact be an interference with the effect he intends. If the images are taken together, the descriptive words—*rising* flowers, lie *lightly*, *earliest* tears, *silver* wings—combine to create the impression that, without allowing us to forget that this is a tomb and that we are concerned with death, is at the same time suggestive of the opposites—of springtime and life. The mind is thus not distracted by the necessity of dwelling on the vision of a special plot of earth, but is led to reflect on the vivifying influence of certain people even in their deaths and while one is grieving for them. Though the description is general, the thought is particular; we are made to understand what death is in relation to the Lady.

That death can be vivifying is an idea that is as old and familiar as martyrdom, and does not need to be laboured. But that the living are really dead is more startling, and consequently requires startling images to impress it on the mind. So the diction in the passage describing 'most souls' is altogether more striking. The souls 'peep' out from 'the body's cage'; they are not only dull but sullen, that is, unwilling to do more. They are 'Useless, unseen,'—the rhythm drags on the long vowels and the inverted foot—and then, still more unexpectedly, they are eastern kings confined to their palaces. The total effect of the mounting images is complex—absurd (consider the use of the word 'peep'), and yet at the same time majestic; there is comedy and tragedy in fusion.

The correctness for which Pope was praised at the time and for which he has been so much criticized since was in him the condition of extreme poetic economy, and therefore instrumental to his force. In him it was a discipline to his passion; in his imitators, it became the means usurping the end, and hence was discarded by the romantics. And one needs to remember that his public was a society with highly formalized standards. To such a public, even the theatrical opening probably had its strength. In a society whose criteria of taste are agreed, we are to expect artistic presentation to be staged; the entrance, when the poem is a challenge to contemporary social conventions, may well impress another generation as 'stagey'.

S. T. COLERIDGE

Christabel

Charles Tomlinson

Part I

'Tis the middle of night by the castle clock,
And the owls have awakened the crowing cock;
Tu—whit!—Tu—whoo!
And hark, again! the crowing cock,
How drowsily it crew.

Sir Leoline, the baron rich,
Hath a toothless mastiff bitch;
From her kennel beneath the rock
She maketh answer to the clock.
Four for the quarters, and twelve for the hour;
Ever and aye, by shine and shower,
Sixteen short howls, not over loud;
Some say, she sees my lady's shroud.

Is the night chilly and dark?
The night is chilly, but not dark.
The thin grey cloud is spread on high,
It covers but not hides the sky.
The moon is behind, and at the full;
And yet she looks both small and dull.
The night is chill, the cloud is gray:
'Tis a month before the month of May,
And the Spring comes slowly up this way.

The lovely lady, Christabel,
Whom her father loves so well,
What makes her in the wood so late,
A furlong from the castle gate?
She had dreams all yesternight
Of her own betrothed knight;
And she in the midnight wood will pray
For the weal of her lover that's far away.

She stole along, she nothing spoke,
The sighs she heaved were soft and low,
And naught was green upon the oak,
But moss and rarest mistletoe;
She kneels beneath the huge oak tree,
And in silence prayeth she.

The lady sprang up suddenly,
The lovely lady, Christabel!
It moaned as near, as near can be,
But what it is, she cannot tell.—
On the other side it seems to be,
Of the huge broad-breasted, old oak tree.

The night is chill; the forest bare;
Is it the wind that moaneth bleak?
There is not wind enough in the air
To move away the ringlet curl
From the lovely lady's cheek—
There is not wind enough to twirl
The one red leaf, the last of its clan,
That dances as often as dance it can,
Hanging so light, and hanging so high,
On the topmost twig that looks up at the sky.

Hush, beating heart of Christabel!
Jesu, Maria shield her well!
She folded her arms beneath her cloak,
And stole to the other side of the oak.
    What sees she there?

There she sees a damsel bright,
Drest in a silken robe of white,
That shadowy in the moonlight shone:
The neck that made that white robe wan,

87

Her stately neck, and arms were bare;
Her blue-veined feet unsandal'd were,
And wildly glittered here and there
The gems entangled in her hair.
I guess, 'twas frightful there to see
A lady so richly clad as she—
Beautiful exceedingly!

Mary mother, save me now!
(Said Christabel) And who art thou?

The lady strange made answer meet,
And her voice was faint and sweet—
Have pity on my sore distress,
I scarce can speak for weariness:
Stretch forth thy hand, and have no fear!
Said Christabel, How camest thou here?
And the lady, whose voice was faint and sweet,
Did thus pursue her answer meet:

My sire is of a noble line,
And my name is Geraldine:
Five warriors seized me yestermorn,
Me, even me, a maid forlorn:
They choked my cries with force and fright,
And tied me to a palfrey white.
The palfrey was as fleet as wind,
And they rode furiously behind.
They spurred amain, their steeds were white,
And once we crossed the shade of night.
As sure as Heaven shall rescue me,
I have no thought what men they be;
Nor do I know how long it is
(For I have lain entranced I wis)

Since one, the tallest of the five,
Took me from the palfrey's back,
A weary woman, scarce alive.
Some muttered words his comrades spoke:
He placed me underneath this oak,
He swore they would return with haste;
Whither they went I cannot tell—
I thought I heard, some minutes past,
Sounds as of a castle bell.

Stretch forth thy hand (thus ended she),
And help a wretched maid to flee.

Then Christabel stretched forth her hand
And comforted fair Geraldine:
O well bright dame may you command
The service of Sir Leoline;
And gladly our stout chivalry
Will he send forth and friends withal
To guide and guard you safe and free
Home to your noble father's hall.
She rose: and forth with steps they passed
That strove to be, and were not, fast.
Her gracious stars the lady blest,
And thus spake on sweet Christabel;
All our household are at rest,
The hall as silent as the cell,
Sir Leoline is weak in health
And may not well awakened be,
But we will move as if in stealth
And I beseech your courtesy
This night, to share your couch with me.

They crossed the moat, and Christabel
Took the key that fitted well;
A little door she opened straight,
All in the middle of the gate;
The gate that was ironed within and without,
Where an army in battle-array had marched out
The lady sank, belike through pain,
And Christabel with might and main
Lifted her up, a weary weight,
Over the threshold of the gate:
Then the lady rose again,
And moved, as she were not in pain.

So free from danger, free from fear,
They crossed the court: right glad they were.
And Christabel devoutly cried
To the lady by her side,
Praise we the Virgin all divine
Who hath rescued thee from thy distress!
Alas, alas! said Geraldine,
I cannot speak for weariness.

So free from danger, free from fear,
They crossed the court: right glad they were.

Outside her kennel, the mastiff old
Lay fast asleep, in moonshine cold.
The mastiff old did not awake,
Yet she an angry moan did make!
And what can ail the mastiff bitch?
Never till now she uttered yell
Beneath the eye of Christabel.
Perhaps it is the owlet's scritch:
For what can ail the mastiff bitch?

They passed the hall, that echoes still,
Pass as lightly as you will!
The brands were flat, the brands were **dying**,
Amid their own white ashes lying;
But when the lady passed, there came
A tongue of light, a fit of flame;
And Christabel saw the lady's eye,
And nothing else saw she thereby,
Save the boss of the shield of Sir Leoline tall,
Which hung in a murky old niche in the wall.
O softly tread, said Christabel,
My father seldom sleepeth well.

Sweet Christabel her feet doth bare,
And jealous of the listening air
They steal their way from stair to stair,
Now in the glimmer, and now in gloom,
And now they pass the Baron's room,
As still as death with stifled breath!
And now have reached her chamber door;
And now doth Geraldine press down
The rushes of the chamber floor.

The moon shines dim in the open air,
And not a moonbeam enters here.
But they without its light can see
The chamber carved so curiously,
Carved with figures strange and sweet,
All made out of the carver's brain,
For a lady's chamber meet:

The lamp with twofold silver chain
Is fastened to an angel's feet.
The silver lamp burns dead and dim;
But Christabel the lamp will trim.
She trimmed the lamp and made it bright,
And left it swinging to and fro,
While Geraldine, in wretched plight,
Sank down upon the floor below.

O weary lady, Geraldine,
I pray you, drink this cordial wine!
It is a wine of virtuous powers;
My mother made it of wild flowers.

And will your mother pity me,
Who am a maiden most forlorn?
Christabel answered—Woe is me!
She died the hour that I was born.
I have heard the gray-haired friar tell,
How on her death-bed she did say,
That she should hear the castle bell
Strike twelve upon my wedding day.
O mother dear! that thou wert here!
I would, said Geraldine, she were!

But soon with altered voice, said she—
'Off, wandering mother! Peak and pine!
I have power to bid thee flee.'
Alas! what ails poor Geraldine?
Why stares she with unsettled eye?
Can she the bodiless dead espy?
And why with hollow voice cries she,
'Off, woman, off! this hour is mine—
Though thou her guardian spirit be,
Off, woman, off! 'tis given to me.'

Then Christabel knelt by the lady's side,
And raised to heaven her eyes so blue—
Alas! said she, this ghastly ride—
Dear lady! it hath wildered you!
The lady wiped her moist cold brow,
And faintly said, ''tis over now!'
Again the wild-flower wine she drank:

Her fair large eyes 'gan glitter bright,
And from the floor whereon she sank,
The lofty lady stood upright;
She was most beautiful to see,
Like a lady of a far countrée.

And thus the lofty lady spake—
All they, who live in the upper sky,
Do love you, holy Christabel!
And you love them, and for their sake
And for the good which me befell,
Even I in my degree will try,
Fair maiden, to requite you well.
But now unrobe yourself; for I
Must pray, ere yet in bed I lie.

Quoth Christabel, so let it be!
And as the lady bade, did she.
Her gentle limbs did she undress,
And lay down in her loveliness.

But through her brain of weal and woe
So many thoughts moved to and fro,
That vain it were her lids to close;
So half-way from the bed she rose,
And on her elbow did recline
To look at the lady Geraldine.

Beneath the lamp the lady bowed,
And slowly rolled her eyes around;
Then drawing in her breath aloud,
Like one that shuddered, she unbound
The cincture from beneath her breast:
Her silken robe, and inner vest,
Dropt to her feet, and full in view,
Behold! her bosom and half her side—
A sight to dream of, not to tell!
O shield her! shield sweet Christabel!

Yet Geraldine nor speaks nor stirs:
Ah! what a stricken look was hers!
Deep from within she seems half-way
To lift some weight with sick assay,
And eyes the maid and seeks delay;

Then suddenly, as one defied,
Collects herself in scorn and pride,
And lay down by the Maiden's side!—
And in her arms the maid she took,
    Ah, wel-a-day!
And with low voice and doleful look
These words did say:

In the touch of this bosom there worketh a spell,
Which is lord of thy utterance, Christabel!
Thou knowest tonight, and wilt know tomorrow
This mark of my shame, this seal of my sorrow;
    But vainly thou warrest,
      For this is alone in
    Thy power to declare,
      That in the dim forest
    Thou heardest a low moaning,
And found'st a bright lady, surpassingly fair:
And didst bring her home with thee in love and in charity,
To shield her and shelter her from the damp air.

Conclusion to Part I

It was a lovely sight to see
The lady Christabel, when she
Was praying at the old oak tree.
    Amid the jagged shadows
    Of mossy leafless boughs,
    Kneeling in the moonlight,
    To make her gentle vows;
Her slender palms together prest,
Heaving sometimes on her breast;
Her face resigned to bliss or bale—
Her face, oh call it fair not pale,
And both blue eyes more bright than clear,
Each about to have a tear.

With open eyes (ah woe is me!)
Asleep, and dreaming fearfully,
Fearfully dreaming, yet I wis,
Dreaming that alone, which is—
O sorrow and shame! Can this be she,
The lady who knelt at the old oak tree?

And lo! the worker of these harms,
That holds the maiden in her arms,
Seems to slumber still and mild,
As a mother with her child.
A star hath set, a star hath risen,
O Geraldine! since arms of thine
Have been the lovely lady's prison.
O Geraldine! one hour was thine—
Thou'st had thy will! By tairn and rill,
The night-birds all that hour were still.
But now they are jubilant anew,
From cliff and tower, tu-whoo! tu-whoo!
Tu-whoo! tu-whoo! from wood and fell!

And see! the lady Christabel
Gathers herself from out her trance;
Her limbs relax, her countenance
Grows sad and soft; the smooth thin lids
Close o'er her eyes; and tears she sheds—
Large tears that leave the lashes bright!
And oft the while she seems to smile
As infants at a sudden light!

Yea, she doth smile, and she doth weep,
Like a youthful hermitess,
Beauteous in a wilderness,
Who, praying always, prays in sleep.
And, if she move unquietly,
Perchance, 'tis but the blood so free,
Comes back and tingles in her feet.
No doubt, she hath a vision sweet.
What if her guardian spirit 'twere,
What if she knew her mother near?
But this she knows, in joys and woes,
That saints will aid if men will call:
For the blue sky bends over all!

Part II

Each matin bell, the Baron saith,
Knells us back to a world of death.
These words Sir Leoline first said,
When he rose and found his lady dead:
These words Sir Leoline will say,
Many a morn to his dying day.

And hence the custom and law began,
That still at dawn the sacristan,
Who duly pulls the heavy bell,
Five and forty beads must tell
Between each stroke—a warning knell,
Which not a soul can choose but hear
From Bratha Head to Wyndermere.

Saith Bracy the bard, So let it knell!
And let the drowsy sacristan
Still count as slowly as he can!
There is no lack of such, I ween
As well fill up the space between.
In Langdale Pike and Witch's Lair,
And Dungeon-ghyll so foully rent,
With ropes of rock and bells of air
Three sinful sextons' ghosts are pent,
Who all give back, one after t'other,
The death-note to their living brother;
And oft too, by the knell offended,
Just as their one! two! three! is ended,
The devil mocks the doleful tale
With a merry peal from Borrowdale.

The air is still! through mist and cloud
That merry peal comes ringing loud;
And Geraldine shakes off her dread,
And rises lightly from the bed;
Puts on her silken vestments white,
And tricks her hair in lovely plight,
And nothing doubting of her spell
Awakens the lady Christabel.
'Sleep you, sweet lady Christabel?
I trust that you have rested well.'

And Christabel awoke and spied
The same who lay down by her side—
O rather say, the same whom she
Raised up beneath the old oak tree!
Nay, fairer yet! and yet more fair!
For she belike hath drunken deep
Of all the blessedness of sleep!
And while she spake, her looks, her air
Such gentle thankfulness declare,

That (so it seemed) her girded vests
Grew tight beneath her heaving breasts.
'Sure I have sinned!' said Christabel,
'Now Heaven be praised if all be well!'
And in low faltering tones, yet sweet,
Did she the lofty lady greet
With such perplexity of mind
As dreams too lively leave behind.

So quickly she rose, and quickly arrayed
Her maiden limbs, and having prayed
That He, who on the cross did groan,
Might wash away her sins unknown,
She forthwith led fair Geraldine
To meet her sire, Sir Leoline.

The lovely maid and the lady tall
Are pacing both into the hall,
And pacing on through page and groom
Enter the Baron's presence room.

The Baron rose, and while he prest
His gentle daughter to his breast,
With cheerful wonder in his eyes
The lady Geraldine espies,
And gave such welcome to the same,
As might beseem so bright a dame!

But when he heard the lady's tale,
And when she told her father's name,
Why waxed Sir Leoline so pale,
Murmuring o'er the name again,
Lord Roland de Vaux of Tryermaine?

Alas! they had been friends in youth;
But whispering tongues can poison truth;
And constancy lives in realms above;
And life is thorny; and youth is vain;
And to be wroth with one we love,
Doth work like madness in the brain.
And thus it chanced, as I divine,
With Roland and Sir Leoline.

Each spake words of high disdain
And insult to his heart's best brother:
They parted—ne'er to meet again!
But never either found another
To free the hollow heart from paining—
They stood aloof, the scars remaining,
Like cliffs which had been rent asunder;
A dreary sea now flows between,
But neither heat, nor frost, nor thunder,
Shall wholly do away, I ween,
The marks of that which once hath been.

Sir Leoline, a moment's space,
Stood gazing on the damsel's face;
And the youthful Lord of Tryermaine
Came back upon his heart again.

O then the Baron forgot his age,
His noble heart swelled high with rage;
He swore by the wounds in Jesu's side,
He would proclaim it far and wide
With trump and solemn heraldry,
That they, who thus had wronged the dame,
Were base as spotted infamy!
'And if they dare deny the same,
My herald shall appoint a week,
And let the recreant traitors seek
My tournay court—that there and then
I may dislodge their reptile souls
From the bodies and forms of men!'
He spake: his eye in lightning rolls!
For the lady was ruthlessly seized; and he kenned
In the beautiful lady the child of his friend!

And now the tears were on his face,
And fondly in his arms he took
Fair Geraldine, who met the embrace,
Prolonging it with joyous look.
Which when she viewed, a vision fell
Upon the soul of Christabel,
The vision of fear, the touch and pain!
She shrunk and shuddered, and saw again
(Ah, woe is me! Was it for thee,
Thou gentle maid! such sights to see?)

Again she saw that bosom old,
Again she felt that bosom cold,
And drew in her breath with a hissing sound:
Whereat the Knight turned wildly round,
And nothing saw, but his own sweet maid
With eyes upraised, as one that prayed.

The touch, the sight, had passed away,
And in its stead that vision blest,
Which comforted her after-rest,
While in the lady's arms she lay,
Had put a rapture in her breast,
And on her lips and o'er her eyes
Spread smiles like light!
                              With new surprise,
'What ails then my beloved child?'
The Baron said—His daughter mild
Made answer, 'All will yet be well!'
I ween she had no power to tell
Aught else: so mighty was the spell.
Yet he, who saw this Geraldine,
Had deemed her sure a thing divine,
Such sorrow with such grace she blended,
As if she feared she had offended
Sweet Christabel, that gentle maid!
And with such lowly tones she prayed,
She might be sent without delay
Home to her father's mansion.
                              'Nay!
Nay, by my soul!' said Leoline.
'Ho! Bracy the bard, the charge be thine!
Go thou, with music sweet and loud,
And take two steeds with trappings proud,
And take the youth, whom thou lov'st best
To bear thy harp, and learn thy song,
And clothe you both in solemn vest,
And over the mountains haste along,
Lest wandering folk, that are abroad,
Detain you on the valley road.
And when he has crossed the Irthing flood,
My merry bard! he hastes, he hastes
Up Knorren Moor, through Halegarth Wood,
And reaches soon that castle good
Which stands and threatens Scotland's wastes.

Bard Bracy! bard Bracy! your horses are fleet,
Ye must ride up the hall, your music so sweet,
More loud than your horses' echoing feet!
And loud and loud to Lord Roland call,
Thy daughter is safe in Langdale hall!
Thy beautiful daughter is safe and free—
Sir Leoline greets thee thus through me.
He bids thee come without delay
With all thy numerous array,
And take thy lovely daughter home;
And he will meet thee on the way
With all his numerous array
White with their panting palfreys' foam,
And, by mine honour! I will say,
That I repent me of the day
When I spake words of fierce disdain
To Roland de Vaux of Tryermaine!—
—For since that evil hour hath flown,
Many a summer's sun have shone;
Yet ne'er found I a friend again
Like Roland de Vaux of Tryermaine.'

The lady fell, and clasped his knees,
Her face upraised, her eyes o'erflowing;
And Bracy replied, with faltering voice,
His gracious hail on all bestowing:—
Thy words, thou sire of Christabel,
Are sweeter than my harp can tell,
Yet might I gain a boon of thee,
This day my journey should not be;
So strange a dream hath come to me:
That I had vowed with music loud
To clear yon wood from thing unblest,
Warned by a vision in my rest!
For in my sleep I saw that dove,
That gentle bird, whom thou dost love,
And call'st by thy own daughter's name—
Sir Leoline! I saw the same
Fluttering, and uttering fearful moan,
Among the green herbs in the forest alone.
Which when I saw and when I heard,
I wondered what might ail the bird:
For nothing near it could I see,
Save the grass and green herbs underneath the old tree.

And in my dream, methought, I went
To search out what might there be found:
And what the sweet bird's trouble meant,
That thus lay fluttering on the ground.
I went and peered, and could descry
No cause for her distressful cry;
But yet for her dear lady's sake
I stooped, methought, the dove to take,
When lo! I saw a bright green snake
Coiled around its wings and neck.
Green as the herbs on which it couched,
Close by the dove's its head it crouched;
And with the dove it heaves and stirs,
Swelling its neck as she swelled hers!
I woke; it was the midnight hour,
The clock was echoing in the tower;
But though my slumber was gone by,
This dream it would not pass away—
It seems to live upon my eye!
And thence I vowed this self-same day,
With music strong and saintly song
To wander through the forest bare
Lest aught unholy loiter there.

Thus Bracy said: the Baron, the while,
Half-listening heard him with a smile;
Then turned to Lady Geraldine,
His eyes made up of wonder and love;
And said in courtly accents fine,
Sweet maid, Lord Roland's beauteous dove,
With arms more strong than harp or song,
Thy sire and I will crush the snake!
He kissed her forehead as he spake,
And Geraldine in maiden wise,
Casting down her large bright eyes,
With blushing cheek and courtesy fine
She turned her from Sir Leoline;
Softly gathering up her train,
That o'er her right airm fell again;
And folded her arms across her chest,
And couched her head upon her breast,
And looked askance at Christabel—
Jesu, Maria, shield her well!

A snake's small eye blinks dull and shy,
And the lady's eyes they shrunk in her head,
Each shrunk up to a serpent's eye,
And with somewhat of malice, and more of dread
At Christabel she looked askance!—
One moment—and the sight was fled!
But Christabel in dizzy trance,
Stumbling on the unsteady ground—
Shuddered aloud, with a hissing sound;
And Geraldine again turned round,
And like a thing, that sought relief,
Full of wonder and full of grief,
She rolled her large bright eyes divine
Wildly on Sir Leoline.

The maid, alas! her thoughts are gone,
She nothing sees—no sight but one!
The maid, devoid of guile and sin,
I know not how, in fearful wise
So deeply had she drunken in
That look, those shrunken serpent eyes,
That all her features were resigned
To this sole image in her mind:
And passively did imitate
That look of dull and treacherous hate,
And thus she stood, in dizzy trance,
Still picturing that look askance,
With forced unconscious sympathy
Full before her father's view—
As far as such a look could be,
In eyes so innocent and blue!
And when the trance was o'er, the maid
Paused awhile, and inly prayed,
Then falling at her father's feet,
'By my mother's soul do I entreat
That thou this woman send away!'
She said; and more she could not say,
For what she knew she could not tell,
O'er-mastered by the mighty spell.

Why is thy cheek so wan and wild,
Sir Leoline? Thy only child
Lies at thy feet, thy joy, thy pride,
So fair, so innocent, so mild;
The same, for whom thy lady died!

O by the pangs of her dead mother
Think thou no evil of thy child!
For her, and thee, and for no other,
She prayed the moment ere she died:
Prayed that the babe from whom she died,
Might prove her dear lord's joy and pride!
   That prayer her deadly pangs beguiled,
      Sir Leoline!
   And would'st thou wrong thy only child,
      Her child and thine?
Within the Baron's heart and brain
If thoughts, like these, had any share,
They only swelled his rage and pain,
And did but work confusion there.
His heart was cleft with pain and rage,
His cheeks they quivered, his eyes were wild,
Dishonoured thus in his old age;
Dishonoured by his only child,
And all his hospitality
To th'insulted daughter of his friend.
By more than woman's jealousy,
Brought thus to a disgraceful end—
He rolled his eye with stern regard
Upon the gentle minstrel bard,
And said in tones abrupt, austere—
Why Bracy! dost thou loiter here?
I bade thee hence! The bard obeyed;
And turning from his own sweet maid,
The aged knight, Sir Leoline,
Led forth the lady Geraldine!

Conclusion to Part II

A little child, a limber elf,
Singing, dancing to itself,
A fairy thing with red round cheeks
That always finds and never seeks,
Makes such a vision to the sight
As fills a father's eyes with light;
And pleasures flow in so thick and fast
Upon his heart, that he at last
Must needs express his love's excess
With words of unmeant bitterness.

Perhaps 'tis pretty to force together
Thoughts so unlike each other;
To mutter and mock a broken charm,
To dally with wrong that does no harm.
Perhaps 'tis tender too and pretty
At each wild word to feel within
A sweet recoil of love and pity.
And what, if in a world of sin
(O sorrow and shame should this be true!)
Such giddiness of heart and brain
Comes seldom save from rage and pain,
So talks as it's most used to do.

1. *The context*

*C*HRISTABEL is a tale of terror. It was written, that is to say, within a certain literary convention. Although this convention was not, artistically, a particularly successful one, its nature has some bearing our reading of the poem. The genre was a European phenomenon. It expressed, or tried to express, a contemporary state of mind reacting to profound social changes and it did so, not by dealing with them directly, but by appearing to ignore these changes. Walpole said that he wrote *Otranto* 'glad to think of anything rather than politics'. But the politics, or rather the feelings which the external events gave rise, reappeared on the plane of fantasy in the combined expression of nostalgia for, yet fear of, the past.

One modern writer, M. André Breton, in his essay *Limits not Frontiers of Surrealism*,[1] has traced the significance, in this light, of the ubiquitous ruins, the inevitable ghost and the subterranean passages of the convention and suggests even that 'in the stormy night can be heard the incessant roar of cannon'. Be this as it may, one can agree with M. Breton's formulation of the basic conflict which is played out against this turbulent background, a background 'chosen', as he says, 'for the appearance of beings of pure temptation, combining in the highest degree the struggle between the instinct of death on the one hand . . . and, on the other, Eros who exacts after each human hecatomb, the glorious restoration of life.'

[1] In *Surrealism* edited by Herbert Read (Faber and Faber).

In the fragmentary *Christabel* there is no 'glorious restoration of life' as, for example, in the business of the long-lost child of *Otranto* who is found at last and rules in the tyrant's stead. All the other elements of the tale of terror, however, are present—elements which Coleridge had admired in Mrs. Radcliffe (see his review of *Udolpho* of 1794[1]) and was to guy later on when he sent to Wordsworth a satirical 'recipe'[2] on the subject of Scott's *Lady of the Lake*. His list of requirements (too lengthy for quotation here) is present, almost in its entirety, in *Christabel*. The surprising thing is that *Christabel*, though a minor work, is an entirely successful one within its particular limits.

We have in *Christabel* perhaps the only tale of terror which expresses with any real subtlety the basic pattern of the genre, the struggle between the instinct of death and Eros. This struggle centres on the relationship of Geraldine, the 'fatal woman' (one of M. Breton's 'beings of pure temptation'), with Christabel herself, 'the maid devoid of guile and sin'. Geraldine does not appear among Dr. Mario Praz's fatal women in his *The Romantic Agony* and one feels that she provides a far more compelling example than many of those we find there. She clearly belongs under Dr. Praz's heading of 'La Belle Dame Sans Merci' (the genesis of Keats's poem of this title Dr. Praz traces to Coleridge's ballad *Love*), her characteristics being those of the fated and fatal men and women of Romantic literature, characteristics which are primarily the dramatization of an inner disturbance such as we find commented on by M. Breton. This condition, as Dr. Praz shows, finds expression either in the inflicting of, or the passive submission to, pain. Both attitudes of mind are present in *Christabel*.

2. The text

In *Christabel* the struggle of evil and innocence is examined, although within the framework of the typical tale of terror, for the purposes of moral realization of the manner in which evil works upon and transforms innocence. Coleridge's success in achieving this realization by poetic means is due to a dramatic tension building up to a final, irrevocable climax and skilfully regulated by its background of symbols from the natural world.

---

[1] In the Nonesuch *Coleridge*, p. 203.
[2] In *Selected Letters*, edited by Kathleen Raine, p. 172.

As far as the poem goes (it is a 'fragment') it is complete.[1] The climax of,

> And turning from his own sweet maid
> The aged knight, Sir Leoline,
> Led forth the Lady Geraldine.

leaves Christabel in that condition of pathological isolation which the Mariner also feels and which Coleridge must himself have known. It follows upon the carefully ordered series of psychological shocks to which Christabel has been subjected and beneath which her innocence is crushed. Mr. Humphry House says of the poem in his excellent book on Coleridge that it is 'fragmentary and finally unsatisfying' and that its mystery remains both incomplete and clueless. If one feels a certain incompleteness about the poem it is because we are left with Christabel's pathological isolation which is never, unlike that of the Ancient Mariner, to be resolved. (Indeed, of the Mariner's, it would perhaps be more true to say that it is only partially resolved.) The 'story', of course, was never completed and the elements concerning the broken friendship between Sir Leoline and the father of Geraldine, relevant as they are to the poem's theme of the division of the inmost being and of the most intimate relationships, were never knit up into a more organic significance. *Christabel* offers, however, despite its abrupt conclusion in psychological stasis, a completeness concerning what *does* happen, if only we pay attention to the premonitory nature of the symbols at the opening and see the poetic interest as centering on the uncertain balance which is represented here between health and disease, good and evil, and the end as a tragedy in which neurosis, not death, strikes the final blow. One has in *Christabel*, in allegorical form, that same concern which tormented the self-analyst of the notebooks and the reader of John Webster's Folio on *The Displaying of Supposed Witchcraft*: 'the mind's failure to guide the Will.'

[1] On Coleridge's insistence that 'in my very first conception of the tale I had the whole present to my mind, with the wholeness, no less than the loveliness, of a vision', we have Wordsworth's comment: 'I am sure that he never formed a plan or knew what was to be the end of *Christabel*, and that he merely deceived himself when he thought, as he says, that he had the idea quite clear in his mind.' (Recorded in Crabb Robinson's Diary, Feb. 1st., 1836.)

For Christabel, bewitched, suffers simultaneously with the disintegration of personality the disintegration of the will.

Let us begin with the first important symbolical passage of
the poem:

> The thin grey cloud is spread on high,
> It covers but not hides the sky.
> The moon is behind and at the full
> And yet she looks both small and dull.

Everything hangs in this state of precarious uncertainty, of
incipient disease. The cloud threatens the sky, but the sky still
shows through, and to counterpoint this, the moon has achieved
its most fruitful phase yet remains without the bright appearance of a full moon. Coleridge thus reinforces the idea of potentialities in Nature which are never finally to be realized in the
story:

> 'Tis a month before the month of May,
> And the Spring comes slowly up this way.

The light of the moon is 'cold' and where it falls, it illumines a
further symbol of decay, the toothless mastiff. In Christabel's
room 'not a moonbeam enters here' and here she—ironically
enough—feels safe.

Behind the moon in *The Ancient Mariner* there is the association of the Queen of Heaven, 'the holy Mother' as Coleridge
calls her. In *Christabel* the diseased condition of the moon links
suggestively with the inability of Christabel's dead mother, her
guardian spirit, to operate in her defence. This symbolical use
of the moon to reinforce the presentation of a psychological
condition is characteristic of Coleridge's natural effects. 'In
looking at objects of Nature,' as he writes in *Anima Poetae* (Ed.
E. H. Coleridge, 1895, p. 136), 'I seem rather to be seeking,
as it were asking for, a symbolical language for something
within me that already and forever exists, than observing anything new.' The sky—again, symbolically, a potential which
remains frustrate—should offer Christabel the feeling of freedom and of free will:

> All they who live in the upper sky
> Do love you, holy Christabel

106

says Geraldine; and Christabel herself knows

> in joys and woes
> That saints will aid if men will call:
> For the blue sky bends over all.

But the sky is not blue during the time of the action of the poem: its sphere no longer operates upon that of the world below although, 'covered but not hidden', one can see it. Its presence adds to our appreciation of Christabel's growing feelings of helplessness and isolation. The diseased moon prepares us for her transition from a condition of organic innocence to one of complete division. What is the nature of this division and how is its appearance developed in the poem? The development, it should be noticed, takes place through instances of what happens *to* Christabel rather than what she does. Evil works upon her and by the time she feels *possessed* by it and, 'with forced unconscious sympathy' perhaps even becoming evil herself, she has lost her own free will.

It is worth while here to bear in mind Coleridge's interest in psychological phenomena, in Mesmerism, and also in witchcraft, where a powerful idea working upon the human psyche produces the feeling of guilt followed by mental deterioration. An interesting and relevant indication of Coleridge's interests as a psychologist occurs in the preface to his unsuccessful poem *The Three Graves*. After the inevitable Coleridgean apologia for the subject, the metre and the fragmentary nature of the piece, he goes on to tell us that at the time of its composition he 'had been reading Bryan Edward's account of the effect of the Oby witchcraft on the Negroes in the West Indies, and Hearne's deeply interesting anecdotes of similar workings on the imagination of the Copper Indians.' In settling on a story of psychological obsession brought about by a blasphemous curse (a story Coleridge says is 'positive fact, and of no very distant date') he had wanted to show 'the possible effect on the imagination from an Idea violently and suddenly impressed on it.' 'I conceived the design', he says, 'of showing that instances of this kind are not peculiar to savage or barbarous tribes, and of illustrating the mode in which the mind is affected in these cases, and the progress and symptoms of the morbid action on the fancy from the beginning.' All three protagonists in the poem are reduced to a condition of morbid introversion and their minds possessed by the image of the woman who has delivered the curse. Coleridge, despite a certain psychological acuteness, handles the affair somewhat clumsily as poetic material and we must return to Geraldine's onslaught upon Christabel to see what he is really capable of in dealing with this kind of subject.

To begin with, Christabel finds herself alone. Her lover is absent, her mother dead, her father sick:

> Each matin bell, the Baron saith,
> Knells us back to a world of death . . .
> These words Sir Leoline will say
> Many a morn to his dying day.

Here is the position of the typical persecuted woman of the tale of terror, defenceless and vulnerable, her isolation being intensified by its juxtaposition with the fine image of 'the one red leaf, the last of its clan',

> That dances as often as dance it can,
> Hanging so light, and hanging so high,
> On the topmost twig that looks up at the sky.

In this condition Christabel finds the Lady Geraldine who, according to her own story, has been abducted, then abandoned, and takes her into the castle. Coleridge conveys Geraldine's character of fatal woman in a cumulative series of startling touches. At the outset he gives no hint of the evil in her nature and Christabel sees her as 'Beautiful exceedingly'. The first hint—and it is scarcely even that until we re-read the poem—comes with her unwillingness to join in Christabel's prayer:

> Praise we the Virgin all divine
> Who hath rescued thee from thy distress!
> Alas, alas! said Geraldine,
> I cannot speak for weariness.

Christabel's first disquiet occurs as they go into the castle and past the sleeping mastiff:

> The mastiff old did not awake
> Yet she an angry moan did make . . .

But even this disquiet seems connected rather with the circumstances of the night than with the actual character of Geraldine.

The third stroke is more direct. It takes up the motif of Geraldine's eye which is to be dramatically reintroduced at the climax of the poem. As they are passing the almost extinguished hall fire,

> . . . when the lady passed, there came
> A tongue of light, a fit of flame;
> And Christabel saw the lady's eye,
> And nothing else she saw thereby.

The fourth leaves us in no doubt. Geraldine, fearing the spirit of Christabel's dead mother, the young girl's guardian spirit, bursts out in a tirade against its presence. Coleridge gives the situation an added uncertainty by withholding from us as yet Geraldine's exact intentions. Indeed, whatever they may be, the fatal woman, aware of her own fatality, seems half to regret what she is about to do—

> Even I in my degree will try,
> Fair maiden, to requite you well.—

and as she undresses,

> Beneath the lamp the lady bowed
> And slowly rolled her eyes around . . .

As she lies down to sleep beside Christabel, she has put by all her scruples:

> In the touch of this bosom there worketh a spell,
> Which is lord of thy utterance, Christabel.

They sleep and the suggestions crystallize into a final irony:

> . . . lo, the worker of these harms,
> That holds the maiden in her arms,
> Seems to slumber still and mild
> As a mother with her child.

—Christabel has lost her natural father and has found an unnatural mother: the guardian spirit has been worsted. The important final image of this passage of the sleeping mother embracing her child comes to mind once more, as we shall see, when we hear Bracy's dream of the same night.

In Part One the ground has been prepared: in Part Two the evil of Geraldine begins to operate within Christabel herself.

Geraldine, 'nothing doubting of her spell/Awakens the lady Christabel.' Christabel has, on the level of the conscious mind, reassured herself and sees her tormentor as 'fairer yet! and yet more fair!', but her unconscious fears become conscious once more as her father embraces Geraldine and the latter prolongs the embrace 'with joyous look':

> Which when she viewed a vision fell
> Upon the soul of Christabel,
> The vision of fear, the touch and pain!
> She shrunk and shuddered, and saw again . . .
> Again she saw that bosom old,
> Again she saw that bosom cold
> And drew in her breath with a hissing sound.

It is the hissing of a horrified intake of breath, but its significance becomes deepened when Bracy the Bard tells his story and with what follows. During the night he has dreamed that he saw the tame dove which bears Christabel's name

> Fluttering, and uttering fearful moan . . .
> I stopped, methought the dove to take,
> When lo! I saw a bright green snake
> Coiled around its wings and neck . . .
> And with the dove it heaves and stirs,
> Swelling its neck as she swells hers!

This moment is one of the most startling and suggestive touches in the poem. We are recalled by the image to that of the two sleeping together; we see in the movement of the snake an attempt to *imitate* that of the bird as well as to prevent its flight; we remember that the sound Christabel herself made resembled that of a snake. Just as the full moon that is dulled, holds in a frightful balance the image of health with the image of disease, the latter overpowering the former, so now there is a further frightful balance: we are on the brink of the suggestion that the identity of Christabel is coveted by Geraldine and that Christabel has unconsciously assumed something of the evil identity of the other. We come now to the most important dramatic climax of the whole, when Geraldine is kissed by Sir Leoline and the significance of Bracy's dream jestingly ignored by the Knight:

Geraldine looks askance at Christabel:

> A snake's small eye blinks dull and shy,
> And the lady's eyes they shrunk in her head,
> Each shrunk up to a serpent's eye . . .
> One moment and the sight was fled!

Our worst suspicion is now confirmed by what follows:

> But Christabel in dizzy trance,
> Stumbling on the unsteady ground—
> Shuddered aloud, with a hissing sound.

She shudders with horror still, but she emits the sound a snake would make. Her imagination is so overpowered by 'those shrunken serpent eyes',

> That all her features were resigned
> To this sole image in her mind . . .

And not only does she see the image, she feels herself *becoming* the image:

> . . . And passively did *imitate*
> That look of dull and treacherous hate,
> And thus she stood, in dizzy trance;
> Still picturing that look askance
> With *forced unconscious sympathy* . . .

The idea has rooted itself in her mind. Despite this fact, she still fights against Geraldine's spell by asking her father to send her tormenter away, instead of which he 'leads forth the Lady Geraldine', symbolically rejecting his own daughter. There is an extremely dramatic propriety about this incident as Sickness and Evil move off together. It completes the psychological fable with a succinctness in juxtaposition with which Coleridge's tacked-on conclusion to the second part sticks out uncomfortably from the rest.

One might note finally that Coleridge makes use of the old and familiar material of folk tale: the ageing ruler ignores his wise counsellor, rejects his 'natural' daughter and prefers his unnatural. None of the protagonists in Coleridge's narrative is in him- or herself complex: all are stock figures and therefore near to allegory and to what J. F. Danby, speaking of *King Lear* where Shakespeare uses the same fable, calls 'the unambiguous

Morality statement' (*Shakespeare's Doctrine of Nature*). One is compelled to see the characters as symbols relating to Everyman's condition of inner psychological tension—the evil preying on the good, the sick undermining the healthy—which brings one back to M. Breton's statement of the symbolical conflict of the tale of terror, and to the fact that Coleridge's poem, limited though it is by its inability to resolve the conflict, presents an extremely individual variant on this basic pattern.

WILLIAM WORDSWORTH

Resolution and Independence

W. W. Robson

I

There was a roaring in the wind all night;
The rain came heavily and fell in floods;
But now the sun is rising calm and bright;
The birds are singing in the distant woods;
Over his own sweet voice the Stock-dove broods;
The Jay makes answer as the Magpie chatters;
And all the air is filled with pleasant noise of waters.

II

All things that love the sun are out of doors;
The sky rejoices in the morning's birth;
The grass is bright with rain-drops;—on the moors
The hare is running races in her mirth;
And with her feet she from the plashy earth
Raises a mist; that, glittering in the sun,
Runs with her all the way, wherever she doth run.

III

I was a Traveller then upon the moor;
I saw the hare that raced about with joy;
I heard the woods and distant waters roar;
Or heard them not, as happy as a boy:
The pleasant season did my heart employ:
My old remembrances went from me wholly;
And all the ways of men, so vain and melancholy.

IV

But, as it sometimes chanceth, from the might
Of joy in minds that can no further go,
As high as we have mounted in delight
In our dejection do we sink as low;
To me that morning did it happen so;
And fears and fancies thick upon me came;
Dim sadness—and blind thoughts, I knew not, nor could name.

V

I heard the sky-lark warbling in the sky;
And I bethought me of the playful hare:
Even such a happy Child of earth am I;
Even as these blissful creatures do I fare;
Far from the world I walk, and from all care;
But there may come another day to me—
Solitude, pain of heart, distress, and poverty.

VI

My whole life I have lived in pleasant thought,
As if life's business were a summer mood;
As if all needful things would come unsought
To genial faith, still rich in genial good;
But how can He expect that others should
Build for him, sow for him, and at his call
Love him, who for himself will take no heed at all?

VII

I thought of Chatterton, the marvellous Boy,
The sleepless Soul that perished in his pride;
Of Him who walked in glory and in joy
Following his plough, along the mountain-side:
By our own spirits are we deified:
We Poets in our youth begin in gladness;
But thereof come in the end despondency and madness.

VIII

Now, whether it were by peculiar grace,
A leading from above, a something given,
Yet it befell that, in this lonely place,
When I.with these untoward thoughts had striven,
Beside a pool bare to the eye of heaven
I saw a Man before me unawares:
The oldest man he seemed that ever wore grey hairs.

IX

As a huge stone is sometimes seen to lie
Couched on the bald top of an eminence;
Wonder to all who do the same espy,
By what means it could thither come, and whence;
So that it seems a thing endued with sense:
Like a sea-beast crawled forth, that on a shelf
Of rock or sand reposeth, there to sun itself;

X

Such seemed this Man, not all alive nor dead,
Nor all asleep—in his extreme old age:
His body was bent double, feet and head
Coming together in life's pilgrimage;
As if some dire constraint of pain, or rage
Of sickness felt by him in times long past,
A more than human weight upon his frame had cast.

XI

Himself he propped, limbs, body, and pale face,
Upon a long grey staff of shaven wood:
And still as I drew near with gentle pace,
Upon the margin of that moorish flood
Motionless as a cloud the old Man stood,
That heareth not the loud winds when they call;
And moveth all together, if it move at all.

XII

At length, himself unsettling, he the pond
Stirred with his staff, and fixedly did look
Upon the muddy water, which he conned,
As if he had been reading in a book:
And now a stranger's privilege I took;
And, drawing to his side, to him did say,
'This morning gives us promise of a glorious day.'

XIII

A gentle answer did the old Man make,
In courteous speech which forth he slowly drew:
And him with further words I thus bespake,
'What occupation do you there pursue?
This is a lonesome place for one like you.'
Ere he replied, in flash of mild surprise
Broke from the sable orbs of his yet-vivid eyes.

XIV

His words came feebly, from a feeble chest,
But each in solemn order followed each,
With something of a lofty utterance drest—
Choice word and measured phrase, above the reach
Of ordinary men; a stately speech;
Such as grave Livers do in Scotland use,
Religious men, who give to God and man their dues.

XV

He told, that to these waters he had come
To gather leeches, being old and poor:
Employment hazardous and wearisome!
And he had many hardships to endure:
From pond to pond he roamed, from moor to moor;
Housing, with God's good help, by choice or chance;
And in this way he gained an honest maintenance.

XVI

The old Man still stood talking by my side;
But now his voice to me was like a stream
Scarce heard; nor word from word could I divide;
And the whole body of the Man did seem
Like one whom I had met with in a dream;
Or like a man from some far region sent,
To give me human strength, by apt admonishment.

XVII

My former thoughts returned: the fear that kills;
And hope that is unwilling to be fed;
Cold, pain, and labour, and all fleshly ills;
And mighty Poets in their misery dead.
—Perplexed, and longing to be comforted,
My question eagerly did I renew,
'How is it that you live, and what is it you do?'

XVIII

He with a smile did then his words repeat;
And said that, gathering leeches, far and wide
He travelled; stirring thus about his feet
The waters of the pools where they abide.
'Once I could meet with them on every side;
But they have dwindled long by slow decay;
Yet still I persevere, and find them where I may.'

XIX

While he was talking thus, the lonely place,
The old Man's shape, and speech—all troubled me:
In my mind's eye I seemed to see him pace
About the weary moors continually,
Wandering about alone and silently.
While I these thoughts within myself pursued,
He, having made a pause, the same discourse renewed.

XX

And soon with this he other matter blended,
Cheerfully uttered, with demeanour kind,
But stately in the main; and, when he ended,
I could have laughed myself to scorn to find
In that decrepit Man so firm a mind.
'God,' said I, 'be my help and stay secure;
I'll think of the Leech-gatherer on the lonely moor!'

'*RESOLUTION and Independence*,' says Coleridge, 'is *especially* characteristic of the author. There is scarce a defect or excellence in his writings of which it would not present a specimen.' It is also characteristic of the author in its method. Wordsworth chooses an episode which would seem, abstractly described, to be of small transmissible significance. His success lies in convincing us of the significance *he* found in it, one essentially particular and personal. He imposes conviction by means of that characteristic medium *through* which we are made to see and judge all that Wordsworth wishes us to see and judge, and *of* which the figures and situations he presents seem so completely to be.

This medium is verse of a *timbre* we recognize at once as Wordsworthian: the medium of *The Ruined Cottage* and *Hart-Leap Well* and *Michael*. *Resolution and Independence* perhaps belongs more fully with the first of these than with the other two; Wordsworth (we can divine without knowing any external facts about the personal crisis that underlies it) is more deeply involved in the experience he offers for our contemplation. The point can be made by remarking on the quality of

117

those poems. When we compare, for instance, *Michael* with Crabbe's best work, we feel that Crabbe has the advantage. *Michael* is a very fine poem, finer than Tennyson's *Dora*; but, in comparison with Crabbe, *Michael* and *Dora* go together. But *Resolution and Independence* is, in an important sense, more profoundly personal than *Michael* or *The Brothers*; or, to say this in more strictly literary terms, it is more immediate; though it is on a larger scale, it has the same immediacy, as it has substantially the same method, as the 'Lucy' poems. A comparison of it with Crabbe would not be helpful—except as showing how far removed is its structure and its significance from anything appreciable by the eighteenth-century mind.

I said that *Resolution and Independence* was profoundly personal. Certainly it has biographical value—whether we judge its impulsion to have come chiefly from Wordsworth's worry about Coleridge, or about his own resolve to marry and settle down, or about his tendencies to recurrent depression. Certainly, too, it has its humanitarian aspect, as an example of poetic 'field-work among rustics'; and in this aspect also it is very typical of its author. But *Resolution and Independence* is not the anecdote related, in faithful detail, in Dorothy Wordsworth's Journal. For one thing, Dorothy is not there; and, though William of course is there, that sober, prosaic individual with the traditionally northern virtues, a child of the English eighteenth century, common-sensical, pious and *bourgeois* (while Dorothy, with her simple grace, is like the heroine of *Persuasion*), he is only fully asserted, and vindicated, at the poem's close; the core of the poem is the 'unknown modes of being': and in calling this poem personal we are testifying primarily to an experience of them, and to Wordsworth's way of resolving and validating that experience. *Resolution and Independence* is a poem, self-sufficient and existing in its own right. It is a poem describing a psychological event which issued in a moral attitude. Our judgment that it is a 'public' poem follows closely upon the judgment that this moral consequence—this more general significance—is felt to spring rightly and naturally from Wordsworth's own interpretation of the psychological event. In *Strange Fits of Passion* Wordsworth comes very close to offering only the statement of a vividly evoked psychological curiosity: there is a tacit admission of limited significance ('But in the

Lover's ear alone'). *Strange Fits of Passion*, nevertheless, is also a poem; but it is clearly a border-line case; 'border-line' between the private and the public, or (the distinction is often much the same where Wordsworth is concerned) between the successful poem and the unsuccessful one. *Resolution and Independence*, which has a really similar method and subject-matter, implicitly claims more for itself than the shorter poem; it is conceived on a grander scale; and we are asked, in judging it, to apply to it—and apply it to—much more of our experience. Dorothy wrote gravely to an uncomprehending critic of the poem within the Wordsworth circle: 'When you happen to be displeased with what you suppose to be the tendency or moral of any poem which William writes, ask yourself whether you have hit upon the real tendency and true moral, and above all never think that he writes for no reason but merely because a thing happened—and when you feel any poem of his to be tedious, ask yourself in what spirit it was written.' (Letter to Sara and Mary Hutchinson, June 1802.) The 'real tendency' and 'true moral' of *Resolution and Independence*, together with the 'spirit in which it was written', make it clear that *Resolution and Independence* was meant to be important and general. If we cannot find it to be either, its failure must be judged to be more than technical; nothing in the poem will survive that failure of intention. However, I address myself here to readers for whom the poem does not so fail; wishing to examine more closely the grounds and conditions of its success.

The poem seems to begin artlessly enough, with a series of statements, in the specious present, that might be casual remarks introducing a very different kind of poem, 'lyrical' and careless of before and after. The shift to the past tense in III, going with the introduction of the poet (who brings in, though for the moment he has forgotten about them, 'all the ways of men, so vain and melancholy'), changes our sense of what the poem is to be; III, though so fully in the happy key of I and II, makes it certain that this key cannot honestly be maintained. Nevertheless, the opening stanzas play their part in our final impression. Their 'presentness' is quite right: as we can see if we turn them, for experimental purposes, into statements about the past. This *is* Nature—as Nature is when Nature is happy; and there is, too, anticipatory contrast, not only between the happiness of Nature and the sudden sadness of Wordsworth, but between the bright light, the pleasant sounds, the gay movements of living creatures, and the sudden bareness, silence and stillness of the setting in which we see the leech-gatherer. (Compare the effect of 'Runs with her all the way, wherever she doth run' with 'And moveth all together, if it move at all.') Finally, when we go back to that opening having taken the poem as a whole, it seems a kind of proleptic clarification; Wordsworth, in 'laughing himself to scorn', laughs himself back to a happiness which is felt to be still there. The simple patterning of statements, then, turn out to be less artless than we might suppose from considering those stanzas in isolation. But the 'artless' effect is important; there is, we feel, no arranging; the objects of delight simply presented themselves so, freshly and naturally, in their innocent irresponsibility; their 'mirth' is not to be distinguished from the spectator's delighted motions of identification. The nature of *his* satisfaction is made explicit enough in one of Wordsworth's own pieces of 'practical criticism': 'The stock-dove is said to *coo*, a sound well imitating the note of the bird; but, by the intervention of the metaphor *broods*, the affections are called in by the imagination to assist in marking the manner in which the bird reiterates and prolongs her soft note, as if herself delighting to listen to it, and participating of a still and quiet satisfaction, like that which may be supposed inseparable from the continuous process of incubation.' (Preface to Poems, 1815.) What follows the opening verses reminds us, of course, of another shade of meaning in 'broods'.

The satisfactions of I–III—those of Nature indistinguishable from those of the poet ('with joy' in III can be taken indifferently with 'the hare that raced about' or 'I saw')—are explicitly associated with childhood ('as happy as a boy'); so that we cannot say, when we reach 'all the ways of men' at the end of III, whether the 'old remembrances' suggest to the poet the contrast between 'men' and Nature or the contrast between 'men' and boys; clearly intending to remind himself of the former, he succeeds all the more in reminding us of the latter. Thus in V the sky-lark, like the hare, is no doubt a 'Child of earth' irrespective of its age; so are human beings; but in view of what has gone before we are inclined to give a slight extra stress to 'Child'. It is a commonplace that Wordsworth (as in *Tintern Abbey* and *The Prelude*) associates Nature with the Child; but the association here, taken with the emphasis laid on the problems of adult living in VI, introduces a *kind* of contrast with the Man unusual in Wordsworth. For the theme of *Resolution and Independence* is maturity; or rather, the recognition of a fact of moral experience without which there cannot be full maturity; that is, a successful emergence from the world of the Child.

But though the critical attitude towards a prolonged childhood is felt in the gloomy anticipations of V ('Solitude, pain of heart, distress and poverty') and the retrospect and self-searchings of VI, the transition to the Poets in VII ('Poets' cannot be poets without an ability to recapture the emotions of the Child) states it, if not ambiguously, at any rate with some doubt. Chatterton—of whom Wordsworth, in his prose moods, had no very high opinion—was only a Boy ('It is wonderful', said Johnson, 'how the whelp has written such things') but 'marvellous'; 'The sleepless Soul' cannot mainly mean his insomnia due to guilt at being found out, it is the Poet's eternal alertness that is relevant here; 'perished in his pride' might imply a doubt about the moral legitimacy of Chatterton's suicide, but the line sounds triumphant in itself, and it leads into the quite unequivocal 'glory and joy' of Burns, which cannot be separated from his 'Following his plough' as a child of Nature. The fifth line 'By our own spirits are we deified' therefore comes in oddly—oddly when we ask ourselves just what, for all its familiarity, it means. It serves its purpose, however; without it, the stanza would run the risk of smugness ('We Poets'); just being a Poet, and young, and glad, is enough to bring on eventually 'despondency' and 'madness' (why 'madness', we might ask?). 'Our own spirits', however, brings in the essential criticism, and, through 'deified', prepares the way for the surprising 'madness', while retroactively qualifying 'pride', 'glory', and 'joy'; one's spirits here are one's genius, or one's conviction of it, but 'spirits' also suggests the dispositional 'genial faith' and the more ephemeral 'high spirits' (Burns's whisky, I'm afraid, is irrelevant); the line condenses a fundamental criticism of Romantic poetry all the more effectively because embedded in a Romantic stanza.

121

VIII, the turning-point of the poem, gives us an immediate contrast, in its Wordsworthian tentativeness and embarrassed syntax, with the rhetorical, poetical verse of VII; the 'peculiar grace' and the 'eye of heaven', carrying a further criticism of 'deified': the Poet has disappeared from the centre of interest in this stanza, with its characteristic starkness; in the next, there is nothing human at the centre at all. Of the two famous similes which occupy IX, Wordsworth observes: 'In these images, the conferring, the abstracting, and the modifying powers of the Imagination, immediately and mediately acting, are all brought into conjunction. The stone is endowed with something of the power of life to approximate it to the sea-beast; and the sea-beast stripped of some of its vital qualities to assimilate it to the stone; which intermediate image is thus treated for the purpose of bringing the original image, that of the stone, to a nearer resemblance to the figure and condition of the aged Man; who is divested of so much of the indication of life and motion as to bring him to the point where the two objects unite and coalesce in comparison.' (Preface to Poems, 1815.) Wordsworth indicates by what in such a context are themselves unusual metaphors ('stripped' and 'divested') the workings here of his metaphoric technique. It achieves an effect, after the explicit emotionalisms, the exhilarations and depressions ('joy' and 'dejection') in the first part of the poem, of an extraordinary dehumanization and spareness. 'Beside a pool bare to the eye of heaven'—that 'bare' is the keyword (cf. 'Couched on the bald top of an eminence'). Something existing by itself, obedient to its own mysterious laws, totally independent of the onlooker—this single figure now fills up the landscape that had formerly been so populous with 'blissful creatures'; that now, we realize for the first time, is a 'lonely place'. Instead of the metaphoric language 'clothing' the thought (as we should normally say) it seems to operate by a process of 'stripping' and 'divesting'. Even what might seem merely an ungainly Wordsworthianism, 'The oldest man he seemed that ever *wore* grey hairs', perhaps helps, by the negative suggestion of 'wore', to reihforce 'bare to the eye of heaven'. It is the mere existence of the old Man which is so impressive (speaking of an earlier version of this stanza, in which Wordsworth indulged his 'mystical feeling for the verb "to be"'—'By which the old

Man *was*, etc.', the poet laid great stress on the importance, for his purposes, of the sudden unexplained appearance of this being in his primal simplicity). And it is this mere existence which the odd similes of IX co-operate to define. The first simile, indeed, if followed through strictly with an eye to its prose content, compares the old Man to something that only *'seems* a thing endued with sense'. The father-figure unquestionably is present, but we do not yet know in which of his embodiments; he seems certainly to be 'from some far region sent', but we do not yet know just what his 'apt admonishment' will be: it might be something terrifying. The 'huge stone', 'Couched on the bald top of an eminence', so that we don't know how it got there, and the 'sea-beast crawled forth', while serving, as Words-worth says, to establish the intermediate status of the old Man, are themselves directly evocative, and of something nearer terror than awe.

In X the old Man is still impressive, but is now a recog-nizable, if very Wordsworthian, human being, a character of the *Prelude*, with the 'more than human weight' of his past upon him. That 'more than human', while seeming to make a greater claim on our capacity for awe than the non-human similes of IX, actually makes less; it prepares us for the transition to XII–XV, the part of the poem that has been adversely criti-cized, but which is none the less not only justifiable but essential. The simile which concludes XI, while reminding us of the extreme difference between Wordsworth's sensibility and Shelley's, serves two purposes; its idiosyncrasy helps to rein-force the oddity of the previous similes of the stone and the sea-beast, but, in being so much less disturbing, it induces our acceptance of the old Man as a simple, dignified, and patient human figure, a 'resigned solitary'; and in 'That heareth not the loud winds when they call' we have both a direct evocation (again by negative suggestion) of the old Man, and a subtle hint of the imperious emotional demand of the poet (compare XVII, 'Perplexed, and longing to be comforted, My question eagerly did I renew'). The old Man is by now a recognizable old Man—however cloud-like, he has more than a figurative 'human weight': 'Himself he *propped*, limbs, body, and pale face, Upon a long grey staff of shaven wood'—'propped', taken with the simile that closes the stanza, is an important word, helping as it does to counteract some part of the effect of 'cloud', and giving a prosaic grounding to the summing-up line, 'And moveth all together, if it move at all.'

The 'conversation' which follows brings forcibly to our attention the criticism levelled at *Resolution and Independence.* Coleridge, in illustration of his general thesis about Wordsworth, complains (in the *Biographia Literaria*) of the incongruities of style; citing the contrast between the diction of XVII and XIX on the one hand, and XVIII ('Yet still I persevere, and find them where I may') on the other. Admittedly he had an earlier, and still more prosy version of XVIII in mind; as well as lines, later cancelled, such as

> Close by a pond, upon the further side,
> He stood alone; a minute's space, I guess,
> I watched him, he continuing motionless;
> To the pool's further margin then I drew,
> He being all the while before me full in view.

('The metre', Coleridge had remarked a little earlier, 'merely reminds the reader of his claims in order to disappoint them.') But it seems a very unintelligent reading of the poem as it stands that merely finds in the manner of XII–XV and XIX–XX a Wordsworthian lapse into prosaicism. The awkwardnesses have point; but a point that cannot be brought out if one confines oneself to considering proprieties of diction. The mode of *Resolution and Independence* as a whole has to be understood. *Resolution and Independence* is a poem which casts some doubt on the theory, made current by I. A. Richards in *The Principles of Literary Criticism*, that great poetry must in some way immunize itself to irony, by 'containing' or neutralizing unsympathetic reactions, or by anticipating them. The corollary to this theory, that great poems cannot be successfully parodied, is also made to seem doubtful. For *Resolution and Independence* has been successfully parodied, by Lewis Carroll; and no doubt the parody, in its final form (in *Through the Looking Glass*), makes a pointed comic criticism of the poet's self-absorption and his tactlessness, and of the poem's superficial inconsequence. But when you enjoy the parody, and take its point, you cannot feel that it damages the original. To understand the mood and intention of *Resolution and Independence* is to see why it is not an adverse or qualifying criticism to admit that it contains no irony or humour, or that it is open to parody.

The justification for the banalities and gawkinesses of the central stanzas can be brought out by way of considering a parody of them that does not, on the whole, come off, though it is amusing; the earlier version (1856) of Lewis Carroll's *Looking Glass* parody. (Its author thought that its 'appearance' must be 'painful . . . to the admirers of Wordsworth and his poem of Resolution and Independence.') The earlier version is much more severe on what, in speaking of the 'White Knight' parody, I called Wordsworth's tactlessness; what is burlesqued here is patronizing snobbery and a comically brutal egotism and self-preoccupation.

> I met an aged, aged man
> Upon the lonely moor:
> I knew I was a gentleman,
> And he was but a boor.

(Yet compare 'But now a stranger's privilege I took'); Wordsworth's approach, and his handling of the spoken dialogue, are no doubt comically ungainly, but the whole point is that the old Man isn't a boor ('solemn order', 'lofty utterance', 'choice word and measured phrase', 'a stately speech', etc.). And Wordsworth shows no condescension towards him, rather a bewildered and at first only half-comprehending respectfulness.

> I did not hear a word he said,
> But kicked that old man calm,
> And said, 'Come, tell me how you live!'
> And pinched him in the arm.

This has more point, in so far as it fixes upon the inanity of Wordsworth's question. 'How is it that you live, and what is it you do?' *is* a flat line, and it does not cease to be flat when we see why it is there; but we need not find the poet's insistence ('My question eagerly did I renew') a complacent Wordsworthian indulgence of the kind here satirized. Wordsworth's personal need, his demand for reassurance, issuing in that oddly inappropriate question, is not so much for a reassurance *from* the old Man as for a reassurance *about* the old Man. When this is realized, the prosaicisms seem quite justified; they perform an essential function, in contrasting the public world of everyday human experience and human endurance with the inner world into which Wordsworth has taken the figure of the leech-gatherer, and made of it a quantity which cannot be apprehended without uncertainty and dread.

> While he was talking thus, the lonely place,
> The old Man's shape, and speech—all troubled me;

'Troubled' is the key word here. The significance of the old Man—one that is not finally grasped till the last stanza—is a very personal significance for the poet; there is no hint of anything like the self-indulgence of

> I knew I was a gentleman,
> And he was but a boor

—whatever we may think about some other short poems of Wordsworth. And we might note that in the later version of the parody (in *Through the Looking Glass*) the 'Wordsworth' figure becomes a sympathetic character (the White Knight) and many of the satiric touches are softened into Carrollian fantasy: so that many readers have enjoyed it without realizing that it is a parody at all.

The movement of the later part of *Resolution and Independence* may now be summarized. The old Man in XIII–XV, now seen in close-up, is a credible figure, with his endurance and his simple dignity (the victim of 'an unjust state of society', Wordsworth remarked in a letter defending the poem). He stands for an important element in Wordsworth's own temperament and character; Walter Pater used the expression from XIV, 'grave Livers', to suggest the social and moral habit of Wordsworthian verse. We might say, indeed, that the poem as a whole gives us the two contrasting aspects of Wordsworth himself: his strength of character and prosaic simplicity in the leech-gatherer, his 'blank misgivings of a creature' and sense of 'unknown modes of being' in the poet-interlocutor. The conclusion of the poem gives us the reconciliation or 'resolution' of the two attitudes: an achieved integrity.

The way in which the resolution is effected is characteristic. The mood of XVI—standing, as it does, in extreme and plainly deliberate contrast with XV—is of reversion to the experience of the stanzas in which the old Man first appears; he is an internalized figure, of uncertain significance:

126

> And the whole body of the Man did seem
> Like one whom I had met with in a dream.

His voice is 'like a stream Scarce heard'; the simile associates him again with the non-human. But by now we have, as we had not in IX, an alternative estimate of him to set against that. Wordsworth, we know, attached great importance to the trance-like condition described in XVI; but, even if we agree with Mr. F. W. Bateson that he was mistaken in so doing, we can see the dramatic effect of the contrasting stanzas XV and XVI; the contrast, we note, is repeated in the juxtaposing of XVIII and XIX:

> While I these thoughts within myself pursued,
> He, having made a pause, the same discourse renewed.

The 'troubling' and uncertain significance of the old Man is one appropriate to the child's vision; the 'admonition' he represents to the child is morally ambiguous and disturbing. Recognition of the real nature of the 'admonition'—what the old Man really is and stands for—means achievement of 'so firm a mind'; the 'true moral' of the poem is not only that awareness of the greater suffering of others helps one to deal with one's own, but that *achieving* that awareness—that recognition of others' 'independence' of one's own fantasies, and of what one's fantasies make of them—is itself a moral discovery of the greatest importance: so that the last stanza comes with both a resolving and a validating effect. The old Man, existing in his own right, is himself a 'help' and 'stay' against the encroachments of fantasy; his solidity is guaranteed by the firmness and rectitude of that placid verse.

Resolution and Independence, then, has a structure, and it is this structure which makes it a successful and public poem. Properly viewed, the incongruities disappear, or seem to be functional; the artlessness and clumsiness serve to high-light, to dramatize a contrast which the poem intends to bring out (the 'Two Voices' in the same poem); they are intentionally set against a formal deliberateness of manner so noticeable that it suggests a stylization: one based upon a personal rehandling of the medium of Spenser—a poet with whom Wordsworth has much in common. (Wordsworth had been reading a Spenserian poem, Thomson's *Castle of Indolence*, about this time.)

The setting and presentation of the old Man may, indeed, show the influence of Spenser's Despair. But the significance of the leech-gatherer for Wordsworth is not only that he stands, of course, for something quite other than Despair, but that, in an important sense, he does not 'stand for' anything, but is just a normal and natural, though exceptionally dignified, patient, and resolute, human being. This is quite as important as the more obvious 'message' of the poem; and plays quite as large a part in the type-experience which the poem describes. But even if we take from it only the more obvious message (as Mr. Empson puts it, 'The endurance of the leech-gatherer gives Wordsworth strength to face the pain of the world') we are taking what is certainly there, and what, even stated abstractly, is by no means contemptible.

> He had also dim recollections
> Of pedlars tramping on their rounds;
> Milk-pans, and pails; and odd collections
> Of saws, and proverbs; and reflections
> Old parsons make in burying-grounds.

Shelley's smile is justified; but this element is essential to *Resolution and Independence*; it is part of the central Wordsworthian sanity and strength.

To a Waterfowl

Donald Davie

Whither, 'midst falling dew,
While glow the heavens with the last steps of day,
Far, through their rosy depths, dost thou pursue
   Thy solitary way?

Vainly the fowler's eye
Might mark thy distant flight to do thee wrong,
As, darkly seen against the crimson sky,
   Thy figure floats along.

Seek'st thou the plashy brink
Of weedy lake, or marge of river wide,
Or where the rocking billows rise and sink
   On the chafed ocean side?

There is a Power whose care
Teaches thy way along that pathless coast,—
The desert and illimitable air,—
   Lone wandering, but not lost.

All day thy wings have fanned
At that far height, the cold thin atmosphere,
Yet stoop not, weary, to the welcome land,
   Though the dark night is near.

129

And soon that toil shall end;
Soon shalt thou find a summer home and rest,
And scream among thy fellows; reeds shall bend,
    Soon, o'er thy sheltered nest.

Thou'rt gone, the abyss of heaven
Hath swallowed up thy form; yet, on my heart
Deeply hath sunk the lesson thou hast given,
    And shall not soon depart.

He who, from zone to zone,
Guides through the boundless sky thy certain flight,
In the long way that I must tread alone,
    Will lead my steps aright.

IT is convenient to point to the sixth stanza as the point at which we feel a more than usual honesty in the poet. 'And scream among thy fellows . . .' Screaming, with its connotations of rage and terror, seems not at all appropriate to Bryant's intention in this place, where 'rest' in the line before, and 'sheltered' in the following line, carry the idea of earned repose, wings folding, and the fall to rest. But the moment is beautifully controlled; for the implications of earned repose are there, but qualified and sharpened by the word 'scream'. We are only too ready to lapse with the bird into shelter, into the arms of a comfortable Providence; but Bryant will not allow it, demanding that we remain alert, aware of the bird in itself as a foreign creation, not only as a text for the poet's discourse. How easy, and how dishonest, would have been the word 'cry', falling fitly into place with the tired lapse upon the lap of nature. But in that case it would have been a tired child that lapsed upon a mother's lap, the lap of 'mother Nature' or a maternal God. And the cry would not have been what it purports to be, the cry of a bird, but a human cry, or a bird's cry treated as if human. Water-fowl *do* scream. Yet it is not true that the word denotes only. It carries connotations, though not the ones expected. It connotes the bird's 'beastliness', its otherness, its existence in and for itself, as well as in the eyes of man. There is no question of our entering into this otherness by an effort of sympathy. We are only to remember that a bird is not a man. So we are not invited to identify ourselves with the bird, only, while keeping our distance, to take it for a sign. 'Summer home' has the same effect.

This is enough to show Bryant disowning the indulgence of the neo-Georgian poet. It is just as important to notice how he avoids the self-indulgence of another kind of poet, how the surprising word draws no attention to itself, how the temptingly *recherché* epithet is avoided, so that the momentary pungency does not halt the exposition. So I said that it is convenient to regard this point as the one at which our attention is forced to be close. It is convenient so to regard it. But in fact there is no forcing here or anywhere else. The demand for attention does not assert itself. It is easy to read this poem carelessly and pass it off as merely creditable or even dull.

One could for instance equally well take the last line of the fourth stanza, 'Lone wandering, but not lost'. If we look back on this from the end of the poem, we perceive that 'lost' is something not far short of a pun. Here the word has the homely tang of 'Lost in a wood'; but after the rest of the poem has been read, it takes on also the other meanings or the other shades of meaning represented by 'the lost tribes', or even by 'lost' = 'damned'. For the moment what is pleasing is the approach to popular idiom in a poem up to this point couched in rather literary diction. The word demands once again an alertness in the reader, a keeping of one's wits about one, a refusal to go all the way after the easily cheapened emotional appeal of 'lone'. And on the other hand the pun or near-pun is submerged, refusing the opposite temptation to stand and preen upon a slick smartness. The poet can have it both ways.

It may be here, then, that the careful reader first becomes aware of having to deal with something more than a didactic set-piece. Certainly the first stanzas seem to promise no more, if even so much. 'Rosy depths' is weak, and so is 'crimson sky', while it is only the vagueness of the second line which prevents the reader from asking whether 'steps' is the right word for a progress which leaves a glow. At this point we do not know what we are in for, and later, when we realize that it is no part of the poet's intention to be vivid or 'concrete', our objections to 'rosy depths', for instance, may disappear. (Of course if we are of those readers for whom all poetry must be 'concrete', we shall continue to object; but that is our funeral.) Still, the language of the first two stanzas is no more than tolerable at best. And 'Thy figure floats along' is perhaps unacceptable on any terms. 'Falling dew' may be called artificial, in the sense that it does not appeal to sense-experience (no one sees the dew falling) but to deductions from that experience. 'Thy figure floats along' is artificial in another and less excusable sense. It does not appeal beyond experience to a known fact. It does not appeal to experience, for 'floating' does not adequately represent the experience of seeing a bird in flight; it is as vague as 'figure'. Still less, on the other hand, does it appeal to a known fact, belying experience, about the flight of a bird. The appearance is of ease, the fact is effort. But neither ease nor effort is represented by 'floats'. Moreover there is the disagreeable association of the 'Gothick' heroine seen as a floating form down a perspective of dank arches. This precariousness has its own charm; but it is charming not to the reader of poetry but to the antiquarian amateur. And the image causes discomfort.

What I have called 'precariousness' may deserve a harsher name. At any rate the third stanza explains and confirms it. For this stanza dates the poem and so establishes its convention. It substantiates the Gothick lady. 'Weedy lake' and 'rocking billows' are locutions which show the poet still in touch with the characteristic diction of the eighteenth century; yet 'plashy' and 'marge of river wide', with their Spenserian air, place the poem very late in that tradition, when it was no longer sure of itself. I will play fair here and admit that one of the few things I know about Bryant is that he read and admired Blair and Kirke White, poets in whom the Augustan diction has become corrupted. And of course one of the principal ingredients of that diction, even so early as Dryden, was borrowings from the language of Spenser. Still I think it true that the diction of this third stanza is enough to place the poem at or about the end of the eighteenth century tradition. It could have been written quite a long time after 1800, but only by a poet who was behind the times or out of touch, a sort of provincial. If we were ignorant of the author, I believe we could go so far as this towards dating the piece on internal evidence. But by 'dating' I do not mean so much assigning a period in time. Rather it is a matter of assigning the poem to its appropriate tradition, so that we may know what conventions are being observed, what to look for and what not to expect, what sort of objective the poet is aiming at.

But it is just here that we run into difficulties. For if my analysis holds so far, it appears that this poem appeals clearly to no one tradition, and abides unreservedly by no one system of conventions. It exists in a sort of hiatus between two traditions and in a makeshift convention compounded of elements from both. This is the secret of that precariousness which manifests itself in such uneasy locutions as 'Thy figure floats along'; and it is this that makes the right reading of the poem such an exacting test of taste, difficult but also salutary.

'Weedy lake', for instance, goes along with the 'falling dew' of the first line. It appeals beyond sense-experience in just the same way. 'Rushy' or 'reedy' would have been the Romantic word. And bullrushes are weeds. But to call them so shuts out Sabrina and Midas and their whispering, and places them firmly in the vegetable kingdom, where, for this poet as for the botanist, they belong. 'Chafed' does just the same. The chafing of land by the sea is not an observed fact, but a deduction from many observed facts. 'Chafed' is a dry, merely descriptive word. 'Weedy' and 'chafed', then, belong to one convention, as the appropriate diction of an age concerned not so much with experience as with the lessons to be drawn from it. 'Plashy', on the other hand, and 'marge', familiar archaisms, seem to invite just those legendary and literary associations that the other epithets so sternly suppressed. These are not *dry* words at all; they yearn out at the reader, asking him to colour with inarticulate feeling the things to which they refer. They thus appeal to quite another convention. Some readers may feel this betwixt-and-between air unsettling; others may think the poet deserves credit for bringing the two conventions into harmony. I will say only that the harmony, if it is achieved, is precarious, in the sense that while the poet may sustain it throughout his poem (and the reader feels that it is touch and go with him all the way), his success will not help him with the next poem he writes—he is as far as ever from perfecting a style that he can trust, a reliable tool. He is even further from himself contributing to a tradition in the shape of a heritable body of techniques; no later poet will be able to take his procedure as a model.

One sort of poet works his way to God by learning the lessons of experience, drawing conclusions from it, and so coming upon the moral laws behind it. Another sort of poet leaps up to God by dwelling with a fervent intensity upon experience as it is offered to him, not for the lessons it can give, but for what it is in itself. In the first stanzas of this poem, the reader is uncertain which sort of poet he is dealing with, so uncertain that he wonders if the poet himself knows. But the balance of probability was always towards the first alternative, because of the ceremonious tone and stately movement, and the rigidity of the metrical arrangement. For the leap to God would have to be made in the verse, and so it would demand, not Bryant's stanza, but some larger unit which would provide for a gathering impetus and *élan*.

Poet and reader alike begin to move with more assurance in the fourth stanza. Here, for the first time in the poem, we encounter something in the nature of Mr. Empson's ambiguities. For 'teaches thy way' appears as an impurity, an awkward construction forced upon the poet by the exigencies of metre and rhyme, until we remember the usage 'teaching the way to do'. And this, once remembered, gives to the phrase the sense not only of guiding along a navigated track, but of teaching wings how to fly. In the same way, the sea-coast is not pathless, but only the coast imagined as duplicated at the altitude of the bird's flight. And once the idea of altitude is introduced, there is the merest hint, no more, of that other 'coast' which comes with 'coasting', so obviously a better word for the flight of a bird than that 'floating' of six lines before.

Only now can the point of the pun on 'lost' be properly taken. For in the third line of this stanza the equable flow and the subdued tone are abandoned. 'The desert and illimitable air'—a reverberation, a powerful élan; and fine, but at once controlled and valued by the earthy and quaint tang of the colloquial 'lost'. The Miltonic blast has been worked for, and is paid for; at the same time it asserts magnificently the importance and the glory of what the poet has in hand. And so it is possible to talk in a heightened tone, to move into 'that far height, the cold thin atmosphere', and for the wings to grow into sails, into a dragon's vans, 'fanning' the air. So the subsidence is effected upon several different levels. First the movement subsides after

the beautiful break at 'weary'. Second, the flight subsides to the
nest. Third, the vaulting human thought subsides, to a need
for shelter. And finally, with 'scream among thy fellows', the
bird subsides, from a dragon or an angel, fanning the wheat
from the chaff in lofty speculation, to being, precisely, once more
a bird, a brute creature.

Thus, when,

> Thou'rt gone, the abyss of heaven
> Hath swallowed up thy form,

not only is the flying bird lost to sight, but the symbol too is
lost to the eye of the mind. The abyss is not only the blue depth,
but also the profundity of paradox in which the questions of
destiny evade answer. Only so, having realized the incomplete
and arbitrary nature of the 'lessons' given, can Bryant's certainty
('And shall not soon depart') appear heroic and admirable,
more than a windy gesture. The certainty of conviction impresses the more, not because of the uncertainty of the revelation, but because of the poet's acknowledgment of what in it
would seem uncertain to others.

Or so we might have said, were it not for the last stanza.
It is difficult to be fair to this. The moral is thumped home very
pat indeed, but I think we deceive ourselves if we suppose that
this is what offends us. We should not mind the certainty if
the moral itself were more acceptable. Perhaps most readers
will agree with me in thinking the migratory instinct in birds
is no just analogy for the provisions made by divine solicitude
for the guidance of the human pilgrim. And Bryant seems to
assert something closer than analogy. In fact he seems now, at
the end, to approach that identification of himself with the bird,
that earlier he took care to avoid. Yet we cannot but think that
the human being has a margin of choice for good and evil, that
a bird has not. Hence divine guidance in the human soul must
work in a way very different from the automatic and undeviating
operation of instinct in migratory birds. To think otherwise is
to cheapen alike the idea of Providence and the idea of human
dignity—a dignity which depends, by the traditional paradox,
upon the possibility of human depravity.

All this, however, is quite extraneous to the poem as poem.
In raising these objections, we are in fact asking Bryant, not

only to write a different poem from the one he has written, but to believe in a different god from the 'Power' that he offers to us. My disappointment with the last stanza is relevant to the poem as poem, only if I can show that the expectations which it disappoints are such as earlier passages have entitled me to entertain. Only then can my objections stand as a valid criticism of the poem.

I think this can be shown. For if the lesson to be drawn is as straightforward as this, if supernatural guidance in human life is no more of a mystery than the migratory instinct in waterfowl (mysterious as that is), then 'the abyss of heaven' is surely not deep enough. It is no longer the profundity of paradox, only those 'rosy depths' of the first stanza, which have grown, in the interim, no ruddier and hardly any deeper. 'Abyss' now comes to seem a pretentious word, too effusive, making promises that cannot be redeemed.

Thus the piece is seriously flawed both first and last. It is not a great poem, it is only just, perhaps, a good one. Just for that reason it demands very careful reading. When a poet's achievement is precarious at best, he requires in especial degree the co-operation of his readers. Not that he should be repeatedly given the benefit of the doubt; that would be not co-operation but indulgence. Rather it is a question of permitting the poem to establish its own convention; and where a poet is himself uncertain about the convention he is writing in (having perhaps to express something for which the established conventions are inadequate, yet lacking the energy to break wholly free of them), the reader has to be patient while the poet feels his way towards the convention he wants. Bryant feels his way through three or four stanzas.

Ultimately every poem establishes its own convention, dictates its own terms. But in a period when certain conventions (of diction, for instance) are shared by almost all the poets of one or more generations, the reader can with ease take his first rough bearings, and the poet can rely upon his doing so. When poets and readers agree, for instance, that certain metres, certain rhetorical figures, a certain vocabulary, go along with elegy, certain others with satire, the poet can expect his reader to understand quite quickly how any one poem he writes is to be 'taken'. But in periods such as our own, or Bryant's, when the genres are being reshuffled so that they are no longer mutually exclusive, the poet finds it much harder, not just to hold, but to direct the reader's attention, so that he shall know what to look for, what not to expect. Even in these cases, however, the poem establishes a convention for itself by, in effect, challenging comparison with certain poems and not with others. We begin to get somewhere with Bryant's poem only when he brings it home to us (and perhaps to himself) that, although this poem could never have been written in the eighteenth century, yet it belongs, and is to be taken, along with an eighteenth century poem such as Gray's 'On the Spring', not with Shelley's 'To a Skylark'.

From this point of view, to offer to read a poem 'in isolation' is really a piece of trickery. For a great part of any careful reading consists in setting the poem among its fellows, that is, with those poems, in that genre, where it belongs. This has the effect, not of multiplying the meanings to be found, but rather of limiting the meanings to those which are really there, excluding those that come from reading it in the wrong way, expecting things that the poem (not the poet) tells us, by implication, not to expect.

G. M. HOPKINS

The Windhover

To Christ our Lord

Dennis Ward

I CAUGHT this morning morning's minion, king-
   dom of daylight's dauphin, dapple-dawn-drawn Falcon, in his riding
   Of the rolling level underneath him steady air, and striding
High there, how he rung upon the rein of a wimpling wing
In his ecstasy! then off, off forth on swing,
   As a skate's heel sweeps smooth on a bow-bend: the hurl and gliding
   Rebuffed the big wind. My heart in hiding
Stirred for a bird,—the achieve of, the mastery of the thing!

Brute beauty and valour and act, oh, air, pride, plume here
   Buckle! AND the fire that breaks from thee then, a billion
Times told lovelier, more dangerous, O my chevalier!

   No wonder of it: shéer plód makes plough down sillion
Shine, and blue-bleak embers, ah my dear,
   Fall, gall themselves, and gash gold-vermilion.

This essay is an attempt to probe the question: What did *The Windhover* mean to Hopkins? This is not the place to argue the

value of such an approach; it must suffice that I state quite
baldly my opinion that such a struggle for bearings as that illustrated in the body of this essay shows the best possible way into
the poem—the essential first step in encompassing its experience.

I CAUGHT this morning morning's minion, king-
    dom of daylight's dauphin, dapple-dawn-drawn Falcon, in his riding
    Of the rolling level underneath him steady air, and striding
High there, how he rung upon the rein of a wimpling wing
In his ecstasy!

The poet catches sight of the Falcon flying high and solitary
in the early morning sky and responds with a burst of sensuous
delight. The movement of the verse follows first the upward
surge of the poet's spirit, then turns away to lift and swing with
the bird's flight as it 'rides' the wind, a monarch—'kingdom of
daylight's dauphin'. The immediacy of the verb 'caught' conveys
exactly that first swift shock of delight. From the initial impact
it is as though the poet—in spirit at least—is himself snatched
up to fly with the Falcon. The movement of this opening is one
of lift and pause and lift. The three *m*'s emphasize the running
stress-words 'morning', 'morning's', 'minion'; but of first importance is the *grading* of the stresses. 'Morning's' takes a more
emphatic stress than 'morning' and forces a pause between the
two words. This pause allows the stress variation full play and
emphasizes the progression from the temporal 'morning' to
the possessive impersonification[1] 'morning's'. 'Minion' takes the
lightest stress of the whole of this first phase, and, as a result, the
natural grammatical pause between it and 'king-' is lengthened

---

[1] 'This most peculiar attitude towards self—whether joined to a rational
or to an irrational nature—immediately proceeding from his habitual
search for the inscape of things, drove Hopkins instinctively to their
impersonification, a personification, that is, of the irrational selves on the
level of sensitive perception, unconscious therefore, in so far as Hopkins
neither reflected upon it nor intellectually accounted for it. I wish to
stress the words "on the level of sensitive perception"; this restriction
implies that the impersonification did not take place by an explicit act
of comparison by and in which the intellectual presented the irrational
object as a person. For this reason I have chosen the term " impersonification", and I preserve the term "personification" for that figure of speech
which cannot exist without a conscious act of intellectual reasoning.'
(Peters, *Gerard Manley Hopkins.*)

into a full breath-pause, so that the exceptionally heavy stress on the latter—which ends the rising movement and which takes some of its force from the echo of the two preceding slack -*ing*'s—can be fully marked.

From there the movement follows the course of flight and dips and swings and lifts with it. The chivalric terms 'dauphin' and 'minion' seem appropriate to such a creature as the 'riding', 'striding' Falcon, who is certainly the morning's darling and prince of daylight. Two interpretations are possible for the image 'dapple-dawn-drawn Falcon'. Isolated, it may seem to imply that the Falcon is drawn—outlined, etched—against the dappled dawn; but this is too static, too lifeless. In its context, it gives rather the impression of movement; and the most satisfactory explanation is that the Falcon is 'dawn-drawn' in the sense of being attracted, of being drawn upwards, *into* the 'dapple-dawn'—as a royal 'minion' might well be attracted into the royal presence. The romance terms 'minion', 'dauphin' and, later, 'chevalier'—combined with the description of the Falcon's *riding* of the rolling level underneath him steady air, and *striding* high there'—carry connotations of the mediaeval chivalry, knight-errantry and active pride. The very movement of the verse here seems to sway to the movement of a charger.[1] Here is the 'pride' and 'valour' and 'plume' of the bird; and its struggle against the elements becomes symbolic of the struggle of the Christian knight (Christ—to whom the sonnet is addressed) against the forces of evil.

In the adjectival compounds 'dapple-dawn-drawn' and 'rolling level underneath him steady', Hopkins has inscaped his objects. The Falcon is not simply a falcon—any falcon—seen at a certain time of day, performing a certain action in a particular setting. The Falcon is not separable from any of these circumstances; they are the outward expression of its essential features, part of its being, and are inseparable either from the Falcon or each other. It is the same with the inscaping of the 'air'; the significant thing about it is its complete identification with the Falcon's flight, which, as it were, renders it visible. The compound image provides an excellent example of how an oral reading will bring out the sense of a difficult passage. Sight-read it appears almost unintelligible; but when read aloud it resolves

[1] Peters, *Gerard Manley Hopkins*, pp. 105–6.

itself into a complex of three movements, which combine in expressing the control and supremacy of the 'dauphin' in his skyey kingdom, and we get: 'his riding of the rolling . . . level underneath him . . . steady air'. The air is rolling, but the Falcon's command is such that it appears level beneath him, and the final impression is of 'steady' (subdued—conquered) air. This·emphasis on the Falcon's supremacy and control is further heightened later in the sonnet when his long, turning glide appears to have 'rebuffed the big wind'.

Now that the Falcon has been identified with the idea of the Christian knight, it is tempting to relate part of the next image to that concept and to interpret it on those terms. W. A. M. Peters, S.J., provides the extreme example: 'rung', he says,

calls up the ringing bells with which the reins are adorned as befits a royal charger. But 'rein' is a homophone of 'reign' and this recalls once again that the hawk is a dauphin, is a prince.[1]

W. H. Gardner gives a more sober·and convincing reading:

The technical term 'rung upon the rein' compares the sweeping curves of the bird's flight to the circle described by a horse at the end of the trainer's long rein.[2]

This certainly does more justice to the sense of movement that is an important aspect of the Falcon's flight and its effect upon the poet. But even this is too earthbound and hardly does justice to a 'dawn-drawn' flight. R. V. Schoder, S.J., has offered the best explanation[3] in his reminder that 'rung' is the correct hawking term for describing a spiral climb. *The Oxford English Dictionary* quotes an example of this use of the term from the *Pall Mall Gazette* of August 20th, 1869:

When flown at a rook, both birds at times 'ring' into the sky, the rook striving its utmost to keep above its pursuer.[4]

If this sense of 'rung' is combined with Professor Gardner's explanation of the 'running rein', the result is a vivid image of

[1] *Gerard Manley Hopkins*, W. A. M. Peters, S.J., p. 105.
[2] *Gerard Manley Hopkins*, W. H. Gardner, Vol. I, p. 180.
[3] *What Does The Windhover Mean?*, *Immortal Diamond*, pp. 290–1.
[4] *Oxford English Dictionary*, Vol. 8, p. 692, col. 2.

the Falcon's lifting flight: the control of the bird pulling against the curve of its climb would give exactly that impression of being held on a 'running rein'. Yet a still further refinement is in order. As will be seen later (in the interpretation of the sestet) the important thing about the flight of the Falcon is that it is controlled in a double sense—is expressive of both determinate and indeterminate action. Its course is determined by the will of the bird in relation to the directing forces. Therefore it is worth while bearing in mind the idea of 'rein' contained in such phrases as 'giving the rein' or Shakespeare's:

> When she will take the rein, I let her run[1]

—which conveys the idea of *controlled freedom* or, less paradoxically, of governed impulse. According to Hopkins, man's actions are influenced by God; man, in a sense, is also on a 'running rein', though his free-will allows him the power to acknowledge or deny God's leading stresses.

Father Schoder says of the description 'wimpling wing':

The falcon's wing is described as 'wimpling' because of the way the feathers appear in graceful folds when seen from below (as Hopkins recalls from closer observation before), and also because the mechanics of banked flight require the pivotal wing to be contracted so that its shortened span forces the surface into bulging ripples.[2]

This is very convincing, and it is exactly the sort of detail that Hopkins would have seized upon to inscape the Falcon's flight. Even so, I feel that the important thing is the movement that is suggested by the term 'wimpling'—especially when spoken aloud, as it should be.[3] 'Wimpling' suggests a rippling motion like the flickering of feathers in a wind, or like the shuddering movement of a wing held at tension, kite-like, against a stiff

---

[1] *The Winter's Tale*, Act II, iii, 51.

[2] *Immortal Diamond*, p. 291.

[3] In a letter to Coventry Patmore, Hopkins wrote: 'Such verse as I do compose is oral, made away from paper, and I put it down with repugnance.' (*Letters*, Vol. 3, p. 231.) Again, in writing to Bridges about the poem *The Leaden Echo and the Golden Echo*, he defended his rhythmic subtleties with: 'The long lines are not rhythm run to seed: everything is weighed and timed in them. Wait till they have taken hold of your ear and you will find it so.' (*Letters*, Vol. I, 154–5.)

breeze—the sort of movement that a flapping wimple would make, rather like the ruffle of a flag, which Hopkins described in his Journal:

and indeed a floating flag is like wind visible, and what weeds are in a current; it gives thew and fires it and bloods it in.[1]

'In his ecstasy' again calls to mind the struggle of the Falcon in relation to the Christian knight. As the bird battles against the wind, he seems to rejoice in his strength as does the knight in his battle against evil; it is as though the protagonist can find his true strength only in the *trial* of strength and purpose, as though his might is drawn from the force of the opposition. Then the Falcon turns:

. . . then off, off forth on swing,
As a skate's heel sweeps smooth on a bow-bend: the hurl and gliding
Rebuffed the big wind.

The simile of the 'skate's heel' persuades Father Schoder[2] that 'bow' should be understood as representing the 'figure 8'—the skating figure—and that the curve of the Falcon's flight is expressed in terms of the curve made by the heel of the skate on the loop-bend. But the idea of a precisely skated figure hardly conveys the speed and strain of the turn into the wind. It is important that this sense of stress and strain should be fully realized, and it seems better caught in the image of an English long-bow held at tension.

Hitherto it has been the bird itself that has dominated the poet's thought—'the achieve of, the mastery of the thing!' Now his thoughts turn inward to relate the experience to his own state of being, to his own struggle and aspiration. In a mere bird he has seen the image of Christian endeavour, 'caught' the essence of its spirit: the struggle and the achievement in face of all difficulties, the courage and pride in singleness of purpose that allows its possessor to triumph equally in open conflict or willing submission. Even as the Falcon can beat the wind beneath him or turn with it, submitting only to defeat it through its own impetus:

. . . the hurl and gliding
Rebuffed the big wind.

[1] *Notebooks*, p. 178.
[2] *Immortal Diamond*, p. 292.

—so the true Christian knight, the ideal of the Jesuit priest, is He who brought his followers the offer not of peace but of strife and the trial of persecution—the Christ who could rise in wrath and cast the money-lenders from the temple and as willingly submit to the agony and humiliation of the Crucifixion. What Hopkins is saying in 'My heart in hiding stirred for a bird' is that the Falcon's example has re-animated his failing purpose. But he is saying much more than this. In exciting the poet's emulative desire, the bird has become the instrument of God (here it is worth remembering that a 'minion' is an instrument of the supreme monarch) and has brought the flash of recognition of God's stress. But this requires elaboration, which can best be done with a few extracts from Hopkins's other writings, especially from his *Comments on the Spiritual Exercises of St. Ignatius Loyola*—a work that has much to offer the commentator on the *Windhover*. First, a note on inspiration:

The word inspiration need cause no difficulty. I mean by it a mood of great, abnormal in fact, mental acuteness, either energetic or receptive, according as the thoughts which arise in it seem generated by a stress and action of the brain, or to strike into it unasked.[1]

Now, for Hopkins, inspiration derives from God, is in fact God's 'assisting grace'; its function is 'elevating', and it:

. . . lifts the receiver from one cleave of being to another and to a vital act in Christ: this is truly God's finger touching the very vein of personality, which nothing else can reach and man respond to by no play whatever, by bare acknowledgement only, the counter stress which God alone can feel ('subito probas eum'), the aspiration in answer to his inspiration.[2]

Directly after this passage Hopkins remarked, 'Of this I have written above and somewhere else long ago.' Mr. Humphry House, the editor of the *Notebooks and Papers of Gerard Manley Hopkins*, suggests, quite rightly, that the 'somewhere else' is the first part of *The Wreck of The Deutschland*; but the elevating function of God's 'assisting grace' is a common theme in Hopkins's poetry; it is, in fact, the theme of *The Windhover*. However, the phrase 'aspiration in answer to his inspiration' invites

[1] Letter to A. Baillie, Sept 16th, 1864.
[2] *Comments, Notebooks*, p. 309.

comment, and the fifth stanza of *The Wreck of The Deutschland* provides a good starting point:

> I kiss my hand
> To the stars, lovely-asunder
> Starlight, wafting him out of it; and
> Glow, glory in thunder;
> Kiss my hand to the dappled-with-damson west:
> Since, tho' he is under the world's splendour and wonder,
> His mystery must be instressed, stressed;
> For I greet him the days I meet him, and bless when I understand.

In short, this realization of God in natural phenomena must be made actual in the person by a contributive effort of acceptance; for:

as mere possibility, passive power, is not power proper and has no activity it cannot of itself come to stress, cannot instress itself.[1]

Hopkins, then, in his reaction to the natural beauty of the Falcon, has felt God's stress, but so far his reaction has been passive, and to become active it must be 'instressed, stressed'. From this observation we may proceed to the sestet of the sonnet.

The sestet opens:

Brute beauty and valour and act, oh, air, pride, plume, here Buckle!

Here Hopkins calls on the qualities of the bird that have excited his admiration and inspired a 'heart in hiding' to come together in that heart and condition it for his life's purpose of struggle and sacrifice. It is not the refinements of the bird that are significant; it is the inspiration that is realized *through* them. The verb 'Buckle' has long been a debating point. If read as an indicative and not, as above, as an imperative, the meaning of the poem is changed completely and tends to become the weary surrender of the poet to the ascetic demands of the priest that many critics believe it to be. In such a reading, the sheer delight, the whole initiative and magnificent upward sweep, fails as the 'Brute beauty', 'valour' and 'act', the 'pride' and the 'plume' are made to crumble before the wearily submissive recollection of the priestly vocation. A variant of the imperative reading of

---

[1] *Comments, Notebooks*, p. 309.

'Buckle' is that the bird represents only the 'valour' and 'pride' of 'brute beauty', which is purposeless, and that the poet-priest calls upon these qualities to submit—that is, his delight in these qualities—to the sterner demands of a spiritual life of plodding action: 'sheer plod makes plough down sillion shine'. This would again throw the emphasis upon the incompatibility of the poetic and priestly vocations. But neither of these readings is satisfactory. Hopkins rejects neither the natural beauties of the bird nor the sensuous delight that he finds in them; indeed, they are the source of his inspiration and strength. They must not be denied; they must be stressed—made more. Hopkins's 'here' in 'here Buckle' is not primarily temporal, less 'at this moment of recollection' than 'here in this place'—that is, *in my heart*—as later analysis will show.

The next problem is the reading of:

... AND the fire that breaks from thee then, a billion
Times told lovelier, more dangerous, O my chevalier!

Why did Hopkins write 'AND' in capitals? Professor Gardner has the answer pat; it is, he says, a metrical subtlety:

A very curious expedient was the writing of 'AND' in capitals. This could only be to point out that although the word counts in the scansion merely as a slack syllable, in the actual reading aloud it must be pronounced with speed and stress; by this means the poet hoodwinks the academic exciseman and slips in what is virtually a six-stress line under cover of a pentameter.[1]

It is a pleasant thought, this hoodwinking of the 'academic exciseman'; but surely Hopkins's device has more to it than that. Again Father Schoder's observations point in the right direction and deserve quotation:

The very way in which 'AND' is emphasized reveals its imporance in the development of the thought. It is the 'and' of consequence, equivalent to 'and as a certain result'; for the preceding line is really the protasis, to which this is the apodasis—*if* this struggle is re-enacted in the poet's soul, *then in consequence* a glory, 'fire' will break forth from him too.[2]

[1] *Gerard Manley Hopkins*, W. H. Gardner, Vol. I, pp. 99–100.
[2] *Immortal Diamond*, p. 298.

As has already been suggested, I believe that the important thing is not that the struggle—or for that matter any of the physical attributes of the bird—should be *re-enacted* in the heart or soul of the poet. Again it is the *significance* (the latent possibilities in relation to the poet) of the struggle—its implications when apprehended as God's 'assisting grace' and the exercising of that 'more particular providence' that incites the emulative desire of the 'receiver':

When a man has given himself to God's service, when he has denied himself and followed, he has fitted himself to receive and does receive from God a special guidance, a more particular providence.[1]

It is this realization of God's purpose that provides the motivation for the *active* life in Christ. The function of this emulative desire is explained in the *Comments*:

For prayer is the expression of a wish to God and, since God searches the heart, the conceiving even of the wish is prayer in God's eyes. For there must be something which shall truly be the creature's in the work of corresponding with grace . . . correspondence itself is on man's side not so much corresponding as the wish to correspond, and this least sigh of desire, this aspiration, is the life and spirit of man.[2]

So, too, in the poem *To what serves Mortal Beauty?*, which expressly deals with this subject, we get:

What do then? how meet beauty? Merely meet it; own,
Home at heart, heaven's sweet gift; then leave, let that alone.
Yea, wish that though, wish all, God's better beauty, grace.

There we have it; it is the perception of that 'better beauty', God's grace, which lies behind the mortal beauty, that provides the incentive and is the end to be sought. And this again throws the emphasis on that key-word 'Buckle'; for now we realize that in the very act of engaging the 'receiver's' heart, the physical attributes, the 'mortal beauty', will give way, be elevated, to the spiritual. Our reading of this ambiguous 'Buckle' will, then, carry connotations both of 'engaging' and of 'giving way'

[1] *Letters*, Vol. II, p. 93.
[2] *Comments*, *Notebooks*, p. 333.

From this we can continue the explanation of the sestet. The mortal beauty of the Falcon, the energy and valour and pride, will be a 'billion times told lovelier' when apprehended as the outward and visible sign of the creative force, God, which is 'under the world's splendour and wonder'. 'Then' (which is stressed and means 'when this has been accomplished') it not only will be immeasurably more beautiful; it will prove a source of spiritual strength, 'more dangerous' in that it will be actuated, will be stressed (made more) by 'corresponding' aspiration. The dangerous and active end to which this kind of inspiration draws the priest is the absolute submission to God's will, the effect of which is expressed in the Jesuit prayer:

Dearest Lord, teach me to be generous; to serve Thee as Thou deservest, to give and not to count the cost, to fight and not to heed the wounds, to toil and not to seek for rest, to labour and not to ask for reward—save that of knowing that I am doing Thy will.

It is not easy for those of us who do not share Hopkins's faith to appreciate the thrill of that 'dangerous'; it carries something of the primitive force of our earliest Christian poetry—*The Dream of the Rood*, for instance, where Christ is revealed as the ideal of heroic action, and his sacrifice is expressed in militant phraseology:

Ongyrede hine þā geong hæle,
þæt wæs God ælmihtig,
strang and stīðmōd
gestah hē on gealgan hēanne
mōdig on manigre gesyhðe,
þā hē wolde mancyn lȳsan.

Then the young Hero, who was Christ Almighty, brave and unflinching, stripped Himself. He mounted on the high Cross, brave in the sight of many, when he was minded to redeem mankind.[1]

Whom or what is Hopkins addressing with his 'thee' and his 'O my chevalier!'? According to our interpretation so far, it must be the re-animated heart; but this opinion, which is shared by Father Schoder but not by many other readers, is rather

[1] *Dream of the Rood*, lines 39–40.

startling without further support; generally, it is considered easier and more logical to believe that he is addressing Christ, or perhaps the Falcon. Our help here may be a passage from the *Comments* which describes fully the ideal state of correspondence with God. As it is relevant to the whole idea of 'assisting grace' it will be worth while quoting the full passage:

For grace is any action, activity on God's part by which, in creating or after creating, he carries the creature to or towards the end of his being, which is self-sacrifice to God and its salvation. It is, I say, any such activity on God's part, so that so far as this action or activity is God's it is divine stress, holy spirit, and, as all is done through Christ, Christ's spirit; so far as it is action, correspondence, or the creature's it is *acto salutaris*; so far as it is looked at in *esse quieto* it is Christ and his member on one side, his member in Christ on the other. It is as if a man said That Christ is playing at me and me playing at Christ, only it is no play but truth, That is Christ *being me* and me being Christ.[1]

To which might be added another quotation, this time from his poetry:

. . . for Christ plays in ten thousand places,
Lovely in limbs, and lovely in eyes not his
To the Father through the features of men's faces.[2]

With these extracts as support, I suggest that Hopkins is addressing Christ *and* his heart *and* the Falcon; for they are inseparable. In achieving that state of correspondence where the bird is recognized as the 'mortal' representation of the divine presence, he has achieved that perfect condition of 'Christ being me and me being Christ'. Now we can understand why the sonnet is addressed (and it is *addressed*, not merely dedicated) to Christ. It does not matter that the sub-heading 'To Christ Our Lord' was not in the original draft and was added years later; for the address is essential to its creation and is an integral part of the poem. 'Chevalier' is equally apt as the form of address for the high-riding Falcon, the hero Christ, or the newly dedicated knight and priest. 'Chevalier' echoes the chivalric

[1] *Comments, Notebooks*, p. 332.
[2] 'As kingfishers catch fire, dragonflies draw flame'.

terms 'dauphin' and 'minion', which it supersedes; for a 'dauphin' is less than a monarch and appears, with the first introduction of the bird, in conjunction with 'minion'—in other words, in the opening of the sonnet, the Falcon is at once the symbol of Christ, the intermediary of God, and of earthly beauty, as far as it represents God's influence or 'inspiration'. The comprehensive term of address, 'Chevalier', symbolizes the consummation of the whole process of 'correspondence'—of 'aspiration in answer to His inspiration'.

'Honour', Hopkins tells us in the sonnet *In Honour of St. Alphonsus Rodriguez*, 'is flashed off exploit', and so, too, in *The Windhover* there is 'no wonder'—nothing surprising—that the highest Christian qualities should be struck out of conflict. It is the 'sheer plod', the sheer effort, involved in driving the ploughshare through the 'sillion' (selion) that makes it (Hopkins surely means the plough-share, not the 'sillion') shiny and bright; it flashes brighter for its use and friction. So also do 'blue-bleak embers' strike their brightest fire ('gold-vermilion' —blood colour) when they break from the self-consuming heat of the fire and gash and gall themselves against the outer world. It is usual to emphasize the laboured movement of the poem—what has often been described as the 'heavy, weary movement'.[1] But *The Windhover* was not conceived in the self-damning mood of *Carrion Comfort*, and it is completely wrong to force it into compliance with the spirit of that and other 'agony' sonnets; nothing could be farther from the truth. Father Schoder may be right when he says that the close of *The Windhover* brings out the contrast between the high ideals and the earthbound struggle of the priest; but he is surely mistaken when he suggests that the contrast is realized in a spirit of 'weary' submission. Rather has the contemplation of the higher flights of spiritual and worldly endeavour in the supreme example of Christ given *purpose* to the priest's humble struggle. 'Weary' is absolutely wrong; 'purposeful' better expresses the spirit and movement of this final phase:

> No wonder of it: sheer plod makes plough down sillion
> Shine, and blue-bleak embers, ah my dear,
> Fall, gall themselves, and gash gold-vermilion.

[1] *Immortal Diamond*, p. 303.

'Sheer plod makes plough down sillion shine, and blue-bleak embers . . .'—the weight of the stresses and the alliterated explosives in 'plod . . . plough' and 'blue-bleak' give the impression of push and effort, while the slash and thrust of 'fall, gall themselves, and gash gold-vermilion' recaptures the battling spirit of the Falcon and the knight (dangerous indeed!—the essential spirit of the poem) and, which cannot be emphasized too strongly or repeated too often, is expressed not in the writhing agony of a 'terrible pathos' (Bridges unwittingly did Hopkins considerable disservice when he coined that phrase) but in the spirit of militant zeal and sheer delight that animates the *St. Alphonsus Rodriguez* sonnet:

> And those strokes once that gashed flesh or galled shield
> Should tongue that time now, trumpet now that field,
> And, on the fighter, forge his glorious day.

The Windhover is a declaration of Christian purpose and a triumphant confirmation of the poet's personal faith—the faith that was his very existence:

I have not only made my vows publicly some two and twenty times but I make them to myself every day.[1]

—we need not marvel that the sonnet was so dear to him.[2] In this sonnet we have the poetic expression of that intensely personal awareness of God's 'stress' that, in his tortured prose, he tried to analyse in his Comments on *The Spiritual Exercises of St. Ignatius Loyola*—the tremendous impulse of his religious faith acting upon that Self 'more distinctive than the taste of ale or alum, more distinctive than the smell of walnutleaf or camphor'[3]:

> Each mortal thing does one thing and the same:
> Deals out that being indoors dwells;
> Selves—goes itself; *myself* it speaks and spells;
> Crying *What I do is me*; for that I came.[4]

[1] *Letters*, Vol. II, p. 75.
[2] 'I shall shortly send you an amended copy of *The Windhover*; the amendment only touches a single line, I think, but as that is the best thing I ever wrote I should like you to have it in its best form.' (*Letters*, Vol. I, p. 85.)
[3] *Comments, Notebooks*, p. 309.
[4] *Poems*, p. 95.

WORKS QUOTED

Notebooks and Papers of Gerard Manley Hopkins, edited by Humphry House (O.U.P., 1937).

Letters:

Vol. I, *Letters of Gerard Manley Hopkins to Robert Bridges,* edited by Claude Colleer Abbott (O.U.P., 1935).

Vol. II, *Correspondence of Gerard Manley Hopkins and R. W. Dixon,* edited by Claude Colleer Abbott (O.U.P., 1935).

Vol. III, *Further Letters of Gerard Manley Hopkins,* edited by Claude Colleer Abbott (O.U.P., 1938).

Poems of Gerard Manley Hopkins, 3rd Edn., edited by W. H. Gardner (O.U.P., 1948).

Comments on the Spiritual Exercises of St. Ignatius Loyola (incl. in *Notebooks and Papers,* as above).

W. A. M. Peters, S.J.: *Gerard Manley Hopkins: A Critical Essay towards the Understanding of his Poetry* (O.U.P., 1948).

Norman Weyand, S.J. (Editor): *Immortal Diamond: Studies in Gerard Manley Hopkins* (Sheed and Ward, 1949).

R. V. Schoder, S.J.: *What Does The Windhover Mean?* (Essay in *Immortal Diamond,* as above).

W. H. Gardner: Gerard Manley Hopkins: *A Study of Poetic Idiosyncrasy in Relation to Poetic Tradition* (Secker and Warburg) Vol. I, 1944; Vol. II, 1948.

LIONEL JOHNSON

The Dark Angel

Iain Fletcher

Dark Angel, with thine aching lust
To rid the world of penitence:
Malicious Angel, who still dost
My soul such subtile violence!

Because of thee, no thought, no thing,
Abides for me undesecrate:
Dark Angel, ever on the wing,
Who never reachest me too late!

When music sounds, then changest thou
Its silvery to a sultry fire:
Nor will thine envious heart allow
Delight untortured by desire.

Through thee, the gracious Muses turn
To Furies, O mine Enemy!
And all the things of beauty burn
With flames of evil ecstasy.

Because of thee, the land of dreams
Becomes a gathering place of fears:
Until tormented slumber seems
One vehemence of useless tears.

When sunlight glows upon the flowers,
Or ripples down the dancing sea:
Thou, with thy troop of passionate powers,
Beleaguerest, bewilderest, me.

Within the breath of autumn woods,
Within the winter silences:
Thy venomous spirit stirs and broods,
O Master of impieties!

The ardour of red flame is thine,
And thine the steely soul of ice:
Thou poisonest the fair design
Of nature, with unfair device.

Apples of ashes, golden bright;
Waters of bitterness, how sweet!
O banquet of a foul delight,
Prepared by thee, dark Paraclete!

Thou art the whisper in the gloom,
The hinting tone, the haunting laugh:
Thou art the adorner of my tomb,
The minstrel of mine epitaph.

I fight thee, in the Holy Name!
Yet, what thou dost, is what God saith:
Tempter! should I escape thy flame,
Thou wilt have helped my soul from Death:

The second Death, that never dies,
That cannot die, when time is dead:
Live Death, wherein the lost soul cries,
Eternally uncomforted.

Dark Angel, with thine aching lust!
Of two defeats, of two despairs:
Less dread, a change to drifting dust,
Than thine eternity of cares.

Do what thou wilt, thou shalt not so,
Dark Angel! triumph over me:
Lonely, unto the Lone I go;
Divine, to the Divinity.

I T may seem perverse to devote an essay of the type that follows to *The Dark Angel*. Normally, the poem that receives this treatment, for example a Blake lyric, presents us with a deceptively simple surface; or alternatively it may be snarled with allusions, like the *Gerontion* of Mr. Eliot. *The Dark Angel* falls between such extremes: without being charged, like many lyrics of Blake, with a purely personal symbolic energy, it can be said to contain rich and even challenging allusions. But these allusions do not play upon one another and reverberate like the muffled echoes and contrasts in a poem of Eliot. With Johnson, they subserve the two or three dominant themes; their role is not simply decorative. At the same time, though, it is possible to imagine the poem being carried through without them: they are not altogether organic.

Johnson's poem belongs, of course, to a literary period near enough to us in time, but distant from us spiritually. Yet the evaluation of a poem of the *fin de siècle* may for that reason provide as much of a test of critical method as the evaluation of a metaphysical poem of the earlier seventeenth century, a period distant from us in time, with whose perplexities and conventions of style we are readily sympathetic. On a poem that so neatly expresses the essence of its decade as *The Dark Angel* we should be able to do more than pass a motion of indifference or, at the most, of anger at the remaindered quality of its diction.

My own approach to the poem may seem to be overmuch in terms of theology. If a defence for so unfashionable an approach is required it is simply that *The Dark Angel* is couched entirely in religious language; its subject is metaphysical despair; its object, complete clarity about the self. The sickness it describes is despair at being oneself, proceeding from immediacy to self-reflection and so to the more complex forms of the religious dialectic. And we can plot in the poem this development down to the *peripeteia* of 'Do what thou wilt . . .', the acceptance of despair, the fear of assimilation in and the confronting of the Dark Angel, the Shadow-self; though, of course, the contingent cause of the poem lies in the weakness of the will when faced by certain temptations.

155

What is most evident at a cursory reading is the *pervasive* quality of the evil. The Devil of theology is limited in that he can affect us only through the senses, can control the disposition of our bodies, can count on one's being weakened by illness (like Johnson), by melancholy or poverty; but he cannot touch the will directly, even though by nature the will is corrupt. Should we, so far as the total symbolism is concerned, rule out dualistic pessimism (of a Manichaean order), it is clear that the Dark Angel must be part of Johnson's psyche; not something which can in the last analysis be distinguished from it. This other part of the psyche, this other self, is the shadow without which the substance would no longer cohere. Johnson wants apparently to unmask the Devil. But what if having done so he finds his own face behind the mask? And how will he escape the other or lower self; by redemption or annihilation?

I may at this point seem to be putting the question in psychological terms. After all, descriptions of the inner life are no more than convenient working generalizations. One can simply enough substitute the descriptive abstracts of psychology for the theological drama of the soul. But to do this would be to lose sight of the poem's moral structure. Moral theology, assuming a God who created us and on whom we are absolutely dependent, deals with absolute obligations; psychology, even though it is as fundamentally suasive as moral theology, is more flexible and modest. It seeks to make men accept themselves and fit in with society; it brackets off the question whether either selves or society are ever what they ideally ought to be. One set of concepts, then, tends towards transforming the individual, the other proceeds on a care and maintenance level. The poem, though, is clearly a reflection not merely of a theological, but a psychological situation: an adjustment not only to God's demands, but to the demands of the late nineteenth century social order. With both of these the self is at variance. In its detail, the poem resembles what might be described in Jungian terms as an attempt at 'individuation', a harmonious relation between the components of the self.

Where actual interpretation of lines is in question, I have rather unscrupulously gone behind the back of the poem and used two other, latin poems of Johnson's—*In Honorem Doriani Creatorisque Eius* and *Satanas*—to which *The Dark Angel* is pretty clearly filiated. This in itself is a form of condemnation and I have had recourse to it purely in the interest of exegesis, not of evaluation. But it is still relevant to compare the poem addressed to Wilde with *The Dark Angel*. What was seen only as a warning in the earlier poem comes home later with horrible triumph. *The Dark Angel* is at once a justification of failure, an attempt at reassurance, an exploration of lost territory.

> Dark Angel, with thine aching lust
> To rid the world of penitence:

The 'dark' of this vocative serves two purposes: dark as the darkened Seraph, but dark too in the sense of 'unknown'. To unmask Satan is to conquer him. You tabulate the positions he has attacked already: art, nature, personal relationships, etc., as if that could help. Johnson's life, at this time, had begun to break up and the poem sets out rather desperately in a search for answers. But 'dark' is also the signature of the shadow-self: here as elsewhere the two aspects of the danger interpenetrate: 'we are betrayed by what is false within.'

We know of two passions a fallen spiritual being can experience: pride and envy. By the fact of his fall, the Angel experienced both these passions: pride in his separation from God and apparent autonomy; envy of what he had previously enjoyed, and of the hypostatization of Christ. This 'ache' of envy and pride indicates duration and intensity. Christ was sacrificed from the beginning of the world; there was a metaphysical fall (of Satan) before the moral fall (of man, or of this creation). Intensity, because 'the Devil's despair is the most intense despair; for the devil is sheer spirit, and therefore absolute consciousness and transparency; in the devil there is no obscurity which might serve as a mitigating excuse, his despair is therefore absolute defiance.'[1] In this sense the poem opens, as it finishes, on the eschatological plane. The reference to the Sacrament of Penance confronts us as a large general statement corresponding to the last two lines: 'Lonely to the lone I go:/ Divine, to the Divinity.' If the world be rid of penitence, it will be formally rid of Grace. It will be given over entirely to despair, the second despair of the Tempter. But this vocative 'dark' represents a challenge. However much the shadow

[1] Kierkegaard, *Sickness unto Death*, p. 65.

battens on the substance, it can only reflect it: however wide
the darkness spreads, it remains the absence of light. This is
the extent of your ambition, is it the extent of your power?

> Malicious Angel, who still dost
> My soul such subtile violence!

The statement is held in by the preceding colon. As the poem
begins and ends with a large working generalization of origin
and destination, so, too, the argument proceeds in a fairly rigid
dialectic. 'Who *still* dost', the answers are known already, as
if that were of any use.

> Because of thee, no thought, no thing,
> Abides for me undesecrate:

The onset of metaphysical despair will enforce a turning inward
in the hope of finding the smaller distortion, of ourselves, not
the world. All human activities are wrongly directed, and all
things are indeed 'made double', but not in the harmoniously
connected manner of the book of *Ecclesiasticus*.[1] The 'undesecrate' looks back to the Sacrament of Penance. Ideally speaking,
the view of the world as naturally sacramental might be maintained: It is still God's creation, however wounded, as Satan is
still God's creature, however darkened. No creature can lose its
central goodness: if it did so it would no longer exist. 'Undesecrate' is typical of the negative diction, of the passive constructions, that haunt the poem. Thus, we find 'unfair', 'untortured',
'uncomforted', 'impieties'. This is suggestive of the con-
strictions of the *vie recluse*; but it hints also at the essential
nature of evil as defined in the Fathers and Aquinas—the absence
of real good from a real subject. The characteristic of evil is
that it can only mar what is already existent: it tends towards
non-being, yet never attains it.

> Dark Angel, ever on the wing,
> Who never reachest me too late!

The Dark Angel is naturally depicted in his realm—Prince of the
Air. He appears here as a bird of prey moving, on the authority
of Aquinas, with a velocity far in excess of light. We cannot *see*

[1] *Ecclesiasticus* 42, vv. 22–25. 'All things are double one against
another: . . . One thing establisheth the good things of another.'

the evil, we can only translate from experience the terms used by the enemy. The paranomasia 'ever' and 'never' may seem to start a paradox. Clearly it refers to the double *role*, Angel and Shadow. The pattern of inner and outer has been established by 'thought' and 'thing'. This, then, can imply: I am warned by temptation that you as Devil are on the wing; *but as shadow you are already there.* The stationary quality of the victim means both that additional grace never seems to be given me to avoid you, and the enclosed life I live gives me little opportunity of hiding from you in society or through diversion.

> When music sounds, then changest thou
> Its silvery to a sultry fire:
> Nor will thine envious heart allow
> Delight untortured by desire.

Why should we begin with music here? Music is the most accessible emotionally of all the arts; the art which has the most immediate effect on the senses, on the animal nature. It is also a catalyst—'all art aspires to the condition of music',—the credo of Pater and Verlaine—the condition to which the present poem aspires. Music represents cosmic harmony: The Greeks spoke of 'the harmony of Zeus'; the morning stars sang together; Lucifer fell, star of the morning. This hope that music will lead to purgation is an oblique means of mentioning the Aesthetic heresy. It represents the first of the distractions from despair, proposed in order to avoid recognizing despair and confronting the Shadow. Many trances, including mystical states, are self-induced with the assistance of music, and this might seem an opportunity of arriving at individual harmony without including the lower self. Music suspends the real chaos and permits us to dwell in ambivalence without synthesis. The 'silvery' leaves a sense of cool pure order: the moon against the sun of 'sultry', with its overtones of disturbance and desire. The immediate associations of silvery are not only chastity and repose, the Anima as it were, but also pale, spectral, disembodied, fantasy; in short, the life of the imagination. If one part of recognizing the shadow is despair over one's self, then imagination, 'the possibility of all reflection', is a first, but finally illusory means of escape.

This contrast of coolness and rest with warmth and movement

persists through the poem. But not only lust and chastity are opposed, for 'The ardour of red flame is thine,/And thine the steely soul of ice.' This coolness reflects a passionless withdrawal from human values into the *vie recluse*. For this reason we begin not with the natural world but with human skills. The domain of art represents, for Johnson, a moral problem that is less acute in the domain of social relations.

The 'envious heart' gives us the second spiritual vice. The primary meaning can be shifted along these lines: the devil himself is envious of the beauty of art, since it is a mode of apprehending God. The poet himself is perhaps envious of an art form in which he cannot create, over which he has no control, but which can control him by its sensuous power. The aesthete in him would like to create an autonomous world, according to whim: 'Thou poisonest the fair design/Of nature with unfair device.' Like Satan, he cannot emulate the natural order by creation; or, if he does, through the 'gracious muses' of the following stanza, it remains *mimesis* only; a shadow creation, the fruit of the closed world of the imagination. 'My aim is to write great poetry: but to do so I require liberty of subject-matter and liberty of sensation.' The 'untortured' here looks back to the original latin sense of 'tortured', that is, twisted or distorted.

> Through thee, the gracious Muses turn
> To Furies, O mine Enemy!
> And all the things of beauty burn
> With flames of evil ecstasy.

These 'gracious Muses', then, are not merely courtly and enriching, they are full of Graces in the theological sense: they can sing in Hebrew as well as in Greek. In *Satanas*, these Goddesses are equated with the passions that have rent the soul during its probation in this world:

> Gaudet Rector tenebrarum
> Immolare cor amarum;
> Satiare furiarum
> Rex sorores avidas.

If we knew more of the Furies themselves as they appeared to the ancient world, we might make the other leg of this metamorphosis stand more firmly. They are certainly seen as agents

of damnation and despair, not agents of retribution and restoration in the Aeschylean sense. Instead of purgation, poetry induces forbidden passions. In Dante, the Furies are images of the
fruitless remorse which does not lead to penitence (*Inf.* 9. 49)
—Johnson's 'one vehemence of useless tears'. The second pair of
lines in this stanza seems very much of a ninetyish cliché.
The general statement 'all the things of beauty burn, etc.'
might follow as justly from the previous stanza, or from the
stanza which describes the rhythms of the natural world.
Still, it does show us delight in the actual process of being
tortured by desire.

> Because of thee, the land of dreams
> Becomes a gathering place of fears:
> Until tormented slumber seems
> One vehemence of useless tears.

This is rather fine. The lines as a whole have a stronger
movement, probably by contrast with the rather frail rhymes
'enemy' and 'ecstasy'. Could there be a more positive statement
of the intended healing process? No doubt it would be satisfy-
ingly logical to establish the world of the Unconscious at the
beginning of the poem, or somewhere nearer the 'hinting tones'
and 'haunting laughs' of a later stanza. Still, Johnson lived in
the prelapsarian world, before Freud; and a respectable causal
chain extends from Music and Poetry to the Dream. The
military metaphor of 'a gathering place' is well caught up by
the 'troop' of 'beleaguering' powers in the verse that follows.
He is harping again on the world of fantasy, or the closed
world of nonsense: might it not seem a way of escaping from the
harsh logic of belief? There will be the times, say the manuals
of the Latin Church, when you will wish that none of this were
true. Not even the world of the creative imagination can change
it; nor can the healing trance of sleep. It is from the unconscious, from the chthonic world, the Shadow rises. Your dreams
are more intensely personal than your waking reflections. I may
sleep, but the Shadow is unsleeping.

The last two lines have a certain concision. This 'vehemence'
is a synecdoche by transposition, and the prose meaning is a
shedding of tears that leads not to resolution but to exhaustion.
It is in these lines, I think, that the painful moral insight is for

the first time reinforced by a distinctly personal tone. We have had the general statement that the Angel never reaches him too late: but the sharp syntax and the tensely particular meaning here are more genuinely pathetic.

> When sunlight glows upon the flowers,
> Or ripples down the dancing sea:
> Thou, with thy troop of passionate powers,
> Beleaguerest, bewilderest, me.

For Romantic philosophers the Unconscious and Nature are closely connected.[1] C. G. Carus uses, for example, specimens of intelligence and purposive action in unconscious manifestations of life, human, animal and plant, as proof of an Unconscious (unconscious to us) Mind. For Schelling, nature is an unconscious thinking. We can pass then from the world below sleep to the natural world with the hope that there the power of the Angel will at least be mitigated. Nature can be seen as 'a partial revelation, a participation in, the divine Mind'. I use this elaborate analogy because there is obviously more to the stanza than a mere contrast between the peace of the outer world (away from the Rhymers Club, Irish Nationalist Committees and the Fleet Street bars) and the turbulence of the interior life.

This sunlight glowing and rippling suggests Nature herself to be unimpassioned, apparently unfeeling, but perfectly at peace, because without consciousness as we know it. How does the sunlight ripple down the dancing sea? Are we to grasp some notion of the sunlight rhythmically passing through the dancing surface into the marine twilight beneath? And is there no analogous process continuing through the human eye that sees and the human mind that infers? It reintroduces the relation between waking and sleeping worlds. The ordered movement of dancing contrasts with the rapid vicious movements of the passions and the bewildered movements of their victim. 'Passionate' here is less of a ninetyish cliché than 'flames of evil ecstasy'. It is rather the precise word for these *sorores avidas* kept on the move by the energy, the sting of their damnation. Nothing can be further from the instinctive, happy movements of natural order. But this instinctive blindly happy quality of natural objects can be

[1] *v.* Fr. V. White, *God and the Unconscious*, p. 30 *et seq*.

sinister: it may be a silent hint of withdrawn purpose. There is a tacit analogy between it and the person who is not aware of himself as Spirit, not reflective; incapable of the metaphysical despair which begins the process of healing. The landscape suggests high summer, but the counterpart follows: corruption after innocence; the profile of despair, the darkened archetype of the *Paradisus Voluptatis*:

> Within the breath of autumn woods,
> Within the winter silences:
> Thy venomous spirit stirs and broods,
> O Master of impieties!

The spirit stirs in the breath; broods in the silences; haunts waking and sleeping, society and solitude. The reference to decay and immortality is plain. 'The woods decay, the woods decay and fall,' and the ruin of vegetation is clearly analogous to the ruin the Dark Angel effects in the human soul. The word 'venomous' suggests the Serpent lying in winter sleep, but stirring at a footfall. The last line of this verse adds nothing: it is a pure concession to music.

> The ardour of red flame is thine,
> And thine the steely soul of ice:
> Thou poisonest the fair design
> Of nature, with unfair device.

Lust and pride reappear in this flame and ice; but there is a glance too at the two hells of the Schoolmen: the wilderness of perpetual flame; the icy torment. The damned pass from one extreme to the other; they pass from giving themselves in lust to withdrawing themselves in pride. The red flame connects with the autumn woods, the steely ice with the winter silences. These silences refer back to the 'silvery' of an earlier stanza, suggesting chastity because of a virtual withdrawal from life. It is how such a withdrawal is used, purposively or not, that matters. The 'fair design' of nature is violently contrasted with the 'unfair device' of the Dark Angel. Design here is teleological in the highest sense. Nature is invested with order, purpose, rhythm and beauty. 'Device' hints at more than stratagem: something of a heraldic flourish or challenge superimposed on a durable ground, something decorative, not belonging to the kingdom of essence. The Evil One can only disorder, render aimless, cheapen, distort what is shapely with a lying mirror. The 'poisonest' recalls the 'venomous' of the previous verse; the serpent brooding under the fall of leaves; Eden desolate; the rhythm of the seasons broken.

> Apples of ashes, golden bright;
> Waters of bitterness, how sweet!
> O banquet of a foul delight,
> Prepared by thee, dark Paraclete!

Music, Poetry, communion with the natural world, these are all attempts at diversion from despair. We shall now encounter something more dynamic. For this invitation to an *agape*, a love feast, is more than a distant mockery of the Sacrament of Communion. We must, however, consider it first in this sense. Throughout the poem things are 'made double'. On this outer level of interpretation, then, the *agape* signifies the particular metaphysical horror: of eating and drinking the sacred elements to one's own damnation. Both elements are taken—the terrible marriage of Shadow and Ego is about to be consummated, so that we find Priest, Victim, and real presence in one. In a sense it is an ascent from Nature to Nature's God; a last attempt to discharge the burden of his love before it becomes poisoned. If he cannot communicate with the unreflecting lives round him: if he cannot escape, that is, from consciousness of himself in despair, despair at being himself, can he rely on the offer of Grace? Is resignation, the awareness that eternity is the other part of the dialectic, to be the only refuge? He cannot be present and lose himself at the point where God meets Man most surely, most graciously, most in Person. The offer is made; but in place of the very Body and the very Blood what is offered is the apple of damnation, and wine that does not quench, but stimulates thirst. The apple is a primary sexual symbol. In the poetry of antiquity it refers to the brimming shape of a woman's breast; it is the fruit not merely of intellectual, but of carnal knowledge. Its appearance recalls lost Eden. These apples are 'golden bright', they have a Hesperidean tinge suggesting effort and danger (the kind of effort involved is condemned by society). This epithet 'bright' seems vapid, but it suggests phosphorescence, rottenness. For these apples have been culled from the orchards of Josephus.

'The shadows of the five cities are still to be seen as well as the ashes growing in their fruits, which fruits have a colour as if they were fit to be eaten, but if you pluck them with your hands, they dissolve into smoke and ashes.' Here are the parallel passages from the latin poems:

> Hic sunt poma Sodomorum;
> Hic sunt corda vitiorum;
> > Et peccata dulcia. (*In Honorem*)

> Rex veneficus amorum
> Vilum et mortiferorum. . . .
> > Cor corrumpens suaviter . . .
> Fructus profert; inest cinis:
> Profert flores plenos spinis . . . (*Satanas*)

Like the offer to Faust, the offer to Raphael in Balzac's *Peau de Chagrin*, like Dorian Gray's wish that the portrait may age while he remains perpetually youthful, this banquet is a meeting with the adversary; a mutual recognition; the decisive moment in a lifetime. Art and Nature have been dismissed as distractions; this offer refers to social relationships. Johnson is a little coy about what kind of relationships; but the 'unfair' of the previous stanza, the 'cheap and death-bearing loves' of *Satanas*, clarify matters. The real apple is full of juice, of sap, the movement of life. These dead sea fruits are infertile like love between man and man.

Yet the Lamia's banquet is not for a moment believed in. Not merely is the offer a substitute for the communion with that greater society that transcends the societies of earth, the economy of Christ's mystical Body; the loneliness from which it promises relief is not the cause of metaphysical despair. The question of art or contemplation (of the human scene or natural beauty), or even personal relationships, is not the cause of despair, is quite irrelevant to despair. Despair comes directly from the self.

This recognition is part of the healing process: it means an addition to despair, because consciousness of self is increased. And this brings us to the role of 'the dark Paraclete'. Parakletos means not only comforter, but theologically, 'He whereby the Begotten is loved by the One begetting and loves His Begetter', as Augustine puts it. The Paraklete dwells in man to co-operate

with Grace and here is the dialectically opposed indweller, who
accompanies each decision with his own response. He does not
open out towards Grace but towards the terrifying depths of
the Ego.

> Thou art the whisper in the gloom,
> The hinting tone, the haunting laugh:
> Thou art the adorner of my tomb,
> The minstrel of mine epitaph.

Superficially this refers to scruples, to hypocrisy, to imaginary
and relished fears. *Satanas* gives us:

> Venit autem vitiosa
> Species infamiae:
> Veniunt crudeles visus,
> Voces simulati risus . . .

The real note, though, comes over as pathetic irony and on this
ground one might defend the second pair of lines from any
charge of being rhetorically false. They catch the earlier reference to music and poetry in the mocking way of dreams, but the
deeper meaning seems to be: what the world will see is an
outward pattern of failure which corresponds hardly at all to the
condition of the inner life. The significance of the sacramental
offer is not likely to be understood by others: through the forbidden experience one might express one's feelings towards
one's kind (though it would be an effort to pick people up in
bars); through the trance of alcohol one can come to terms with
objective reality. Resignation is based on a fierce metaphysical
contest. But there is something here of the actor's pleasure in
deception. The adorner adds something to what is known
already: my hidden life has itself something of the depth and
mystery of a work of art. There is something, too, of the perverse pleasure in self-corruption we discover in Dorian Gray
and the Shadow retorts, when one attempts amendment: you
are luxuriating in a new emotion; you are a hypocrite, using
your personal religious feelings as the raw material of art.
Voces simulati risus? In *Satanas* the howl of the damned sounds
like painful hysterical laughter: how seriously we took this
science of debauchery! There must, too, be a vivid reference to
the voluptuousness of hiding a secret that threatens to escape
one's silence, whose existence one hardly admits to oneself.

These voices are the noises in the ear of the dipsomaniac, chiming with the typical feeling of pursuit and persecution. And, if any comfort lay in the reflection: 'I can destroy the shadow by destroying myself,' like a transformation in a nightmare the thought might come: I am deceived. Who is the shadow? am I? is it? For all I know the world may be the sport of an evil demiurge and if virtue is, in the classic definition, 'the love of universal being', then this might dispose of the argument that an evil demiurge could never make me with such a conscience. Everything is made double: the still small voice has its brutal relatives. And these sneering laughs in darkness, smothered echoes suggested by the paronomasia 'hinting' and 'haunting', lead up to the flat statement of despair:

> I fight thee, in the Holy Name!
> Yet, what thou dost is what God saith:

The comma before the Holy Name makes it come out with despairing weight. This is absolute zero: one was tricked. But might one not be consoled, thinking of the Adversary's role in *Job*: God uses evil for his own ends: evil fulfils the purpose of good? This 'saith' can mean either 'as God tells us' (i.e. through the Old Testament) or 'as God ordains it', though by foreseeing evil, as Samuel Clarke tells us, He does not command it to occur: an act is not retrospectively true, it only becomes true when it happens. These lines, then, in plain prose, are despairingly paradoxical: I fight you in God's name, yet you are doing what God tells you to. But have we not been already warned of the Dark Angel's masks?

> Tempter! should I escape thy flame,
> Thou wilt have helped my soul from Death.

Temptation is constructive: it can elicit Grace. From this point he certainly 'accepts the universe' in some broader sense as moral. So on to the eschatological plane:

> The second Death, that never dies,
> That cannot die, when time is dead:
> Live Death, wherein the lost soul cries,[1]
> Eternally uncomforted.

[1] In an earlier version of the poem, published in *The Second Book of the Rhymers Club* (1894), Johnson has 'wherefrom the lost soul cries'. This is perhaps more poignant, but faintly suggests Hell as a place, not a state.

This is the mediaeval (and no doubt patristic) notion of Hell reflected in Donne when he describes it in his fifteenth Sermon as a state of 'Eternall dying, and not dead'. In that eternal instant of horror, the soul imprisons all the content of its past action. (The 'uncomforted' recalls the Paraclete, the veiled sharer of the love feast.) This 'live death' resembles his present condition. Again, the thought might come that he could do without the rewards if he might only feel himself freed from the penalties. To distract, almost, from this thought:

> Dark Angel, with thine aching lust!
> Of two defeats, of two despairs:
> Less dread, a change to drifting dust,
> Than thine eternity of cares.

This 'aching lust' of the first stanza we can read directly with 'the eternity of cares'. *Satanas* gives us:

> Vitae eius mors est finis:
> Crux est eius requies
> Qualis illic apparebit
> Cruciatus, et manebit!
> ·Quantas ista quot habebit
> Mors amaritudines!

'Death is the purpose of his life.' But before non-being can be arrived at, the ground of being must be shattered: the aim of the shadow is night; the end of Lucifer is deicide, death of God. What are these two defeats and consequent despairs? If one refers to *Satanas*, it seems certain that the defeats are the metaphysical Fall and the Cross, while the despairs are deprivation of God and deprivation of death. Lucifer fell by pride and would rise by the same passion. (Suarez in his De Angelis[1] suggests that Satan desired a hypostatic union with God, in the manner of Christ's hypostasis. Aquinas, anticipating this speculation, objects that, for Satan, this would be tantamount to wishing to cease to be, and no one can purpose that in a metaphysical sense. This hypostasis is the counterpart of the dialectical relation between shadow and waking self, the urge of the Unconscious to assimilate the Conscious.) In such a context Johnson's reference to 'drifting dust' becomes considerably

[1] *De Angelis* Lib. 8. Cap. 18, quoted in *Satan*: Etudes Carmélitaines, 1948.

pointed. What the Shadow represents in mystical or, indeed, in average Christian experience, Walter Hilton tells us, is the human burden: Grace does not rid us of the burden, but helps us to bear it: 'the soul is not borne *in* the shadow, though he feel it; but *he* beareth *it.*' Incapable, unlike Baudelaire, of the strength to suffer and be spiritually lucid about his suffering, Johnson does not revolt against it, but becomes resigned. He does not accept his suffering, as a final condition of the whole man; as a *terminus ab quo*, for the artist. The despairing self, at this point, is self-convinced that the 'thorn-in-the-flesh' gnaws so profoundly that it cannot be abstracted, no matter whether this is actually so, or whether his passion makes it true for him. 'The dialectic of resignation is commonly this: in order to will in despair to be oneself there must be consciousness of the infinite (which) is really only . . . the abstracted possibility of the self, and it is this self the man despairingly wills to be, detaching himself from every relation to the Power which posited it . . . by the aid of being the infinite form he wills to construct it himself.' The dialectic of resignation issues in this: 'to will to be one's eternal self, and then with respect to something positive wherein the self suffers, *not to will to be oneself, contenting oneself with the thought that after all this will disappear in eternity, thinking oneself therefore justified in not accepting it in time*, so that although suffering under it, the self will not make to it the concession that it properly belongs to the self . . .'.[1] This 'drifting dust' by no means represents the orthodox sentiment, *cupio dissolvi et esse cum Christo*. Rather, it is a reduction to the atomic universe of Democritus one associates with it, a world of flux, without moral absolutes, so that the poem is resolved by being undercut.

> Less dread, a change to drifting dust,
> Than thine eternity of cares.

The teleological harmonies of 'the fair design' have been forgotten, and Johnson's own deliberate exercise in self-murder becomes logical in this light. In prose, the lines would run: 'Of two defeats, of two despairs, a change to drifting dust is less dreadful than *thine* eternity of cares.' The emphasis on *thine* suggests that the 'change to drifting dust' is, in some sense,

[1] Kierkegaard, *op. cit.*, p. 108 *seqq.*

our lot as against *thine* (the dark angel's) eternity of cares. It happens to bodies, not to spirits. Dust to dust, ashes to ashes . . . In other words the Old Testament is echoing at the back of the poet's mind no less than Epicurean, or modern materialism. But then *thine* eternity of cares may be also the eternity of the cares of the damned which Satan, himself the greatest sufferer among them, presides over.

By the general logic of the poem, though, the first defeat becomes the human defeat by death (the dissolution of the body) and the first despair is perhaps merely despair of the soul's survival, 'Death may be the. end'. The second defeat, which more properly belongs to pure spirit, is the defeat of the wish to die and the second despair is the despair of redemption. 'Materialism may be true after all, and that is consoling, for to people of my temperament the central thing in the Christian religion becomes Hell.' There can be no direct filiation of ideas, but Victorian Broad Church Christians were for ever worrying about eternal torment which, they thought, made Christianity immoral. One thinks of the anecdote about Dean Farrar: 'Drinks on the house, o' man! Old Farrar says there ain't no Hell.'

More broadly the dualism here between body (drifting dust) and spirit (eternity of cares) will help us to the Plotinian eschatology of the last stanza. The drifting dust, as it were, falls away to nothing in the poet's imagination, to moral unreality, and *when* it has done so there is nothing left in his imagination to individuate spirits. What is purely spiritual as such must be good and must of its own nature go back to God. The effect is a psychological one of relaxing, letting go— letting the dust fall far away, the cares, since they are no longer to be the poet's concern. This, then, is the general logic of the stanza: (1) Either materialism is true, in which case I have been worrying myself sick about an illusion—this whole poem has been about nothing, or (2) even if it is not true, it is still true that our human bodies are destroyed and what remains is pure spirit, and (3) I have been imagining pure spirit eternally tormenting itself and seeking to destroy other spirits, but (4) what is really pure in my spirit must be taken up to the source of all purity, and it is right that what is impure should fall away from me and be destroyed:

> *Lonely, unto the Lone I go;*
> *Divine, to the Divinity.*

More profoundly: the immanence of a kind of evil spiritual power in physical existence is the dominant theme of the poem up to the last two stanzas: the notion of the destruction of physical existence, or its transformation to 'drifting dust' brings in, as something of a release, the notion of transcendence. Because the poet can see the situation of damnation, therefore also he is *beyond* it. The pathos here comes partly from the release being somehow mechanical—the Lone to the Lone, the Divine to the Divinity, like iron filings to a magnet, with no more need for worry, effort and self-torment on Johnson's part. The metaphor of gravity, of physical attraction, or of things mechanically arranging themselves into their separate species, underlies both the drifting dust image and the Divine-to-the-Divinity image. It may be only the Dark Angel himself, with his 'eternity of cares', who is left separate, responsible and individuated. From a Freudian point of view it could be said that this is a pure death wish statement: the confidence in this kind of unindividuated immortality is the death wish in a very transparent disguise. The answer to the constant nagging of temptation and remorse, to the inescapable anxiety of being alive, is the certainty that there will come a time when this nagging is no longer relevant, this anxiety no longer necessary.

The first line of the stanza is an epistrophe of the first line of the poem. A radical shift of attitude has taken place, amounting almost to a reversal of fortune. Earlier, the Dark Angel is depicted in majesty, shedding a baleful radiance over the soul. Now Johnson so far forgets himself as to feel pity. This is an analogue of the victim's pity for the tormentor; a pity that was known in German concentration camps. The Angel's suffering is far greater than mine; it is only his own torment which makes him torment me.

But even with our reading of the penultimate stanza the poem is not resolved; or resolved in an odd enough way.

> Do what thou wilt, thou shalt not so,
> Dark Angel! triumph over me:
> *Lonely, unto the Lone I go;*
> *Divine, to the Divinity.*

'If we ask', Santayana remarks, 'what the alternative to these despairs may be, and what will issue from the triumphs he still hopes for, we find nothing positive, nothing specific, but only transcendental spirit, still open to every thought and to every torment, (the) words are the words of Plotinus and the Christian mystics but here we do not feel them backed by either the Platonic or the Christian scheme of the universe; they are floating words.'[1] Still, Johnson might plead the wording of Psalm 82, vv. 6–7: 'I have said, ye are Gods'—words used by Christ (John 10, x. 34) which Coleridge thought referred to the first apostasy, the fall of the Angels.

The actual quotation from Plotinus appears at the end of the *Enneads*. 'That which is Soul can never reach an absolute Unreal. Moving downwards she will come to Evil, and so to an Unreal, but not to Unreality-absolute. And if she hasten upon the contrary road she will come not to another but herself. But to exist in herself alone and not in the universe of Being, is to exist in God. He that sees himself made one with that supreme Self, possesses in himself the counterpart of the Supreme; can he but pass over from himself to God, the Image to the Original, he has reached his journey's end. . . . This is the life of Gods and of the godlike and happy among men; a quittance from things alien and earthly, a life beyond earthly pleasure, a flight of the alone to the Alone.'[2]

Here, then, is the counterpart in personal terms of 'dum veniat Supernum', of the drama of individuation. If we recur to the 'drifting dust', though, it still seems that Johnson attempts to resolve matters by accepting either Materialism, or an ideal Pantheism, to which any idea of personal salvation remains irrelevant. The soul is itself part of the mental history of God recollected at death. This doctrine of the One makes little of the principle of individuation, a principle underlying *The Dark Angel*, without which the poem would be void of significance. Moreover, we cannot defend it on the ground that this confusion is overtly expressed; the poem purports to be an argument directed towards and arriving at an expected conclusion. We are responsible for our actions: we become what our actions

[1] G. Santayana, *The Middle Span*, 1947, p. 67 *f*.

[2] I quote from the translation of E. R. Dodds in his *Selections from the Neoplatonists* (1923), p. 124.

make us. Where otherwise would be the point of the Offer? Yet one can still read the poem entirely in the light of the Plotinian *regressus*. The blight on art, on natural beauty, on human relationships, what more need that signify than the soul's inmost wish to abstract herself from illusion, to 'stand out' of the world of objects; so that rightly using that part in him which is divine, he may bring it back and lose it in the One. He will escape his lower self by being a self no longer. He is not, then, perfecting the self, he is transcending it; he is not over-coming his weakness, but avoiding by rising above the conflict. Our conclusion must be that the public symbolism is altogether at variance with the poem's inward situation.

All this remains a mere preliminary to judging whether the poem succeeds in embodying and communicating the experi-ence. Our own response, as readers, can hardly be restricted to a feeling of sympathy; to sensing the pathos and, to some degree, the slender individual note. We must, if the poem has succeeded, not remain *hypocrites lecteurs*: we too must be un-avoidably caught up in the *desolatio et concors* of the poem's inward situation; must be afraid not for Johnson, but for our-selves: we too must encounter the shadow.

The symbolism of the poem is made more easily accessible to us by its speaking of the Devil of theology. But this brings its own dangers. Johnson's problem is to find public symbols for a private drama, and to present those symbols in action with sufficient vigour, thus establishing them as general truths of the life of the spirit. Whatever symbol is used it must give the impression of containing more than its surface value. And this is where his difficulty begins: by equating the Shadow so firmly with the Devil of theology he not only risks the rigours of the stock response, but involves the poem in a set of un-desired associations. At the time the poem was written, the ordered progress of the nineteenth century, its complacency and materialism, had made the Devil an awkward figure to take seriously as a universal immoral agent. The only place he in-habited familiarly was the interior life of those for whom the social order had no place, not the populace but the practitioners of art. And if one did encounter him in literature he came all too frequently encased in aesthetic frivolity, wearing the patched mask of Catholic Diabolism—a convenient literary fiction for *fin de siècle* neurosis. Johnson would have remained more faithful to his intuition had he described 'Him' in vaguer terms; for the angel was doubly 'Dark', dark with evil and dark because unknown: the shadow is at once so personal and so foreign to the self. Perhaps his haunting anxieties and painful insights are better expressed in *The Precept of Silence*:

> I know you: solitary griefs,
> Desolate passions, aching hours!
> I know you: tremulous beliefs,
> Agonised hopes, and ashen flowers!

But Johnson did, in the last analysis, see the problem as we see it: as an attempt at psychological healing; as an attempt to reconcile the contradiction between private sensibility and institutional religion; between the truths of the visible Church and the truths of the heart. If the poem fails (as it manifestly does) it is not through failure of insight. The premiss has been cleanly enough defined, but the wrong conclusions follow: after contemplating the Angel with horrified intentness, Johnson escapes through the eschatological trap-door.

The Dark Angel, then, records confused feelings and their illogical, but not necessarily dishonest, conclusion. Yet, there is little corresponding tension and confusion in its language, or in its argument. The argument ascends like a series of syllogisms. Whenever a general situation is invoked it is presented in abstract terms and the general clarity and dignity of the design is betrayed everywhere by timidity of diction and rhythmical prettiness. The secondary nature of the imagery, the negative diction, the fondness for passives, all contribute. We have only to compare these suave octosyllabics, predominantly aural in effect, invariably acatalectic, with the tortured syntax, the broken cries of Hopkins in his 'terrible sonnets'. These may seem peculiar to Hopkins's idiom; but certainly some technical equivalent is required to embody violent spiritual states: the beauty of terror. It is the violence of Hopkins's experience, which wrenches his sonnets into those strange strewn shapes as though a hurricane had passed and left the landscape with a precarious face. The relation between experience and expression is more than logical. But, joining the contemporary pursuit of the disembodied lyrical sigh, as in Verlaine or Dowson, Johnson fails as he must do, in trying to embody *terribilità*, in capturing more than a mood, a perilously balanced moment of insight.

In detail, the same story repeats itself. There are two points in *The Dark Angel* where something concentrated and concrete is demanded: namely, in the stanza of the *agape*, and at the point of reversal: 'less dread, a change to drifting dust.' How tepid is the description of the lurking apples as 'golden bright'; granting all its latent richness of allusion, while at the *peripeteia* Johnson relies entirely on the mechanical counterpoint of 'aching lust'. This does force us back to the beginning of the poem, so that we infer the contrast, but as an intellectual, not as an emotional proposition. A line such as 'abides for me undesecrate:' provides an example of the poem's diction at its worst. The word 'abide', despite its Saxon origin, exudes a dry pietistic flavour while the emphatic passive 'abides *for me*' underlines the subjective and pathetic effect. The sombre latinity of 'undesecrate', far from communicating as Johnson intends a ritual and universal quality, merely illustrates Sir Max Beerbohm's remark about Pater, or Mr. Eliot's stricture on Milton, that he is writing English as if it were a dead tongue. Where he places emphasis Johnson does so by these latinisms. Where we might expect the natural rise and fall of the voice, we are disappointed. 'Who still dost' cries out for stress on the 'still', but the dull rhyme word must take some of the weight. These latinisms make the poem neater, but deprive it of strength. By subjecting his general effects to a closed system of ideas, to a pseudo-hieratic diction—the diction is altogether typical of the 1890's in being consciously purged of all non-literary associations—Johnson may establish himself in the reader's eyes as a 'character', as he did in the eyes of Yeats and his other friends; we may say: 'this does sound a stifled note that is oddly his'; but by isolating himself from current ideas and colloquial speech the poet risks losing a source of vitality. Compare *The Dark Angel* with one of Hardy's on the inadequacy of God. When we encounter the hesitant, searching rhythms, the often ugly constructions of Hardy, we hear the man's voice stumbling in perplexity, anger or resignation. He talks to us directly, without any self-conscious ordering of language, and we feel at that moment, however local the occasion or individual the sentiment, that he is also speaking *for* us. The more individual his rhythms and diction, the more they appear to approximate to the common voice.

But as Johnson disguises resignation as affirmation, so he blurs, wherever possible, all distinctions. *The Dark Angel* has no polysyllabic rhymes and this certainly aids the transitions from line to line; enables the argument to move rapidly. Yet consider these pairs: 'enemy, 'ecstasy'; 'silences', 'impieties'; 'me', 'divinity'. 'Penitence' and 'violence' are again typical of these feminine endings, suitable perhaps for suggesting the languid apartments of *The House of Life*, but totally unsuited, so it seems, to the onset of the Angel. One has to stretch the words in one's mouth; not bite them off.

This is all to say that the poem's style corresponds to the life it is recording. It is finicky: it is the product of the unstable invalid Johnson was. Its very purged and closed-in effect reflects faithfully the suffocated qualities of the *vie recluse*, a clouded life, shut in deliberately, lived behind closed doors and heavy curtains. A life where nothing is resolved; nothing is stated; where the frontiers between fantasy and reality are dangerously frail. (And this finds its reflection in the frailty of the rhymes, the poem's too fluid texture.)

If, after reading the poem, we cannot take Johnson seriously as a tragic figure, but simply as, in stature, pathetic: then the poem mirrors his predicament. To his friends, Johnson was something of a self-contrived 'character': his life seemed almost a literary fiction in itself. Yeats tells us of those elaborated imaginary conversations recounted by Johnson so often, but never varying in detail; where Gladstone or Newman or Jowett would deliver themselves of utterances characteristically epigrammatic or sententious. Johnson's life was not lived through literature: in a certain sense it *was* literature: literature was the only discipline to which he responded, by which he was transformed.

Even though this be granted it is difficult to defend the method by which he translates his experience. The poem is not about the *longueurs* of the *vie recluse*; it concerns an experience of metaphysical horror which should change the nature of subsequent experience. The problem of aestheticism; the problem of knowing one's own damnation before death; the problem of dipsomania and grace. Contrast with these vague and abstract descriptions of the seasons, the ruined garden and the memorial love-feast, with something of a similar order from a metaphysical poet writing in a language more ready with abstract general statements. Maurice Scève, the sixteenth-century French poet, is depicting union here and in God, what Plotinus describes in his last *Ennead* and what Johnson hints at in *The Dark Angel* (for the flight from generation to essence is a flight from the imperfect love of objects to the perfect love of God). Scève is insisting, though, on bodily union of lovers in Heaven as promised to us by the resurrection of the flesh, and this Baroque solidity is helpful to the metaphor.

> A si hault bien de tant saincte amytié
> Facilement te debvroit inciter,
> Sinon debvoir, ou honneste pitié,
> A tout le moins mon loyal persister,
> Pour unyment, et ensemble assister
> Lassus en paix en nostre eternel throsne.
>   N'apperçoy tu de l'Occident le Rhosne
> Se destourner et vers Midy courir,
> Pour seulement se conjoindre à sa Saone
> Jusqu'à leur Mer, ou tous deux vont mourir?

Albert Beguin[1] calls attention to the admirable image of the River Rhone leaving its apparent source to rejoin *its* Saone to follow a single path to *their* sea where *both* die. How much this inner geography of souls is reinforced by the familiar geography of Scève's own countryside! And, moreover, this beautiful extended image does not depend on cramped language and complex statement. It leaves an impression of *density*, without sacrifice of music.

Johnson's closed life of fantasy and invalidism is the natural breeding ground of Angels. In silence and darkness these serene terrible creatures from another world of being may be tempted into visitation. The great poets of angelology—Hölderlin, Baudelaire, Rilke—are also poets of loneliness. Though Baudelaire had a wide circle of acquaintances, he possessed scarcely a single friend. Hölderlin lived his life in isolation of madness and Rilke buried himself in a tower to write his greatest poetry.

[1] *v.* A. Beguin, *Sur la 'Mystique' de Maurice Scève.* Fontaine Tome VII, No. 36, 1944, pp. 74–97.

And his use of Christian symbolism also charges Johnson with great responsibility. In the great Christian poets, spiritual experience is mysteriously and finally embodied in the symbol, 'the shining mystery of the Cross', so that from being a descriptive abstract of a personal state, the symbols themselves acquire a vitality of their own. Baudelaire, believing in Hell, dubious of Heaven, records his vision with terrifying truth and power: 'Débris d'humanité pour l'éternité mûrs.' Johnson tries to circumscribe the abyss by his neo-scholasticism, his cultural reference (we may take references subdued and explicit to Dante, Plotinus, Crashaw, as part of the Alexandrian quality of the later nineteenth century). Like Baudelaire, Johnson cannot reconcile what is positive in the secular world, material progress, the triumph of reason, optimism, with the realities of the spiritual world—suffering and evil. But the higher organization of Baudelaire's insight, the voluntary nature of his degradations, remains a measure of the great difference between the two poets. In art, as in religion, there can be no compromise with the destroying Angel, the vision of darkness.

T. S. ELIOT

The Love Song of J. Alfred Prufrock

Joseph Margolis

S'io credesse che mia risposta fosse
A persona che mai tornasse al mondo,
Questa fiamma staria senza piu scosse.
Ma perciocche giammai di questo fondo
Non torno vivo alcun, s'i'odo il vero,
Senza tema d'infamia ti rispondo.

Let us go then, you and I,
When the evening is spread out against the sky
Like a patient etherised upon a table;
Let us go, through certain half-deserted streets,
The muttering retreats
Of restless nights in one-night cheap hotels
And sawdust restaurants with oyster-shells:
Streets that follow like a tedious argument
Of insidious intent
To lead you to an overwhelming question . . .
Oh, do not ask, 'What is it?'
Let us go and make our visit.

In the room the women come and go
Talking of Michelangelo.

The yellow fog that rubs its back upon the window-panes,
The yellow smoke that rubs its muzzle on the window-panes
Licked its tongue into the corners of the evening,
Lingered upon the pools that stand in drains,

Let fall upon its back the soot that falls from chimneys,
Slipped by the terrace, made a sudden leap,
And seeing that it was a soft October night,
Curled once about the house, and fell asleep.

And indeed there will be time
For the yellow smoke that slides along the street,
Rubbing its back upon the window-panes;
There will be time, there will be time
To prepare a face to meet the faces that you meet;
There will be time to murder and create,
And time for all the works and days of hands
That lift and drop a question on your plate;
Time for you and time for me,
And time yet for a hundred indecisions,
And for a hundred visions and revisions,
Before the taking of a toast and tea.

In the room the women come and go
Talking of Michelangelo.

And indeed there will be time
To wonder, 'Do I dare?' and, 'Do I dare?'
Time to turn back and descend the stair,
With a bald spot in the middle of my hair—
(They will say: 'How his hair is growing thin!')
My morning coat, my collar mounting firmly to the chin,
My necktie rich and modest, but asserted by a simple pin—
   (They will say: 'But how his arms and legs are thin!')
Do I dare
Disturb the universe?
In a minute there is time
For decisions and revisions which a minute will reverse.

For I have known them all already, known them all:—
Have known the evenings, mornings, afternoons,
I have measured out my life with coffee spoons;
I know the voices dying with a dying fall
Beneath the music from a farther room.
   So how should·I presume?

And I have known the eyes already, known them all—
The eyes that fix you in a formulated phrase,

And when I am formulated, sprawling on a pin,
When I am pinned and wriggling on the wall,
Then how should I begin
To spit out all the butt-ends of my days and ways?
   And how should I presume?

And I have known the arms already, known them all—
Arms that are braceleted and white and bare
  (But in the lamplight, downed with light brown hair!)
Is it perfume from a dress
That makes me so digress?
Arms that lie along a table, or wrap about a shawl.
   And should I then presume?
   And how should I begin?

      .   .   .   .   .

Shall I say, I have gone at dusk through narrow streets
And watched the smoke that rises from the pipes
Of lonely men in shirt-sleeves, leaning out of windows? . . .

I should have been a pair of ragged claws
Scuttling across the floors of silent seas.

      .   .   .   .   .

And the afternoon, the evening, sleeps so peacefully!
Smoothed by long fingers,
Asleep . . . tired . . . or it malingers,
Stretched on the floor, here beside you and me.
Should I, after tea and cakes and ices,
Have the strength to force the moment to its crisis?
But though I have wept and fasted, wept and prayed,
Though I have seen my head (grown slightly bald) brought in upon a
    platter,
I am no prophet—and here's no great matter;
I have seen the moment of my greatness flicker,
And I have seen the eternal Footman hold my coat, and snicker,
And in short, I was afraid.

And would it have been worth it, after all,
After the cups, the marmalade, the tea,
Among the porcelain, among some talk of you and me,
Would it have been worth while,
To have bitten off the matter with a smile,
To have squeezed the universe into a ball

To roll it toward some overwhelming question,
To say: 'I am Lazarus, come from the dead,
Come back to tell you all, I shall tell you all'—
If one, settling a pillow by her head,
 Should say: 'That is not what I meant at all.
 That is not it, at all.'

And would it have been worth it, after all,
Would it have been worth while,
After the sunsets and the dooryards and the sprinkled streets,
After the novels, after the teacups, after the skirts that trail along the
  floor—
And this, and so much more?—
It is impossible to say just what I mean!
But as if a magic lantern threw the nerves in patterns on a screen:
Would it have been worth while
If one, settling a pillow or throwing off a shawl,
And turning toward the window, should say:
 'That is not it at all,
 That is not what I mean, at all.'

  . . . . .

No! I am not Prince Hamlet, nor was meant to be;
Am an attendant lord, one that will do
To swell a progress, start a scene or two,
Advise the prince; no doubt, an easy tool,
Deferential, glad to be of use,
Politic, cautious, and meticulous;
Full of high sentence, but a bit obtuse;
At times, indeed, almost ridiculous—
Almost, at times, the Fool.

I grow old . . . I grow old . . .
I shall wear the bottoms of my trousers rolled.

Shall I part my hair behind? Do I dare to eat a peach?
I shall wear white flannel trousers, and walk upon the beach.
I have heard the mermaids singing, each to each.

I do not think that they will sing to me.

I have seen them riding seaward on the waves
Combing the white hair of the waves blown back
When the wind blows the water white and black.

We have lingered in the chambers of the sea
By sea-girls wreathed with seaweed red and brown
Till human voices wake us, and we drown.

WE are, as readers, actually led to construct the poetry of
the *Love Song*. It appears quite legible at first but becomes pro-
gressively disjointed. And as we sense its difficulty, seemingly
contradictory features strike our attention. It has no obvious
technical structure, it is in fact quite fragmentary; yet it obliges
our wit to study the impression of a strong and apt order. The
language is leisurely, sometimes merely repetitious, but ultimately we recognize its deliberate compression and great economy; and, though they are frequently diffused, the images convey
the inexorable movement of the entire mood. The language is
vernacular and superficial but suddenly it becomes dark and
filled with savage expressions. It seems casual and ironic but
we sense an underlying urgency. At first two persons seem to
be involved but we discover there is only one; and he is J. Alfred
Prufrock whose name is at once important and slightly absurd.
Yet he is also unknown; we suspect he is Everyman. And his
love song is uncertain too. We are led to believe it is concerned
with a romantic coupling but it soon spreads into the more
social themes of friendship and of the desperate need of sympathetic company. Dante is used to announce the song but at
first we cannot see why. And its themes, which are remarkably
diverse, are offered in contrary pairs: youth and old age, work
and idleness, spiritual life and death, commitment and indecision,
dreams and actuality, action and analysis, courage and fear,
personal needs and social obligations, communion and loneliness,
pride and disgust in the self, sincerity and hypocrisy, interest
and boredom.

Even the casual invitation of the first lines is disjunctive and
disturbed:

> Let us go then, you and I,
> When the evening is spread out against the sky
> Like a patient etherised upon a table

It is coupled with a simile as deliberate as itself which opposes an
image of inertia to the intended activity. We cannot imagine

that it is an actual invitation and we cannot help noticing a certain delicious lingering over the cadence and careful phrasing. We are inclined from the very start to diagnose Prufrock's remarks as symptoms of his own disorder. He is divided against himself; he suffers perhaps from a kind of anesthesia or wishes to possess it; he is preoccupied with inert bodies and has a strange habit of treating the atmosphere as an organic creature.

Yet, in a sense, we are only explicating Prufrock's self-analysis. For he quite obviously distinguishes 'you and I' and constructs his own simile. It is too early to know the meaning of the invitation, but as we follow his soliloquy we learn that each term and phrase has its own specific resonance and that our estimate of Prufrock must adjust constantly to new sets of overtones. It is as if we would attribute to Prufrock an interest in constructing not merely extravagant similes but an apt poetic form for his own probing and self-dissection.

He repeats his invitation and the romantic suggestions dissolve in an air of fatigue and surrender:

> Let us go, through certain half-deserted streets,
> The muttering retreats
> Of restless nights in one-night cheap hotels
> And sawdust restaurants with oyster-shells;
> Streets that follow like a tedious argument
> Of insidious intent
> To lead you to an overwhelming question . . .
> Oh, do not ask, 'What is it?'
> Let us go and make our visit.

Prufrock's question is obviously idle and too familiar. He appears in an alien but attractive setting, a would-be tourist of the vulgar and the commonplace. And, as if in recognition, he steps out of his reverie:

> In the room the women come and go
> Talking of Michelangelo.

Another disjunction! We are at once in a salon where the conversation is self-assured on difficult matters. It is a world which can be summarized in a jingle; we know it certainly to be the world Prufrock understands best, commonplace as well and perhaps hiding its own vulgarity. The invitation was a momentary dream Prufrock had permitted himself amid the busy movements of his own society.

But the couplet is a subtle contrivance; it is in fact the rule of Prufrock's life. We know he must select his companions from this company, ladies apparently impervious to reflection and uncertainty, who 'come and go' with an altogether different attitude. The couplet suggests an endless and familiar routine; and it serves as well as a refrain, repeated once again after another hint at the nature of Prufrock's sickly leisure. It intrudes, unspoken, with each successive exposure; it is presupposed everywhere, isolating Prufrock from the society of the salon as well as from the workmen's quarters of the city. We cannot even be certain where he is standing and dreaming at present, but the lines have confirmed his grooming and his longing. They are lines of sudden wit, almost improvization, yet at the same time the outcome of a sustained and self-absorbed effort; Prufrock's reverie engages both worlds and he is quite alone.

He is at least a talented and self-conscious dabbler in language, an amateur of verse. We always observe a certain careful searching for the apt phrase and for nice modifiers; we are always met with gifted summaries of his own experience. He is aware of the efforts of others to 'fix you in a formulated phrase' but he cannot repress his own clever skill. He makes deliberate literary references, some quite indirect, almost puns on the language of other poets; other references are openly directed to the great literature of the world. And in the very last passages of the *Love Song* he actually composes a short set of verses which could readily be separated as a distinct lyric, an expression growing out of his preoccupied versifying and arranging itself almost automatically. It is as if his invitation were designed to 'invoke the Muse'.

The chatter of the salon is about art. The ladies are concerned with Michelangelo, a hero and an artist of heroes. And Prufrock, whose inspiration has broken down, speaks of himself in mock-heroic terms. The creative community has broken down; the ladies cannot understand him and he cannot express himself. The search through the 'half-deserted streets' is more than romantic, more than inspirational.

Suddenly Prufrock escapes again:

> The yellow fog that rubs its back upon the window-panes,
> The yellow smoke that rubs its muzzle on the window-panes
> Licked its tongue into the corners of the evening,
> Lingered upon the pools that stand in drains,
> Let slip upon its back the soot that falls from chimneys,
> Slipped by the terrace, made a sudden leap,
> And seeing that it was a soft October night,
> Curled once about the house, and fell asleep.

It is as if the casual jingle were too bold—as if, failing to deflect the question, it merely focussed it more precisely. So that Prufrock must attempt an evasion through some invented, non-committal interest. He muses on the weather, he turns his eye to the street, he explores a conceit slowly and lovingly. The postponement is ineffectual. The yellow fog 'slides along the street' like an identifiably corrupting power that finally encircles the house; implicitly Prufrock admits his 'overwhelming question' to be the same for the waterfront and the salon.

We are tempted to regard the image as an unconscious disguise for Prufrock himself; we surely do not sense the passage as a digression. The fog is amorphous, solitary, leisurely, perversely curious, observed in autumn, and finally inert. There is an uncomfortable insistence in the repeated images and their morbid quality, which seems at first random and detached like the initial simile, is inevitably linked to Prufrock's own condition:

> And indeed there will be time
> For the yellow smoke that slides along the street,
> Rubbing its back upon the window-panes;
> There will be time, there will be time
> To prepare a face to meet the faces that you meet;
> There will be time to murder and create,
> And time for all the works and days of hands
> That lift and drop a question on your plate;
> Time for you and time for me,
> And time yet for a hundred indecisions,
> And for a hundred visions and revisions,
> Before the taking of a toast and tea.

All of the earlier themes resound through these lines, still vague and diffused but increasingly focussed on the salon society of which Prufrock is a member. The progress of the fog parallels the progress of the poetic revelation of Prufrock's question as it 'slides along the street' and curls 'about the house'.

The persons of the invitation are informed that there is still 'time for you and time for me'. Prufrock cannot yet bring himself to speak directly of his own career; he hides his concern in polite advice. But in the following passage, beyond the refrain (which stresses now Prufrock's membership and isolation in the society of the salon), he turns abruptly to point the question at himself:

> Do I dare
> Disturb the universe?
> In a minute there is time
> For decisions and revisions which a minute will reverse.

Shortly thereafter he demands:

> Then how should I begin
> To spit out all the butt-ends of my days and ways?

We must associate the image of the question with the curbs and gutters of the city; still later the fog seems to have penetrated the salon itself, for Prufrock finds it 'stretched on the floor, here beside you and me'. The fog is a kind of hallucination present only to the divided soul of Prufrock, for we recall that the women 'come and go' freely; the 'street' and the 'floor' are continuous and reinforce, wherever they appear, our impression of Prufrock's spiritual disorder and isolation. The fog is a kind of Grail, ambiguously characterized as corrupting but actually providing the occasion and the test of spiritual regeneration.

So the question which he finally manages to express as his own deep concern permits us to view a heroic and admirable struggle in the very soul of Prufrock. He has discarded, at least momentarily, the 'you' of earlier reference; he has overcome in part his initial paralysis; he acknowledges frankly the triviality of his existence. We are face to face with a human being of considerable intelligence and humility who is attempting to decide in a serious way the significance of his own life. And, though we are inclined to generalize with Prufrock about the trivial condition of all of human life, we must admit the necessity of an answer to the question. There is a religious dimension here, and the collapse of Prufrock's would-be defence identifies the ultimate futility of arguments drawn to justify the positive commitment of one's own life.

There are, interestingly enough, three arguments offered to prove that he should not 'dare'. They begin and end in the same way; we learn that Prufrock knows the 'voices', 'eyes' and 'arms' of the ladies of the salon. He emphasizes his acquaintance, so to speak, with their organs of communication. Yet we know there never has been a satisfactory communication between them; there is a strong impression of distance, disdain, possible conflict, that invades each of the arguments. It is however the deliberately versified monotony of his remarks that betrays his fatigue most clearly:

> For I have known them all already, known them all
> I know the voices dying with a dying fall
> And I have known the eyes already, known them all
> And I have known the arms already, known them all

But there is more than boredom here; Prufrock is fatigued by his own worldliness and his invitation sought to escape this condition.

If we ask what is this crucial commitment which he postpones and which saps all of his strength, what decision of his might 'disturb the universe', we are met by another question—whether there is

> Time to turn back and descend the stair,
> With a bald spot in the middle of my hair

It is of course a piece of impertinence, a pompous and 'at times, indeed, almost ridiculous' mixture of the trivial and the cosmic. But we cannot dispel the impression of its high seriousness; it is a question whether Prufrock can accept the actual conditions of his existence, his own ageing and the discerning eye of his associates. Does he dare 'disturb the universe', affirm his life courageously amid all of his obvious decline? Ought he to 'descend' once again into the illusions of the salon, having finally pierced through to a clear vision of his career? Does he have a constant hold of that rare 'time' which could sustain him in the changing trivialities of his own world?

There is a pathetic note in his preoccupation with the parts of his own body:

(They will say: 'How his hair is growing thin!')
My morning coat, my collar mounting firmly to the chin,
My necktie rich and modest, but asserted by a simple pin—
(They will say: 'But how his arms and legs are thin!')

We recall the images of surgical dissection and amorphous
living creatures and anticipate the 'voices', 'eyes' and 'arms' of
the ladies. Prufrock is fascinated by his own torment. He turns
the confident 'simple pin' into an instrument of torture:

> And when I am formulated, sprawling on a pin,
> When I am pinned and wriggling on the wall,
> Then how should I begin

and, as he comments on the ladies of the salon, his disgust in
his own awkward and helpless condition secretly mounts; so
that at length he bursts out in a savage and poetically isolated
pair of lines:

> I should have been a pair of ragged claws
> Scuttling across the floors of silent seas.

The duality of his nature is implied by the image and by the
lines themselves which are separated from the principal reverie
by a brief digression. We cannot help contrasting his 'scuttling
across the floors of silent seas' with the assured movement of
the women of that other couplet who 'come and go' across the
floors of the salon. It is in the spirit of this outburst perhaps that
Eliot chose the passage from Dante (Inferno, Canto XXVII) to
introduce the piece; Prufrock is in a sense unsuspectingly over-
heard by the living in an open rejection of himself in his own
private Hell.

But his quite admirable analytic power, as Prufrock himself
very well knows, can neither project him into a new life nor
free him from the old. The tired and somewhat bitter arguments
against the salon relent and he observes rather humorously:

> Is it perfume from a dress
> That makes me so digress?

In fact, all three arguments end in questions and all three emphasize his essential passivity. Prufrock understands that he is
activated chiefly by external forces and he suggests almost
gravitational and mechanical models for his relation to the

salon. His digression is a double movement away from a personally motivated and personally acceptable action; he is constantly attracted to the society pattern that he despises or sidetracked into a fruitless reverie about the world of the poorer classes. No sooner does he admit his tendency, than he is off on another digression:

> Shall I say, I have gone at dusk through narrow streets
> And watched the smoke that rises from the pipes
> Of lonely men in shirt-sleeves, leaning out of windows? . . .

There are surprising associations here that force all that has already passed to echo through these lines. The 'lonely men in shirt-sleeves' reminds us of the 'arms that are braceleted and white and bare', the 'smoke that rises from the pipes' recalls the yellow smoke that 'let fall upon its back the soot that falls from chimneys'. The contrasts are superficial, the question remains always the same.

Nevertheless, in a later passage the two worlds are more deliberately contrasted and their relative merits implicitly compared:

> After the sunsets and the dooryards and the sprinkled streets,
> After the novels, after the teacups, after the skirts that trail along
> the floor

Prufrock's power of summary is nowhere more successful. It is not accidental that the lines end in 'streets' and 'floor'. They confirm the ultimate equality of the two worlds. But the first is somewhat larger, more open, stabler, more robust than the second; the second is fragile and artificial. The first gives an impression of a setting for human life; the second suggests the improbable instruments of a highly specialized kind of life. It is to the first that Prufrock is somewhat romantically inclined, though it is for the second that he has been specifically trained. Prufrock is a spectator of both worlds who cannot participate fully and cordially in either.

His admirable clarity appears to be the outcome of a struggle against his own tendency toward mystification and digression. In a moment of complete openness he remarks:

> Should I, after tea and cakes and ices,
> Have the strength to force the moment to its crisis?
> But though I have wept and fasted, wept and prayed,

> Though I have seen my head (grown slightly bald) brought in
> upon a platter,
> I am no prophet—and here's no great matter;
> And I have seen the eternal Footman hold my coat, and snicker,
> And in short, I was afraid.

All that has preceded this statement now appears as a prolonged hesitation; the violent, pathetic outburst at the end of the digression now serves to dramatize the degree of his final self-control. The trivial and the momentous are linked once again and Prufrock's mock-heroic self-estimate reveals a deeper humility. In fact, his curious habit of comparing himself with certain literary heroes—with John the Baptist, Lazarus, with Hamlet—seems quite proper now and not at all as ludicrous as Prufrock would have us believe.

These may be fairly said to be partial aspects of his own nature. The reference to John is anticipated by his preoccupation with his own baldness and the exposure of his spiritual condition through images relating to dissected, impotent and deformed bodies. We must think of him also as Everyman and therefore as a prophet as well, discovering the disorder of modern man—his alienation and his anxiety. Similarly, he is the new Lazarus, overwhelmed by the revelation of his spiritual death and incapable of communicating his experience to his own society. The assertion

> 'I am Lazarus, come from the dead,
> Come back to tell you all, I shall tell you all'

reminds us of his failure 'to turn back and descend the stair' and his oscillation between his reverie and the actual world of his society. He is baffled finally by the isolating power of his own experience:

> 'That is not what I meant at all.
> That is not it, at all.'

And despite his denial: 'No! I am not Prince Hamlet, nor was meant to be', he is surely Hamlet as well, procrastinating yet moving skilfully among his own reflections. The phrasing here is appropriately clever; 'to be' takes on a peculiarly modern significance: man was not 'meant to be' but to become, to live and endure, to age, to end his career, and to accept these conditions as the boundaries of his existence.

We accept therefore the trivial and the solemn together. We accept the dignity and the power of Prufrock's careful estimate of his own role:

> Am an attendant lord, one that will do
> To swell a progress, start a scene or two,
> Advise the prince; no doubt, an easy tool,
> Deferential, glad to be of use,
> Politic, cautious, and meticulous;
> Full of high sentence, but a bit obtuse;
> At times, indeed, almost ridiculous—
> Almost, at times, the Fool.

This is the only occasion on which Prufrock has attempted to sustain an exact evaluation of his entire career, and the statement—including his denial of heroic pretensions—forms a part of a larger and most remarkable unity. It is a kind of poetic 'passage' from light to dark, from order to disorder. Prufrock begins modestly and with a sense of his own limitations, he defines his career as subsidiary but useful, he observes that it is perhaps also vain and somewhat stupid, he admits it may also be absurd; and in the movement of the lines we feel a growing panic and the impending disorganization of the perilously balanced confidence which could admit 'I was afraid'. The 'passage' is completed with the hysterical couplet

> I grow old . . . I grow old . . .
> I shall wear the bottoms of my trousers rolled.

and the bewildered questions and remarks that follow:

> Shall I part my hair behind? Do I dare to eat a peach?
> I shall wear white flannel trousers, and walk upon the beach.
> I have heard the mermaids singing, each to each.

He has made a complete circuit and returned to his original fantasies. And like the poem itself, these last outbursts are composed of individual, disjunctive items which do not follow each other in any obviously consecutive order. Yet the impression of their order is as strong as their random arrangement. Surprisingly enough, Prufrock had himself commented on this very feature:

It is impossible to say just what I mean!
But as if a magic lantern threw the nerves in patterns on a screen

These are the only lines which comment, as it were, on the very language of the poem. Nothing is to be taken quite literally. Prufrock's remarks are more than deliberate observations; they are also symptoms of a deeper spiritual distress and Prufrock is not unaware of the presence of this level of meaning. We must try to discover, as if with some X-ray technique and as Prufrock himself has attempted, the spiritual pattern which holds all of these separate outbursts together in a convincing way. The requirement marks the *Love Song* as a peculiarly modern invention. The image itself suggests a sort of psychoanalytic technique and aptly recalls once again the Myth of the Cave.

The monologue closes with Prufrock's romantic fantasies about the sea:

> I have heard the mermaids singing, each to each.
> I do not think that they will sing to me.
>
> I have seen them riding seaward on the waves
> Combing the white hair of the waves blown back
> When the wind blows the water white and black.
>
> We have lingered in the chambers of the sea
> By sea-girls wreathed with seaweed red and brown
> Till human voices wake us, and we drown.

This is finally Prufrock's song, mad and sweet, subdued and freed from his earlier hysteria as if his dreaming permitted him to collect himself for an acceptance of the unsatisfactory conditions of his life. There is always present however a constant, if unexpressed, reference to all of the features of his waking life and the fantasy is only a temporary respite. Much reminds us of the fog that 'lingered upon the pools, the music from a farther room'. Prufrock concludes 'we have lingered in the chambers of the sea'; the 'I' suddenly has become again the two persons of the original invitation. It is as if the song were actually composed in that first reverie, as if its fantasies expressed too nearly Prufrock's actual condition and could not be sustained. The final line 'till human voices wake us, and we drown' confuses and inverts the image of the sirens and we are obliged to hear again the labour of that implicit and endless refrain:

> In the room the women come and go
> Talking of Michelangelo.

Among School Children

John Wain

I

I walk through the long schoolroom questioning;
A kind old nun in a white hood replies;
The children learn to cipher and to sing,
To study reading-books and histories,
To cut and sew, be neat in everything
In the best modern way—the children's eyes
In momentary wonder stare upon
A sixty-year-old smiling public man.

II

I dream of a Ledaean body, bent
Above a sinking fire, a tale that she
Told of a harsh reproof, or trivial event
That changed some childish day to tragedy—
Told, and it seemed that our two natures blent
Into a sphere from youthful sympathy,
Or else, to alter Plato's parable,
Into the yolk and white of the one shell.

III

And thinking of that fit of grief or rage
I look upon one child or t'other there
And wonder if she stood so at that age—
For even daughters of the swan can share
Something of every paddler's heritage—

And had that colour upon cheek and hair,
And thereupon my heart is driven wild:
She stands before me as a living child.

IV

Her present image floats into the mind—
Did Quattrocento finger fashion it
Hollow of cheek as though it drank the wind
And took a mess of shadows for its meat?
And I though never of Ledaean kind
Had pretty plumage once—enough of that,
Better to smile on all that smile, and show
There is a comfortable kind of old scarecrow.

V

What youthful mother, a shape upon her lap
Honey of generation had betrayed,
And that must sleep, shriek, struggle to escape
As recollection or the drug decide,
Would think her son, did she but see that shape
With sixty or more winters on its head,
A compensation for the pang of his birth,
Or the uncertainty of his setting forth?

VI

Plato thought nature but a spume that plays
Upon a ghostly paradigm of things;
Solider Aristotle played the taws
Upon the bottom of a king of kings;
World-famous golden-thighed Pythagoras
Fingered upon a fiddle-stick or strings
What a star sang and careless Muses heard:
Old clothes upon old sticks to scare a bird.

VII

Both nuns and mothers worship images,
But those the candles light are not as those
That animate a mother's reveries,
But keep a marble or a bronze repose.
And yet they too break hearts—O Presences
That passion, piety or affection knows,
And that all heavenly glory symbolise—
O self-born mockers of man's enterprise;

VIII

Labour is blossoming or dancing where
The body is not bruised to pleasure soul,
Nor beauty born out of its own despair,
Nor blear-eyed wisdom out of midnight oil.
O chestnut-tree, great-rooted blossomer,
Are you the leaf, the blossom or the bole?
O body swayed to music, O brightening glance,
How can we know the dancer from the dance?

THE main subject of the poem is the relationship or inter-penetration of matter and spirit. Broadly speaking, it is a meditation on the riddle that has puzzled us all when we have thought of it, and to which various answers, theological, philosophical, and psychological, have been proposed. We say that Jones dies and goes to Heaven; but *which* Jones goes there? The squalling infant Jones, the undergraduate Jones, the full-blooded middle-aged Jones as *père de famille*, or the old shrunken Jones who actually dies? Obviously they are all the same, in a sense; but in *what* sense are they all the same? This question is the major preoccupation of the poem, and there is also the secondary theme, present as a strong undertow, which is expressed by the word 'labour'. Our identities—our souls, if you like—manifest themselves in our activities, in our *work*; the heads of the schoolchildren bowed over their reading-books and histories, the hard speculations of the philosophers, the straining of the youthful mother in labour, and finally the blossoming and dancing, the work of beings in a state of perfection and rightness. To show how these themes are interwoven, it is necessary first to cross the *pons asinorum*, to give, as bluntly as possible, the paraphrasable content of the poem (one does not speak, in this connection, of its 'meaning').

The poet, at sixty, is performing part of his public duty by being shown over a school. To the children, he is just one more of the genial fogies who represent age and authority. But inwardly, he is visited by thoughts of the woman he loves, and how, late one night, she spoke of some incident of her own childhood. (There was a 'sinking fire', over which she was 'bent'; it was the hour of confidences. Leda was the mother of

196

Helen, the father being Jove in the form of a swan; as the next stanza makes clear, the woman is Ledaean in the sense that she is like Helen rather than like Leda. The conclusion that the poet is in love with her is, to my mind, inescapable, though it can be contested.[1]) This confidence gave the poet a precious sense of kinship with the woman, which he expresses by an indirect use of Plato's image, from the *Symposium*, of the twin halves of a single sphere.

This train of thought sends his mind back to the schoolchildren, and brings with it the realization that she, too, the daughter of the swan, must have looked something like this. Inevitably, the pendulum swings back at once to 'her present image', which is something like a Quattrocento painting. (She is hollow-cheeked, but I cannot take this as necessarily conveying that she is old; she is just one of those very beautiful women, one sees them everywhere, who look as if they did not get quite enough to eat.) He himself has to repress the dangerous and painful thought that in younger days, before he became an old scarecrow, he was handsome enough. He pulls himself up with the thought that the best thing to do is to put a good face on it, and seem at least to be 'comfortable'.

This cluster of contrasts between youth and age lead on to the next step, which is the first generalized thought in the poem, the first one to have no immediate bearing on the poet's personal situation. A man of sixty would hardly seem worth the trouble of bearing and bringing up, if he appeared before his mother at the moment of parturition. That is the broad sense of stanza V; the detail is complicated. The young mother is in the midst of childbirth; she is being given an anaesthetic, but, since birth has to be at least intermittently conscious or it could not be performed, she is divided between consciousness and recollection (a marvellously exact use of the word). This is for her, unmistakably, an ordeal; she would escape if she could; it was the 'honey of generation', the pleasant activity of conceiving the child, which let her in for this: it 'betrayed' her. The grammar of 'had', in the second line, is ambiguous; it could equally well be 'has', but the pluperfect is more final; none

[1] And was contested, with tremendous cogency, by Mr. Richard Hughes in a conversation with me in November 1954. I bring in his name as a means of offering him an oblique apology for not accepting his argument.

of the other verbs in the stanza is a straight present tense, for
'would' and 'did' are conditional, and 'must' is a verb that does
not change in the preterite.

It is necessary to pause here to consider Yeats's note on this
stanza, which reads as follows:

I have taken the 'honey of generation' from Porphyry's essay
on 'The Cave of the Nymphs', but find no warrant in it for considering it the 'drug' that destroys the 'recollection' of pre-
natal freedom. He blamed a cup of oblivion given in the zodiacal
sign of Cancer.

Here we come head-on against the huge recurrent problem
that faces the reader of Yeats. It is, briefly, the problem of how
much notice to take of Yeats's personal fandango of mysticism
and superstition. To many readers it will seem intolerably
arrogant if I say that I propose simply to brush aside his reading
of his own words. Obviously, they will say, if the poet himself
tells us that it is the 'shape' who is 'betrayed'—it is the child
who loses the remembrance of his ideal pre-natal existence by
having the practical joke of birth played on him—then that is
all; away with this obstinate insistence that it is the 'mother'
who was betrayed by the pleasure of generation.

I can only answer, in absolute seriousness, that I must respect
the poem more than the poet, and try to serve it rather than to
serve him. Substitute Yeats's own rendering, and what becomes
of the argument of the poem? The stanza is absolutely clear; it
relates logically to the rest of the poem; it develops the argument; it is intelligible, compassionate, and human. By contrast,
the interpretation which is proffered as Yeats's 'intention' is an
affair of solemn childishness, a product of the side of his nature
which found it necessary to construct a system of beliefs in
order to write poetry at all. I am not contemptuous of this system; it was valuable for Yeats in that it overcame his despair in
the face of a world which appeared to have no beliefs that he
could share; it was responsible for his change from a minor
'aesthetic' poet into a major human one. But what, in all
humility, I would insist on is this: these beliefs were necessary
for him, *but that does not make them necessary for us.* He had to
have them in order to write his poetry; we do not have to have
them in order to read it.

This is not an attempt to set the critic above the poet; it is merely an attempt to avoid setting the poet above the poem. If we admit the interpretation that is imported by Yeats's note, we give that note an authority which, in the last resort, can only be claimed *by the poem*. A poem must dictate its own meaning, and define for itself the area within which it chooses to operate. In this instance, we have a clear case of attempted interference with the poem; the argument requires the juxtaposed images of the young mother, in painful labour, and the scarred, compromised man of sixty; it requires the painful contrast between the cost of producing him and sending him out into life, and his performance considered as the return for that cost.

Having got so far, I must pause to admit that I do not *like* having to be so peremptory; it is never pleasant to feel that one's interpretation of a poem can be carried through only by pushing against the author's. And indeed, if anyone were to claim that, without going outside the poem at all, the grammar and grouping of the words on the page demand the interpretation that it *must* be the shape that is betrayed, it must be the child who is divided between sleeping, shrieking and struggling to escape—I should not know how to answer him. My own feeling is the other way; but the lines could take that interpretation: Jones does not want to be born; he is happier where he is. In the process of being born, he has flashes of 'recollection', in which his pre-natal consciousness comes back; then he 'struggles to escape'— from the womb. If his mother saw him at sixty, she might regret, not only her labour, but the fact of her having called him from his previous and happier existence to enter upon this unsatisfactory soul-and-body relationship. If any reader insisted on this interpretation, I should have to grant it, though I personally do not find it helpful with regard to the poem as a whole. As for Porphyry and the zodiacal sign of Cancer, of course, I cannot away with them. To invoke them is a mere flourish: the kind of flourish that is sometimes necessary to the writer, never to the reader. If this reading is valid, it is valid simply as a piece of Yeats's familiar pessimism, to document which we need not go outside his verse. We do not need magical explanations for what he found already developed in Sophocles:

Never to have lived is best, ancient writers say :
Never to have drawn the breath of life, never to have looked into
    the eye of day;
The second best's a gay goodnight and quickly turn away.

To return to the argument of the poem: the question has now
been posed, in one at least of its possible forms; and we turn,
naturally, to the philosophers. All these philosophers, as we
realize when he names them, had theories about the soul and
the body, though these theories are not conspicuously set in the
poem. Pythagoras suggests to us the transmigration of souls.
Aristotle is the scientist of the trio, the man who invented logic;
what doctrines of his about the soul Yeats may have had in
mind, I do not know, but that is just my ignorance. As regards
Plato, his doctrine of the existence of archetypal forms, of which
the physical world affords only imitations, has never been so
adroitly captured by a single metaphor. What precise associations the word 'paradigm' had for Yeats, I do not know; in my
experience I have very seldom met it except in the pages of a
Greek grammar, where it meant a *schema* of the principle parts
of a verb: an excellent parallel for the intellectually conceived
framework which gives shape and body to the 'spume' that plays
on it. These two lines alone would prove that Yeats was a
great poet, if nothing else of his had survived. Aristotle, by
contrast, leathered Alexander's bottom; the language becomes
earthy and solid, pointing the contrast between the two. Pythagoras was 'world-famous', which, as Mr. G. S. Fraser remarked,[1] is an odd way to talk of a philosopher; it is more the
sort of description one would expect to hear of an athlete or
film-star; perhaps, Mr. Fraser goes on, it signifies something
about the character of Pythagoras—that he enjoyed being
world-famous, even to the extent of tolerating absurd rumours
about himself, such as that he had golden thighs. Since the tendency of this stanza, taken as a whole, is to make fun of the
philosophers, to reduce them to figures of helplessness, such an
interpretation is very easily admissible, though in fact we learn
from Diogenes Laertius that Pythagoras did have a great personal standing and was not unaware of it:

Indeed, his bearing is said to have been most dignified, and
his disciples held the opinion about him that he was Apollo

[1] 'Yeats and the New Criticism', *Colonnade*, Nos. 1–2.

come down from the far north. There is a story that once, when he was disrobed, his thigh was seen to be of gold; and when he crossed the river Nessus, quite a number of people said they heard it welcome him.

(*Lives of Eminent Philosophers*, tr. Hicks, Loeb edition, vol. II, p. 331.)

The two lines describing what Pythagoras did to earn his place in this *galère* (VI, 6, 7) can be put into non-metaphorical language quite easily; we need not do it for ourselves; what is the *Encyclopaedia Britannica* for?

Pythagoras's greatest discovery was, perhaps, that of the dependence of the musical intervals on certain arithmetical ratios of lengths of string at the same tension, 2 : 1 giving the octave, 3 : 2 the fifth and 4 : 3 the fourth. This discovery could not but have powerfully contributed to the idea that 'all things are numbers'. According to Aristotle, the theory in its original form regarded numbers, not as relations predicable of things, but as actually constituting their essence or substance. Numbers, he says, seemed to the Pythagoreans to be the first things in the whole of nature, and they supposed the elements of numbers to be the elements of all things, and the whole heaven to be a musical scale and a number (*Metaph.* A 986a).

To say, therefore, that Pythagoras 'fingered upon a fiddle-stick or strings What a star sang and careless Muses heard' is a brilliant piece of metaphor-spinning, almost on a level with the superb one about Plato; what it has to do with the immediate question is not clear, but the point is that Pythagoras was a very brilliant and deep-thoughted man, and yet it made no difference; the Muses, who work by being careless, did not allow it to matter to them. All three philosophers are, in fact, given up with a sad shrug; they are nothing but a lot of scarecrows like the poet himself. This is profoundly Yeatsian: he enjoyed reading about people's experiments with ideas, but was at the same time profoundly anti-philosophic. Of course the philosophers could have nothing relevant to say; they were in the same trap themselves; it had taken them so long to work out their ideas that they had become scarecrows in the process. 'Bodily decrepitude is wisdom; young We loved each other and were ignorant.' It is no use asking the old what they think about

these matters, any more than the young. Time has taken away
their physical vitality, and added, after all, nothing very valuable
in exchange. It is, of course, a familiar Yeatsian theme:

> Come let us mock at the great
> That had such burdens on the mind
> And toiled so hard and late
> To leave some monument behind,
> Nor thought of the levelling wind.

And again, one is perfectly well aware that the familiar gesture towards occultism can be seen, by those curious enough
to want to see it, behind this stanza as it could behind the
'youthful mother' stanza. The reason why philosophers are
never allowed a look in (the philosopher in *The Hour Glass*
comes off worst in a speculating match with the village idiot,
for instance) is because they represent something incompatible
with the virtues typified by the three key figures of the Yeatsian
world, 'Hunchback and Saint and Fool'. The poem in which this
hocus-pocus is 'explained', *The Phases of the Moon*, is followed
by a group of others on related themes, and in one of them the
Saint is made to say:

> I shall not cease to bless because
> I lay about me with the taws
> That night and morning I may thrash
> Greek Alexander from my flesh.

As far as we are concerned here, the important fact is that the
philosophers are declared out of the running.

In short, this question of the inter-relation of body and spirit
must be referred at last to those who love. The three kinds of
human love, 'passion, piety and affection', are all present in the
poem; we have already seen the poet with his heart driven wild
as the image of his beloved comes before him; now we see the
two other emblematic figures, the nun and the mother, worship-
ping their own kind of images. What ties the three kinds
together, for the purposes of the poem, is the fact that they
are all *composite* images, depending partly on the memory and
partly on the imagination; a mother thinks of her son simultaneously as he was in his cradle, in early childhood, in boyhood
proper, and fuses these images with his 'present image' in man-
hood. The piety of a nun sees eternity and holiness in the still-

ness of marble or bronze statues; indeed, the actualization of religious truth is for her principally an affair of images. She cannot be disappointed in these images in the way a mother might be disappointed in her son, could she but see him with sixty or more winters on his head, but she can suffer the harshness of a dedicated life; her images can break her heart too, in their own way.

When memory and imagination work in this way on an image, they transform it into a composite thing, with its own order of existence, which Yeats here calls a Presence. The Presences are the composite images of love which are known to the three kinds of lover. But they are not merely called forth by the emotions of the lovers; they are 'self-born'; they existed before the love to which they correspond, or at any rate they are independent of it. They are the symbols of heavenly glory; paraphrase cannot get any closer than that, because if one asks the paraphraser's prime question—'What is the literal truth of which this is the metaphorical expression?'—one is left with the circular answer that heaven, for living men, is itself a metaphor, that its glory is metaphorical, and that a symbol is something that cannot be reduced. The Presences correspond, simply, to 'heavenly glory'—and what *that* may be, we shall find out one day; it lies outside the poem, because it lies outside human life and language. No wonder that the Presences are 'mockers of man's enterprise', especially (one suspects) the sort of enterprise the philosophers have.

At all events, the poet now addresses these Presences directly; not for their information, not to ask them anything, but simply because they are, rhetorically, the only possible audience for his words. And he tells them something about Labour. Labour, here, is the condition of being; it is performing one's function. It is the only continuity that runs through the bewildering series of changes that are the life of Jones. Trees grow leaves and blossoms; men grow hair and nails, but with them it cannot stop there; activity is the expression of identity, and identity is the one link that binds bank-manager Jones with schoolboy Jones. But—and this is part of the problem—something has gone wrong; just as we can never grasp and arrest the Protean identity, so we can never achieve a perfect relationship between activity and nature; between 'labour' and 'blossoming or dancing'

It is unfortunately true that the body has to be 'bruised to pleasure soul'; witness the patient toil of the nun as she teaches the children a few simple lessons, which for them are as arduous as the speculations of the philosophers; witness the asceticism of the nun; witness the 'pang' of the mother in setting the whole process going and making passion, piety and affection attainable in the first place. 'Beauty' also is 'born out of its own despair', in the sense that beautiful poems are written by old scarecrows who had better not even think of the fact that they used to be good-looking. Similarly the philosophers get bleary eyes as they ponder their problems instead of going to sleep, which turns them into scarecrows all the faster. But in a perfect state, such as we are now imagining, all these things would be attainable without paying such a crushing price for them. 'Labour' would be 'blossoming'—simply unconscious growth—or 'dancing'—a natural if stylized activity—in such a state. 'Where' at the end of the first line means either 'in the place where' or 'when such conditions are present'—cf. 'where you've got a good referee, the game is played fairly'; it is a familiar concentration of meanings in the word. 'Labour' means, of course, the act of birth as well as the various activities of work; the two are not, at this level, distinguishable. The Presences are 'self-born'—they do not owe their existence to labour; they are, I suppose, identical with the 'self-begotten' who are elsewhere the subject of a short, but complete, poem (*Words For Music Perhaps*, xxiv).

This would indeed be the perfect state; but even then there is no guarantee that we should escape from the confused relationship of matter and spirit. Even blossoming and dancing are accompanied by this confusion; a chestnut-tree has a massive trunk, cool green leaves, and delicate blossoms; at which point is one most in touch with its essential identity? Again, a dancer is the embodiment of the dance; without the tangible, moving human body, the dance would not exist; nevertheless, it is a perceptible thing in itself. This question is brought up, but it is not the function of the poem to propound a solution; the last two sentences are interrogative, reminding us that a poet differs from other kinds of sage by the fact that he makes his poems out of his ignorances as much as his certainties. So we are left with the question, which it was the purpose of the poem to bring before us: not in order to set us to work finding a solution, but merely to force upon us the realization that the question exists.

Exists, that is, as a reality, something to be humanly reckoned with; and what we are concerned with as literary critics is the success of this actualization and the concrete means employed to bring it about.

It is, of course, far easier to indicate in general terms what these means are, than to instance in detail their manner of action. Anyone can see that the success of the poem is due to the suppleness and force of its language, and the dramatic coherence of its construction. But to illustrate these things in the concrete is to approach the vanishing centre of literary criticism, which, not being an exact science, is bound sooner or later to reach a point at which demonstration breaks down and is replaced by a shared sensibility; though, of course, this point is very much more distant than the anti-critical writers on literature would have us think. It remains true, however, that anyone who does not see, without prompting, the peculiarly Yeatsian excellence of language attained in this poem, will not see it with any amount of prompting. It is an affair of variation within a well-defined area, which the reader must be capable of inhabiting. The area is the area of dignity and passion; the language can become familiar, with its 't'other', 'paddler', 'bottom'; it can name commonplace objects, with its 'reading-books', 'yolk', 'scarecrow'; it can rise to the heights of what is conventionally thought of as 'poetic' language, as in the first four lines of stanza IV; but it remains always within the area. Every word used is consonant with dignity and passion. This Yeatsian style, peculiar to this poet but common in his poems, is a high plateau; it has its valleys and hills, but the traveller can never for an instant forget that he is close to the clouds. One recalls how Edmund Wilson, in *Axel's Castle*, tried to pin down the bare nobility of Yeats's 'middle period' style by using an image of the commonplace transmuted into the priceless: 'His words, no matter how prosaic, are always somehow luminous and noble, as if pale pebbles smoothed by the sea were to take on some mysterious value and become more precious than jewels or gold.' It is 'the proud full sail of his great verse', of course, that does it; that opulence of movement which is the justification both of Yeats's arrogance and of the silly mystery-worship of his disposition. Too much humility, too much common-sense, would have left him incapable of sustaining this loftiness; the parallel case is Milton's. The harmony is so rich—I need not bore the reader by pointing out instances of Assonance, Verbal Music, etc.— that the style can afford its familiarities, can interrupt itself with 'enough of that', can, alternatively, rise to its peaks without losing concreteness. It is the writing of a man who has schooled himself to see everything in concrete terms; a handful of abstractions sown here and there would ruin the poem. This was the fruit of Yeats's fierce simple-mindedness; all the abstractions were concrete in his eyes—poverty was a ragged man with a wooden leg, riches the contemplation of great art in a palace. He had undergone, that is, the essential training of the poet, which is to unlearn the discipline of abstract thought insisted on by modern education, and thus to make himself, by the standards of that education, a simpleton.

> You must become an ignorant man again,
> And see the sun again with an ignorant eye,

as Wallace Stevens has it; and in Yeatsian terms, and a context only slightly different,

> John Synge, I and Augusta Gregory, thought
> All that we did, all that we said or sang
> Must come from contact with the soil, from that
> Contact everything Antaeus-like grew strong.
> We three alone in modern times had brought
> Everything down to that sole test again,
> Dream of the noble and the beggar-man.

Yeats was, in fact, a specialized intelligence; his mind was perfectly adapted to the writing of poetry, and able to invest poetry with a pantherine play of intelligence that animated its ceremony and mystery. Outside poetry, he tended to be an albatross; most subjects of enquiry do call for a certain power of abstract thought, and abstract thought was next door to impossible for Yeats. Owing to the irregular nature of his education, he never learnt it in the first place, and would in any case have had to unlearn it. To conclude this digression, I am not of course saying that Yeats was, or that any poet can afford to be, anything but supremely intelligent; merely that the order of intelligence required in poetry does not usually enable its possessor to shine in other fields.

This use of language, then, was the product of a temperament.
It is a compound of the robust and the fastidious, wedded together by the balance of the verse. This balance, like the poem's
structure, is essentially dramatic; it assumes complete control
of the speaking voice, dictating its pace and pitch. Anyone who
would trouble to read an essay like this would not be interested
in having examples heaped up; the kind of thing I am thinking of
is the free-ranging and varied run of stanza VII: after the easy
flow of the first line, the initial statement, we have the difference
between the stillness of the nun's adoration and the rapid vicissi-
tudes of a mother's emotions, brought out by the fact that the
line

> But those the candles light are not as those

consists mainly of single syllables, and therefore must be spoken
slowly, while

> That animate a mother's reveries

is spoken flowingly, and turns mainly on the softer, tenderer
consonants, m, n, r, v. Then immediately we are back in the
world of bronze and marble with the heavy impact of the single
syllables—

> And yet they too break hearts.

I have not much stomach for this kind of work; it easily becomes
absurd, and can best be done by the reader; and here I leave the
diction of the poem.

With regard to its structure, the first thing one notices is
that the poem breaks into two halves. Of its eight stanzas, the
last four contain all the essential argumentation of the piece;
they could be printed alone, and the result would be a concentrated intellectual poem of the greatest difficulty, but perfectly
coherent, perfectly ready to yield to analysis. What, then (to
begin with the elementary question), do the first four stanzas
contribute to the poem?

Elementary as the question is, the answer to it can be made
to open out much of the poem's essential secret. These four
stanzas serve, in the first place, to make the poem easier to
understand. By presenting the personal situation of the poet, and
the concrete setting in which he is thinking of it, they enable us
to enter on the independent speculation of the second half with

a good head of steam to drive us along. Further, since the essence of poetry is the actualization of the concepts it deals with (what it *feels like* to be two and two making four, or alternatively what it feels like to *understand* that two and two make four), they help us towards participation in the poem. This is a well-understood convention of poetry; *Among School Children* is best put in perspective by seeing it as one of the great romantic odes; it is the culminating achievement in the tradition which begins with the Odes of Wordsworth and Coleridge. And it is of course a common feature of this kind of poem that it begins with the personal, concrete statement:

> Well, if the bard was weather-wise, who made
> The grand old ballad of Sir Patrick Spens,
> We shall have rain to-night . . .

The man is looking through the window of his lonely room, talking to himself between set teeth. The prosaic opening helps to moor down the soaring speculation which this kind of poem deals in. There is, by the way, an adroit use of the device in William Empson's poem *Camping Out*, which begins

> And now she cleans her teeth into the lake,

an opening so prosaic that the poem seems to be challenging itself to get off the ground at all. Yet within a dozen lines we have climbed to

> Who moves so among stars, their frame unties;
> See where they blur, and die, and are out-soared.

Yeats's poem uses this convention in a way that reveals complete mastery of the formal technique of the romantic ode. 'I walk through the long schoolroom questioning' is an exact counterpart to the Coleridgean beginning, just as the vivid realism of his description of the schoolroom is a counterpart to the elaborate scene-setting in *Resolution and Independence*. But whereas it was the tendency of the other Romantics to bring the thing round in a circle, so that

> My heart aches, and a drowsy numbness pains
> My sense

would circle round to its ending in

> Fled is that music; do I wake or sleep?

Yeats abandons the circular technique; after the half-way mark, there is no recurrence of the schoolroom, the children, the nun, the personal situation; the 'I' is banished, having done its work, as if to emphasize that the vagaries of a man's own fate only serve to lead him, by his particular route, to the frontier of that realm of speculation whose problems are universal ones. The first half of the poem has given us the three types of love and of labour, either directly or by implication; children imply the existence of mothers and motherhood; the nun implies the existence of a religion and the emotions appropriate to it; the sexual love felt by the poet involves the existence of a beloved woman. The children learn and grow, the nun teaches and worships, the poet loves, smiles and is a public man, performing his duty to the State. These are the actualities of which the abstract elements in the poem's second half are the shadows.

Within the two halves, separate rhythms are discernible. The first half is circular in the traditional manner; it begins with the concrete and ends with it again, enclosing between the two a contour of impressions and memories; the children, his beloved as she is now, as she was then, Plato, the Quattrocento, his own early days. And, since the subject-matter of the first half is the external, physical manifestations of the question that is being discussed—since it is bounded by the actual situation, the children, the woman, the figure of the poet himself—we have, as a kind of rhythm within the rhythm, a progression from the pre-natal to the all-but-senile. One after another the images peel off: in l.9 he dreams of 'a Ledaean body': Leda, not Helen; the mother, not the daughter. The next image is the egg; 'the yolk and white of the one shell'. From that we go on to the 'daughter of the swan', then to the 'living child', then to 'her present image' and finally to the oldest figure in the tableau—himself. We run heavily to a standstill on the word 'scarecrow'; all that can profitably be said in personal terms has been said. Immediately, the movement of the poem is renewed, with a question; aptly, because questioning will be the keynote of the second half, as reverie was the keynote of the first.

This series of questions is arranged as a movement away from the immediate and personal, towards the universal. The 'youthful mother' is still close to the matter of the first half, though independent of it; then come the philosophers; and finally the poem launches into unaided speculation, questioning in its own voice.

This arrangement cannot be an accident. It suits the poem's central enterprise too well, it has too much dramatic propriety, to be anything but the result of careful contrivance. Instead of circling back on itself, the poem moves forward, in the form of a bridge, then suddenly stops with no opposite shore in sight. It is not a bridge after all, but a pier. It leads nowhere; its purpose is to afford us, before we turn and retrace our steps, a bleak and chastening glimpse into the deep waters.

On the
Interpretation of the Difficult Poem

G. S. Fraser

I

THERE are four lines from Denham which may, perhaps, provide me with a point of departure. They are not difficult, and they are not a poem. They became famous because they are an early successful example of balance and antithesis in the heroic couplet; and because they state very clearly some of what were to become the Augustan standards of 'correct writing' in poetry. They were, Mr. F. W. Bateson tells me, a great deal parodied in the early Augustan period; early admirers of them found no puzzle about the meaning, but found the lucid sense very admirably adapted to the sound, the phrasing beautifully balanced, and so on. The lines are these:

> O could I flow like thee, and make thy stream
> My great example as it is my theme.
> Though deep, yet clear; though gentle, yet not dull;
> Strong without rage, without o'erflowing full.

Denham is comparing the ideal beauty of the poem he would like to write with the real beauty of the river he is writing about. The standards of good writing invoked are those that we think of as beginning to come in, perhaps, with Waller—smoothness, elegance, easiness; at the same time, Denham wants his lines to be 'strong' and 'full', packed with sense and nobly sonorous. But the phrase 'strong lines' was sometimes used in a not wholly favourable sense, of Donne, for instance, to suggest a certain crabbedness and ruggedness. He wanted his lines to be 'strong without rage', to express a *controlled* emotion. He wanted their 'fullness' to be kept in order within, as it were, the banks of the heroic couplet. He wanted his meanings to be 'deep, yet clear', and one may think of the new Cartesian philosophy (Denham had been in France), with its presupposition that a clear idea is a true idea; and of the new scientific prose encouraged by the Royal Society, with its plain simplicity, its avoidance of metaphor. The lines are like a kind of manifesto for a new sort of poetry: 'gentle, yet not dull' suggests the growth of a new poetic tone, a polite public manner in verse. It was as terms of literary criticism, perhaps, that all these epithets had their deepest emotive meaning for Denham; but why, of course, the lines strike us as so neat and memorable is that the terms which have their secondary, or applied, or metaphorical meanings in literary criticism do also apply so neatly—apply, we might be tempted to say at first, in a primary sense—to a river.

The neatness is a little deceptive. At least, two very acute critics, Dr. Johnson and Dr. Richards, think so, and I am not wholly disposed to agree with Mr. Bateson and Mr. Alvarez, who know the critical background of the Restoration period much better than I do (and much better, probably, than Dr. Johnson did or Dr. Richards does) and who tend to think that both doctors are off on a wild goose chase. What, for both Johnson and Richards, these lines bring out is a puzzle about the nature of poetic language. What is it about a use of language that makes one call it poetic? An examination of these neat Augustan lines, and of the reaction of these two fine critics to them, may bring even a critic of my type (whose instrument is verbal analysis) round, perhaps reluctantly, and perhaps further than he would like, in the direction of Sir Herbert Read's contention that 'imagery' is 'the primary instrument of poetic consciousness'.

What Dr. Johnson says about the passage is this (the italics here are mine):

The lines are in themselves not perfect; for most of the words thus artfully opposed are to be understood *simply* on one side of the comparison and *metaphorically on the other*; and, *if there be any language which does not express intellectual operations by material images*, into that language they cannot be translated.

Dr. Richards, in one of the most suggestive chapters of his book on Coleridge, comments (the italics are again mine):

> There is, of course, *no such language*; but that Johnson should be applying such reflections to the analysis of poetry is instructive. A more persistent examination would have shown him that the transferences were sometimes primary, sometimes secondary, *sometimes went from the river to the mind, sometimes from the mind to the river*. And with that the assumptions behind his first remark ('The lines are in themselves not perfect . . .') would have broken down.

As a preliminary to more general observations (not on Denham, his style, or his period, but on the nature of poetic language) let us attempt to carry out the 'more persistent examination' which Dr. Richards recommends. Dr. Johnson's reasons for feeling uneasy about these lines may have been the wrong ones, but I think most sensitive readers share his uneasiness; the lines do somehow seem to work out too neatly, and we have a feeling that there is a trick somewhere. The sense of a trick is partly the sense that two poles of a comparison are alluded to rather than embodied; that the river implies the presence of the poem, the poem of the river, and yet that, as realized objects, both are absent. We have to invent our own river and imagine our own poem. We begin by trying to understand what a poem, or a mental process of poetic creation, should be—which for the purpose of the poet's rhetoric we are presumed not to know— by thinking of (which we are presumed to know) what a stream is; in the end, we find we are instead being asked to construct an ideal stream (which the lines, as I say, do not really evoke for us in any concrete fashion) out of what we really did know, after all, to start with, the ideal nature, for a Restoration poet, a precursor of neo-classicism, of a poem. We are, of course, anachronistic in demanding from a Restoration poet a particularized river, an actual river as perceived, or

in demanding of him any particularized observations of the kind
that came in with the Romantic movement, like Coleridge's

> the western sky,
> And its peculiar tint of yellow green . . .
>
> And those thin clouds above, in flakes and bars . . .

A river, for a Restoration poet, would be primarily either an
emblem of change, or a backcloth for pastoral, rather than an
individuated object of contemplation. Rivers, indeed, even to-
day in poetry (for there has been in recent English poetry an
Augustan influence, though we hear less of it than of the influence of Donne or Blake) have often this primarily emblematic
significance, as in these lines of Auden's:

> It was late, late in the evening,
>   The lovers they were gone;
> The clocks had ceased their chiming,
>   And the deep river ran on.

Auden's 'deep river' is Bergsonian duration, felt, lived time, as
contrasted with mathematical, mechanically clicking clock-time;
it is the concrete flow of life, below the conscious level, not to be
arrested, controlled, or measured by the will. And it has a seaward or deathward flow. May there be, even in these neat and
vapid lines of Denham's, an appeal to similar deep associations
—to associations, at least, whose irrelevance we should be
ready to prove, before we deliberately exclude them?

Let me take first of all a set of associations which I am morally
sure *are* irrelevant to Denham (but which are not at all irrelevant to the wider theme of this essay, the frame of mind in
which we ought to approach a difficult, and particularly a difficult modern, poem). Orpheus, torn to pieces, appropriately
floats down a river—and to be 'sold down the river' is a vivid
idiom of modern speech, reinforced in the United States by
memories of slaves being sent down the Mississippi—because
a river reaching the sea is an apt trope for the individual life
reaching death; yet, at the same time, if we think of a tidal river,
and the tides pulsing back and forward (and the post-Darwinian
idea, totally unknown to Denham, of course, of the sea as the
ultimate source of all life), then river-meets-sea is an equally
apt trope for an idea with apparently opposite emotional

associations, sexual congress. And rivers are individual, and the sea is always the same sea—as it might be, an enormous Mrs. Bloom—and so acceptance of the latter trope suggests fallacious reflections, perhaps, but reflections that have a deep traditional emotional appeal about masculinity and femininity: men (rivers) are individual, separate, always emptying themselves: all women are really woman (the sea, the one sea), are the masks of the one goddess, immortal and perpetually replenished.

To be sure, as I have already said, applying all or any of this to these lines would merely provide a comic demonstration of the dangers of working out associations that are not logically 'in' a poem (a danger illustrated in contemporary criticism by the ease with which 'systems' can be abstracted from, and then read back into, poets like Blake and Yeats). But any or all of these associations might, certainly, be in a modern poem—they may all be there in some degree for Auden, though the (obviously slightly flattened) paraphrastic explication of *his* river is time, change, or history—and that is why (to show that, from however oblique an angle, we are approaching our proper subject) it is more difficult to expound Auden's passage than Denham's, though both, as grammatical statements, are 'clear' and 'simple'. Poetic difficulty, in other words, is not identical with grammatical difficulty (with ellipsis, for instance), nor is the 'New Critic' (though he may sometimes look rather like this) simply the old note-maker writ large. You would not get a *critical* interpretation of a difficult play of Shakespeare's simply by running together the notes at the foot of the page in a Variorum edition into a continuous commentary. The critic, in the real sense, stands farther back; on the other hand, without the kind of special insight or habit of dogged persistence that can track down a topical or abstruse literary allusion, or untangle a knotty grammatical point, the critic of modern poetry (and of much of the denser poetry of the past) is not likely to get very far.

Yet if it is dangerous to read, anachronistically or illogically, too much of collateral implication into the imagery of a poem, it is as dangerous to read too little. Quite certainly, I think, the Heracleitan association—a human life is like a river, apparently always the same, but always changing, you cannot bathe twice (or perhaps even once) in the same place—was working somewhere in the back of Denham's mind. A poem is permanent in one sense, a stable record of a changing state of mind; a river is permanent in another, a form that is perpetually changing its constituents; a human life is permanent in neither. When Denham says,

O could *I* flow like thee . . .

his tone has the sadness of a real but vain aspiration. He does not say, 'Oh, might *my poem* flow like thee', and though that at one level is what he means, at a deeper, unconscious level he means what he says. His life envies two kinds of unliving perfection, that of completed art, and unconscious nature. And moreover if (which I take to be the case) Denham started neither with the river nor human consciousness, but with a traditional trope, the river-as-human-consciousness (or the river-as-the-flow-of-human-life), then both Dr. Johnson and Dr. Richards are taking the situation a little too simply.

The task that both Dr. Johnson and Dr. Richards in their remarks on this passage in practice recommend to us (and, indeed, I think it may be one of the central tasks of the critic of poetry) is that of working out how the key-words get their force. My remarks about some of the primal associations of the idea of a river suggest how 'flow' here may get its force; not primarily from the fact that a river flows (nor, though that may have been uppermost in Denham's mind, from the fact that a 'flowing style' was fashionable in poetry), but from the fact that it is very tempting and obvious to say that a human life flows. Moreover, about the ways that we use the word 'flow' either primarily (of a river) or secondarily (of a life) there does cling a deep emotional ambiguity. To the normal eye, unpurged of the pathetic fallacy, the river looks as if it were making its way forward with a kind of purpose; and, in fact, the water is merely taking the easiest way; and so the notion of human life as 'flowing' might be that of striving towards some consummation or merely of gradually and smoothly declining towards death: 'flowing' might be primarily (in this context) 'flowing away'.

Yet, though I think the broad associations dealt with in the above paragraph are relevant, as the broad associations dealt with earlier were not, they were almost certainly not *consciously* relevant for Denham. He is not consciously comparing the river to the mind (as Dr. Richards makes him do), but merely to his poem; and for him, the 'real' poem is essentially the poem on the page, not (as for Wordsworth and Coleridge, possibly) the subjective poem, the poem in the process of creation. 'Flow', in the secondary sense, as applied to the poem, means merely smoothness, ease, fluency, and in this sense, at least, does not very forcibly retransfer back; for it would be obviously silly to hope that a river might have the fluency of one's own verses; however impressed we are by our own artefacts, however humanist and urban we may be (and the poets of Denham's period certainly were), these artefacts never impress the profound levels of our being, as natural processes (or human inner states) do.

Yet, on the other hand, when we get to 'though deep, yet clear', there perhaps our primary thought is that profound poems are often obscure but ideally need not be so; there is no reason why an actual deep river should not be clear, unless it runs over a muddy bottom. The tendency of the poem to engross Denham's attention at the expense of the river is even more obvious in 'though gentle, yet not dull'; 'gentle' of a river means flowing slowly and smoothly, 'gentle' of a composition mildly urbane, like Addison or Goldsmith, say (though there might be here a more particular reference to the actual *movement* of the verse); 'dull' of a river means the opposite of clear, obscure or turbid (or might mean here, to fit into the pattern more neatly, a river motion so slow as to seem sluggish); 'dull' of a composition means 'not interesting', but if the primary reference is again to the *movement*, Denham is hoping that the cadence of his verses will not be so smooth that they will almost send people to sleep. If we take the specific references as being to the *movement* of both verse and water, the transferences work beautifully both ways. But if we take wider literary critical senses of 'gentle' and 'dull' (and take 'dull' of the river to mean not sluggish in motion but turbid), then we have to do a little cheating. We either say, with a subjective emphasis suddenly introduced, 'Though this river flows slowly, *I* do not find it uninteresting,' or 'Though this is not a fierce, turbulent piece of poetry, it is not untranslucent.' There, when talking about literature we are ignoring the 'literary' sense of 'dull', and when talking about the river we are ignoring its primary application to the untranslucency of water. But if, as I say, we restrict the comparison, or its area, to the *movement* of verse and water this cheating is unnecessary.

Yet, dropping into the calms of the mind like pebbles, words do, after all, open out in rings. 'Gentle' is a very human word (primarily meaning noble, secondarily courteous and forbearing, and these secondary derived senses—outside uses like 'gentle birth', 'gentle breeding'—were by Denham's time probably already becoming primary). When used of nature ('gentle breezes'), it always suggests the pathetic fallacy; the breezes are being so soft, because they are so kind. So 'gentle' here, perhaps, is in its primary associations for Denham a moral word, used of conduct and manners; transferred secondarily, by pathetic fallacy, to the river's slow and even flow; coming a third level to be applied in a technical literary critical sense of 'bland, mild, smooth in movement' ('Waller was smooth . . .') to the poem, but in a way in which the secondary (mechanical, of motion) application of the word does not quite exclude its primary (human, of conduct) associations. 'Waller was smooth' in his verses, but he was also smooth in his manners, and in his conduct (in a not quite flattering sense) a smooth person. Augustan terms of literary criticism get, I think, a lot of their dignity and force from these moral associations which we can never quite rid them of. They get also from these associations (since we may not admire smoothness, blandness, and such social qualities, as much as the early Augustans did) part of their occasional effect for modern readers of unconscious irony.

In the last line the primary force of the words is, at first sight, in their application to the river.

Strong without rage, without o'erflowing full,

and yet 'strong' and 'full' are again for Denham important technical terms of literary criticism, and, on the other hand, in the wider associations of the words there is again a decided element of projected pathetic fallacy. 'Strong' is a word which seems to imply human determination and purpose, a word we use primarily of a person or artefact equipped to resist attack ('a strong fighter', 'a strong castle', but not I think a 'strong mountain', unless from a mountaineer's point of view, and even then it sounds like weak personification or whimsical treating of the natural as an artefact). Similarly, the torrent 'rages', that is what we naturally say of it, but only because it reminds us of a man in a rage. (In Denham's time, the strongest associations of the noun—'Civil rage', 'amorous rage'—were with the idea of natural, and therefore anarchic, forces in society or the individual getting out of control.) Finally—I am thinking about the phrase 'without o'erflowing full'—we human beings bother about filling up a glass to the brim without spilling anything; rivers have not really (except in a fancy that would seem childish to us, or to Denham, if we made it explicit) any similar preoccupation about not overflowing their banks. Denham's river is, in fact, if not exactly a personified, very much a humanized river; just as there may be deep insight in Dr. Richards's apparent carelessness in constantly referring to the other pole of the comparison not as 'the poem' but as 'the mind'.

Thus, though it may remain true (to conglobe both doctors) that 'there is no . . . language' 'which does not express intellectual operations by material images'—and, for instance, for all one knows the raging of a torrent, instantaneously identified by primitive men with human rage, might have supplied them with a word (an unconscious metaphor) for that, and primitive words (or unconscious metaphors) for 'strong' may often literally mean oaklike, mountainous, thunderous—still, the words we use 'naturally', about natural processes (not talking scientifically, but expressing our feelings) are all very humanistic, pathetic-fallacious words, strongly tied to uncriticized subjective attitudes. To take a fanciful example: a word like 'thunderous' as applied by poetic convention to Jove and his rage, the anger of powerful princes, the boom of cannons, the galloping of cavalry, and so on, might for a poet of Denham's period have become so dissociated with any feelings about actual thunderstorms that if, in the early gropings of nature poetry, he had wished, rather eccentrically, to evoke thunder for its own sake, he might have felt that he was saying something about it by calling it 'thunderous thunder'. He would mean that the thing itself was as impressive as the various manifestations of mythical or human power and rage for which it had become a trite metaphor. Denham here is, of course, writing an early nature-poem; and part of what one feels about these famous lines is that the various elegant and trite applications, traditional in poetry, of river-words to literature, the course of life, mental processes, acquire a new piquancy when, ostensibly at least, an actual river is what one is mainly talking about.

But what, it seems to me, makes the lines memorable at a more profound level (and explains the fashion for them, the imitations and the parodies) is that into what is said both about the river and the poem there is projected a complexity of feelings about what, for a poet of the Restoration, life should ideally be. A poem is artificial, a river is natural. Human life is ideally both. A poem should seem to 'flow' naturally, social manners should appear spontaneous, however much 'art' has gone into both. Natural objects, on the other hand, can be accommodated to human sensibility only when they look as if they were the result of design (and, of course, for almost every poet of this period they are, God has designed them). Thus, the words a Restoration gentleman uses are humanistic words, words that have at least their *primary* social application in relation to motives, conduct, manners: words like 'deep' of thought, 'clear' of exposition, 'gentle' of aristocratic compunction and self-control, 'strong' approvingly perhaps of passions (a weak man does not have strong passions) but 'rage' disapprovingly of passions breaking free from control—'amorous rage', 'Civil rage', to take examples I have given already. 'Full' might recall Bacon, 'Reading makes a full man', and 'o'erflowing' like 'rage' suggests a failure of self-containment.

There is a level at which, in fact, Denham's lines can be read as wishes not merely for a supposed poem but for a happy life. And the key-words do not, if we take them in this social context, primarily express *either* 'intellectual operations' *or* 'material images'. They are words of social appraisal: the vocabulary of the *honnête homme*. They can be used, indeed, with some technical exactness to evoke canons of poetic excellence, with rhetorical aptness to suggest a generalized appreciation of the beauty of flowing water, but Denham does not want, in Dr. Leavis's sense, to 'realize' for us an actual poem or an actual river; he relies on our presumed experience of both. What he does 'realize' for us is a complex of social attitudes which through the superimposed river-poem and river-life comparisons he can compactly, though indirectly, exemplify.

The idea which these lines finally leave us with is, at its most concrete, the idea of a way of life (and of a mode of writing, as one of the ornaments of that way of life) in which yielding to pleasing impulses can be combined with a regard for decorum, a sense of 'behaving naturally' with attention to rules, a respect for the sources of power with an acceptance of restraint—the idea, in short, powerfully anticipated by Denham here, of Augustan self-control. The river and the poem, the river and the mind, and the intertransferences of feeling between them, are 'stand-ins' for this idea. The 'real subject' of the lines is not a poem or a river or a metaphorical relation between the two but a complex and not fully objectified social attitude, an attitude that seeks to reconcile, in social life, the polarities of nature and artifice. Thus, our feeling for the social uses, the common emotional overtones of Denham's key words (in, for instance, the prose of his contemporaries), is more important as an aid to grasping his tone and intention than any attempt to sort out the denoting functions of the words too firmly, as applying on the one hand primarily to nature, on the other to art. It is the whole point of Denham's attitude that he wants and needs that blur or overlap, that he does not want to make this distinction too sharply; he wants to be able to feel that his words are flowing like the river, he wants to be able to admire the river as if it were a poem. Is this a special case, or can it teach us something about poetic language in general?

II

Nobody perhaps has ever dealt with four lines of verse (four lines of verse which, at a first glance, any intelligent reader should be able both to 'apprehend' and to 'comprehend') at quite such tedious length as I have dealt with these four lines of Denham's in the first section of this essay. But, like the pirates in *Hamlet*, I 'knew what I did'. My point was partly that, for a conscientious critic, *all* poetry is difficult; it is strange that we should use language at all; it is excessively strange that we should use poetic language; it is almost impossible, even taking the simplest example, to state in general terms just what it is about a use of language that makes us recognize it as poetic. My point was also partly that a really *thorough* 'interpretation' of any poem or passage, an attempt within the limits of one's sensibility, insight, and information to say *everything* relevant, is likely to lead to writing as boring for the general reader as are, say, technical essays in analytical philosophy.

There is a famous essay of this sort, a paper read to some learned society by Professor G. E. Moore, on whether existence is a predicate, in which this distinguished philosopher deals at enormous length, with beautifully laborious exactness, with the meaning, or the lack of meaning, of propositions like: 'Some tame tigers do not exist.' This may be a true proposition. If we express it in traditional syllogistic form as *Some S are not-P* it follows from either of the equivalent propositions, *All S are not-P*, or *No S are P*. (It follows even more elegantly, of course, as the direct converse of a proposition which, in this application, seems obviously not verifiable, *All non-P are S*, or, in this application, 'All non-existents are tame tigers.' But it follows from the propositions used in illustration as the subaltern which is true if the universal is true.) Now, it may very well be true either that all tame tigers are non-existent or that no tame tigers are existent or, in more ordinary usage, that there are no tame tigers. The question, really, is whether grammatical predicates like 'existent' and 'non-existent' can slip quite easily, without any fuss or bother, into the logical S-is-P framework. A probability that they cannot arises from our psychological reaction to the statement, 'Some tame tigers do not exist'—a reaction which might be expressed, 'Oh, so are there two kinds of tame tigers, the kind that exist, and the kind that do not exist?' Professor Moore's essay is fascinating to anybody who is even amateurishly interested, as I am, in philosophical analysis, but to the man with a wider and vaguer approach to philosophy—who wants philosophers to tell him how to be wise and good, for instance (as Santayana or Collingwood, for example, tried to tell him, and as Professor Moore himself perhaps tried to tell him in parts of *Principia Ethica*)—the whole Alice-in-Wonderlandy discussion of tame tigers seems futile and flippant. Such a reader is offended by the joke-example, by the inhumanly patient and detached tone of voice, and does not appreciate that a traditionally knotty problem has been, if not solved, at least brought appreciably nearer solution. The feelings of many readers, I imagine, about modern techniques of close examination of poetic texts are rather like the feelings of the unsympathetic amateur about philosophical analysis.

Such readers feel that the close critic of poetry is often as fundamentally uninterested in the text in front of him as Professor Moore is in actual, possible, or imaginary tame tigers; they feel that the poems, like the tigers, are a pretext for displaying an aptitude, and that this aptitude may be a very superficial one of logical adroitness, it need not involve the critic's whole being. What analysis along Empsonian lines, it is sometimes felt, leaves out is the important thing, the massive and confused experience of taking possession of a poem, living with it, becoming habituated to it, deciding whether one wants to go on living with it or not. Taking poems to pieces and putting them together again can, in fact, become a substitute for *enjoying* poems. I put this case as strongly as I can, feeling that there is something in it.

Thus, let me admit that in the first section of this essay I got considerable pleasure from taking an aptitude out for a ride (from taking it occasionally, I gather from the courteous strictures of Mr. Bateson and Mr. Alvarez, when I read a first version of this paper at Oxford, on a false scent); but I do not think these pages have anything at all to offer to the young student who merely wants to understand and enjoy Denham. They have something to offer, perhaps, to the young student who wants to understand, by seeing a kind of slow-motion film of its workings, the machinery of a critical mind. What I was doing was merely making explicit a number of responses, evaluations, tactful uses of background information and consequent quasi-instinctive weightings of words, which work, on the whole, more efficiently if they are *not* made explicit. Professor Empson at the end of *Seven Types* did not precisely say like Gide at the end of *Les Nourritures Terrestres*: 'Throw away my book!' He did say that we should not try to memorize his machinery, and I would expect a reader whom Professor Empson had really helped, to come from *Seven Types* looking at poems in a new way, with a new flexibility and alertness, but not to be able to say (without looking up the analytical contents-table in the later editions) which type of ambiguity was which. Similarly, what one takes away in practice from *The Structure of Complex Words* is a new notion of the *range* of words—of their emotive range as depending on a combination of their various senses with their various social uses. Professor Empson's ingenious ways of tabulating these ranges with plus and minus signs, capital letters, and exclamation-marks may perhaps be taken up by lexicographers; but for other critics, who lack Professor Empson's familiarity with mathematics and symbolic logic, these devices are likely to remain an ingenious hobby of his own. The point, in fact, of all criticism is to get us to closer and more intelligent grips with an actual work of art. A great deal of what is speculative and theoretical in modern close critics is like scaffolding which we can quite safely pull down and have carted away, once the critics have finished helping us to build our own houses.

What, on the other hand, an example of excessive analysis, of exhaustive and exhausting analysis, like my pages about Denham, may do, sometimes, is not so much to illuminate further the particular poem—Denham's lines carry their own light, and my readers are likely to be made thoroughly sick of them for some time—as to suggest a fruitful generalization. There is (this was my generalization from Denham's example) a kind of poetry whose language is best thought of neither as subjective nor objective, neither as a language of the 'inner' (mental) nor the 'outer' (physical) world, but rather as an interpersonal language of social appraisal; and our approach to this kind of poem will need the combination of qualities—chief among them, perhaps, a courteous yet wary responsiveness, and a sense of proportion—which, in ordinary social relationships, we call tact. Tact is partly the gift of accepting and enjoying superficial qualities for what they are worth; for catching at hints, following up suggestions, and yet not pressing either meanings or promises too hard. It is, for instance, to the tact of the reader that much Augustan poetry most profoundly appeals. There are obviously greater kinds of poetry that ought to make use, in the reader, of more profoundly important sets of human qualities—the qualities that we might describe as imaginative sympathy and sincerity in depth. We obviously need these qualities, also, to respond to the greatest things in Johnson or Pope; but there is a middle range of Augustan poetry which demands from the reader chiefly the kind of social awareness I have been discussing.

How far, however, can this social awareness carry us in the

understanding of contemporary poetry, even where that (like much of the poetry of the 1930s, for instance) may seem to owe something, or to be wanting to owe something, to the Augustan mode? Professor Empson may here, perhaps, provide us with an example from his poems on which we may test some of the tactics we have learnt from his criticism. There is a sense in which, obscure and difficult as much of his poetry is, the vocabulary does seem to be resonant, like that of the Augustans, within a context of social appraisal. He does intend to communicate ideas. There is, under much of his work, an urge towards the moral generalization; and the feeling of it, or the play of feelings, is carried often primarily by what we vaguely call (and yet we know what we are talking about) the poet's 'tone of voice'. How far can tact, combined with that close attention to verbal detail and its puzzles which Professor Empson himself has taught us, assist us in interpreting and evaluating his own poems? The best examination of an Empson poem I know is Mr. John Wain's study of 'The Teasers' in his article on Empson in 'Penguin New Writing', No. 40. We had better, however, have the poem on the page before us:

> Not but they die, the teasers and the dreams,
> Not but they die,
>> and tell the careful flood
> To give them what they clamour for and why.
>
> You could not fancy where they rip to blood,
> You could not fancy
>> nor that mud
> I have heard speak that will not cake or dry.
>
> Our claims to act appear so small to these,
> Our claims to act
>> colder lunacies,
> That cheat the love, the moment, the small fact.
>
> Make no escape because they flash and die,
> Make no escape
>> build up your love,
> Leave what you die for and be safe to die.

The first problem, and one of course that doesn't come up at all with the average Augustan poem, is one about form. Mr.

Wain's feeling is that Mr. Empson is on the verge here of making a magnificent formal invention, but that he sketches out the possibility of such an invention, rather than achieves it. The invention is a new kind of quatrain, made out of three iambic pentameter lines, by breaking the second line into two short lines at the caesura; the carelessness comes in, for Mr. Wain, in the failure to fill out in several instances the full iambic pentameter pattern, and in the irregularity or inconsistency of the rhyme-scheme. I want (deriving my desire to defend these apparent faults from the very powerful total effect of the poem on me) to try to justify these apparent carelessnesses on the grounds, more or less, of *total* dramatic expressiveness.

The rhyme-scheme of the four stanzas is: a, b, c, b: c, *b*, c, b: d, e, *d*, e: b, f, g, b. An italicized letter means a rhyme on a weak syllable, and one might or might not see conscious patterning in the fact that the two middle stanzas have similar two-rhyme (where the first and last stanzas have dissimilar one-rhyme) patterns, and in the fact that the weak rhymes in the middle stanzas have what might be called a mirror-image position *vis-à-vis* each other. The first and last stanzas have, as I say, just one rhyme each, but the first stanza connects itself on to the rest of the poem by the b and c rhymes which are picked up in the second stanza, and by the picking up again of the b rhyme (at a distance, but not I think at such a distance as to make the ear lose the link) in the last stanza. One might say—straining things a bit, no doubt, in one's anxiety to defend the poem against Mr. Wain's accusations of formal carelessness—that the first stanza connects itself on to the totality of the poem by the linking rhymes, and that the last stanza connects itself by picking up the b rhyme, but also disconnects itself by enclosing its two non-rhyming words ('escape', 'love') with a certain air of finality between its rhyming first and last lines. One might claim, in fact, that there is, though not a mechanically regular, a logically justifiable rhyming-pattern which explains itself in terms of sense thus: connecting lead-in to the poem (first stanza); body of the poem (second two stanzas, with their similar forms); end of poem (last stanza, linking on to the first by one rhyme, but making a different metrical gesture). What Mr. Wain thought of as carelessness might have been a genuine adaptation of sound-pattern to sense-pattern; we have a bit of outside information, from Mr. Empson in a broadcast, and I am not sure on whose side it tells, Mr. Wain's or mine. The poem was originally much longer but Mr. Empson cut it down to these four stanzas because developed at greater length it seemed to him flat. The stanzas finally chosen for printing might be four from different parts of the poem that made, Mr. Empson felt, reasonably coherent sense together; or they might be four that did come in a batch, and therefore were patterned from the first together for sound as well as sense; or four chosen from different parts of the poem partly for the reason that there happened to be rhyme-links. Purely subjectively, at least, I do not find, very short though the poem is, that one finds the variations in rhyme-pattern at all displeasing to the ear. But we are, of course, at a disadvantage compared to the Augustans in that in an age of verse experiment we have no canons about such matters; we can never be sure that any apparent technical roughness or irregularity in any poem was not put in on purpose.

Mr. Wain is even more reproachful about what he alleges to be careless irregularities, failures to build up a full decasyllable, in the two enclosed lines (made of one line broken into two) in the second, third, and fourth quatrains. The metrical pattern of the poem *is* certainly basically the iambic pentameter, but what Mr. Wain seems to me to be ignoring is that a strong pause or break in a decasyllabic line may be metrically equivalent to a syllable or a couple of syllables. There are plenty of examples of this in Elizabethan and Jacobean drama; and tiny as this poem is, its tone of voice, I think, is essentially dramatic rather than lyrical. In the two enclosed lines of the first quatrain, which do in fact form a perfect decasyllable,

> Not but they die,
>   and tell the careful flood . . .

there is in fact no prolonged caesural pause; the comma (apart from its semantic implications) indicates that there would be a natural tendency, without it, to speak the line with no marked caesura. The movement is swift. In the second quatrain, on the other hand, there *is* a long, a countable pause, expressive of fascinated disgust, after 'fancy' (Mr. Empson brings this out very well in his own reading of the poem):

> You could not fancy [. . .]
>   nor that mud.

227

In the third quatrain, the broken line needs only one more syllable to be a perfect iambic pentameter:

> Our claims to act
>> [seem] colder lunacies,

and Mr. Wain seems to me wrong, therefore, in describing the line as a 'shapeless nothing': the dropped 'seem' (or the dropped whatever), the gasp, leap, or mumble, gives the effect again of emotional construction, of something unpleasant said with difficulty. In the fourth quatrain, the long pause, equivalent to two syllables, suggests the weariness of exhausted wisdom:

> Make no escape [. . .]
>> build up your love.

The poem, in fact, is no mere 'lyric twelve lines long' but a short dramatic and philosophical monologue; and all the metrical irregularities which Mr. Wain censures are, as I have said, traditional in English dramatic verse.

Let us now take the sense of the poem. I am much more in agreement with Mr. Wain's admirable pioneer analysis here, than I am in agreement with him about Mr. Empson's metrical achievements and purposes, but I think the sense also needs a more tediously close analysis than he has given it:

> Not but they die, the teasers and the dreams,
> Not but they die. . . .

'Not but they die' is a literary and pedantic form (Mr. Alvarez, when I read this paper first, admirably described it as the equivalent of a kind of nervous stutter before starting); in its emotive flavour it has something in common with another favourite quaint locution of Mr. Empson's, 'to be sure'. It means, 'Not that it is not the case that they die', or, 'Allowing, certainly, that they die', and the effect—a favourite effect in Mr. Empson's argumentative prose as well as in his verse—is that of a logical concession rather aggressively made. 'You are drearily insisting that our dreams die. Who was going to deny it anyway, and what do you intend to prove from it?' It is not as explicit as that, but there is a hint of that sort of defensive-aggressiveness.

For 'the teasers and the dreams,' I think Mr. Wain's inter-

pretation of the 'desires of the mind' broadly true, but I think
he should have emphasized the extent to which we find ourselves
thinking at once (partly because of 'teasers', a titillating, flirta-
tious word) of dreams in a specifically erotic Freudian sense
rather than of one's 'dreams of building a better world'; I don't
say the second sense is excluded, but I think 'dreams' in the
social-idealistic sense comes out more easily, later in the poem,
under 'our claims to act'. What Mr. Empson does seem to have
in mind throughout the poem is erotic energy as the lawless
source of a much wider human energy. He is against the puritan
rationalistic attitudes ('colder lunacies') that want to ignore
and belittle, or perhaps to cripple and hold down, this infinitely
transformable erotic urge. So one might say that the phrase
'the teasers and the dreams' covers the notion of love in the most
carnal as well as the most spiritual sense.

(It was with this erotic emphasis in mind that Mr. Anthony
Thwaite, in the original discussion of this paper, suggested an
interpretation of these first three lines very different from Mr.
Wain's or mine, but so ingenious that, though I do not accept
it, I have never been able to keep it out of my head in subsequent
readings of the poem. Roughly, he took 'teasers and dreams' to
refer not to actual dreams but to the sort of young woman who
excites men's sexual desires without intending to satisfy them,
what the French call an *allumeuse*. He consequently took 'die' in
the mid-Seventeenth Century sense—which Mr. Empson, who
has explored this metaphor in Dryden, is interested in—of the
sexual act and particularly its climax (the modern colloquial
equivalent for 'die', in this sense, would be 'come'). He then
took 'the careful flood', of course, as referring to the controlled
emission of male sperm at the climax of the act. The paraphrase
suggested by this interpretation would be, 'Not that it is not the
case that these young women who tease you and frustrate you
do not themselves make love sometimes, so (if you get the
chance) tell the hunger in your loins to give them just what
they want at the right moment, and tell that hunger why they
want it.' I reject this, because it does not seem to me to fit in
with the logic of the rest of the poem; yet, knowing Mr. Empson's taste for ambiguities, I do not suppose one can wholly
reject it as, say, a blind alley which one *is* intended to explore
or as a possible overtone.)

So we could—noting Mr. Thwaite's interpretation, but 'bracketing it off'—paraphrase the first line and a half thus: 'Quite allowing that desire fails at last, that our erotic impulses are in any case flickering and transitory, that love burns itself out. . . .' Then,

> Not but they die,
>   and tell the careful flood
> To give them what they clamour for and why.

Do *they* tell the careful flood, or are *we* being told to go and tell it? The grammar will bear it both ways, but though that they should tell the flood seems more natural, both the comma —not logically necessary on the 'they' interpretation—and something passionate and urgent in the 'tone of voice' suggest an imperative. *We*, I think, on the whole are being told to tell the machinery of our subconscious minds to deal with those desires of ours that cannot be fulfilled. The careful flood takes good care of the teasers and the dreams, and it is full of care because ('Go not to Lethe . . .') all anxieties and frustrations are drowned in it. The careful flood is sleep, forgetfulness, the mechanism of repression, the death-wish. What they, the frustrated erotic impulses, clamour for is oblivion, and why they clamour for it is because, in nearly every case, they have not been able to get what they wanted, or what they wanted has not proved lastingly satisfactory. Behind the mood of this stanza there is either a Buddhistic feeling about Karma, the endless inescapable chain of our desires (the profoundest desire, and the most dangerous to pursue directly, being that for non-being), or Freudian insights built up, a little too speculatively, into Schopenhauerian pessimism.

In the next stanza, Miss Kathleen Raine once suggested to me ingeniously that the verb 'fancy' should be contrasted, in Coleridgean fashion, with the verb 'imagine'; there is a realm of horror which can be explored by the poetic imagination but not by mere 'wit-writing', by poetic fancy playing with its 'fixities' and 'definites'. But what I myself feel is that 'fancy' has partly its ordinary colloquial sense, with a sarcastic overtone of deliberate understatement ('What I would fancy more than anything is a nice cup of tea', 'You wouldn't fancy a clump on the head, would you?'), and partly the older sense, from which that colloquial sense is partly derived, of 'love' ('the young man's fancy!'). We are still on the level of Freudian psychology:

> You could not fancy where they rip to blood. . . .

Where erotic impulses of a lawless kind are not repressed but express themselves sadistically, you, as a sane human being, could not *like it*; and you could not go on talking about the expression of these impulses as *love*. To live with the unchastened blind impulses would make a man ill. But controlling them is not getting rid of them. The possibility of madness, the elements of frustrated lust and aggressiveness, of brutish self-centredness, of 'original sin' in all of us are what Mr. Empson means by the speaking mud that will not 'cake or dry'—and which we cannot wholly forget, however deep the 'careful flood' of Styx runs over it (the river metaphor, the allusion to Styx, runs through the first two stanzas and gives them part of their consistent power). The 'mud' is the animal dirt from which we all rise, the clay of which Adam was made, the dust to which we all return, however lofty our moral or intellectual ambitions may be; and it is also the blind hunger for life of the libido.

So we may now paraphrase the first two stanzas thus: 'Quite allowing (as the man who wants to take a puritanical attitude to sex will insist) that the mechanism of repression itself quite efficiently drives our stray and trivial erotic impulses down into the unconscious, still if you could have a good look at what happens at that level, at the frustration which is the irremediably sordid basis of all our human achievements, you would not, I think, enjoy the spectacle; though repression is, of course, certainly better than sadism.'

The third stanza then says:

> Our claims to act appear so small to these,
> Our claims to act
>   colder lunacies,
> That cheat the love, the moment, the small fact.

This is now fairly simple: 'Compared to the strength of the erotic impulse within us, and the extent to which it consciously or unconsciously shapes our lives—even though there is something irrational and, if you like, insane about that impulse—still one's claim to be a free, independent, rational creature seems even more mad, and more trivial and frigid. For at least the erotic impulse, dangerous as it is, is warm and living, and the source of life; yet through our intellectual and moral self-conceit we cheat ourselves of these moments of satisfaction—flirtations, dates, kisses—which the erotic impulse can give us. These 'small facts', which we feel so morally superior about, may prove in retrospect to have made up the best of our life's happiness.'

The fourth stanza is, as Mr. Wain rightly suggests, teasing and elusive:

> Make no escape because they flash and die,
> Make no escape . . .

'Just because moments of erotic satisfaction are few and far between, and vanish away so soon ('the poor benefit of a be-wildering minute') do not for that reason try to escape from them. Rather

> build up your love,
> Leave what you die for and be safe to die.

Rather, that is, build up a framework of human love within which these flashing and dying moments of satisfaction, these dubious transitory values of 'vitality' and 'immediacy', may have lasting human value—for it is when desire is divorced from affection that it takes strange and perverse forms, that it 'rips to blood'. Leave what you die for—leave, that is, the desire to 'escape' from human passion, the 'colder lunacies' of the stoical attitude, which create a kind of death in the heart, which foster the Freudian death-wish—and be safe to die, when real death naturally and inevitably comes, because you will feel that you have lived, that, like the Wife of Bath, you have had 'your world as in your time'.' That, much diluted and expanded, of course, is, I think, certainly the drift. However, there is a more elegant way of taking the same upshot but a reverse meaning from the last line by reading it as a sarcasm: 'Leave what you die for'—leave the love for which you are dying ('I am dying for a cup of tea', 'I am dying for a kiss') and then 'be safe to die' (because, having renounced love, which is the only thing worth 'dying for', you will then have nothing worth 'living for', so why then worry about dying?)

Let me now, after groping through it in this way, attempt drastically to summarize the total drift, as I see it, of this poem. I have interpreted it so far on very narrowly Freudian lines, but it can also be seen more widely as an argument about thought and feeling, or about intellect and emotion. (It is a kind of poem which could only have been written in the age that invented the phrase 'dissociation of sensibility' and that thought of the schizoid state as the typical occupational risk of intellectuals.) The poem is addressed, I think, to a hypothetical listener who in his humanistic pride is pitching the claims of conscious rational willing too high and saying that our feelings and emotions spring anyway from the lower part of our nature, the animal part, and if we ignore them naturally disappear through the machinery of repression. The poet is replying: 'But if you could see the pain and horror in these depths of ours, when the natural impulses are pressed down too strongly, you would not enjoy the spectacle, any more than you would enjoy the spectacle of their having their lawless fling. Love may be a kind of madness, but the claim of man to be a self-sufficient rational will is madness, too, and a frigid madness, not a warm one with the source of life in it. Of course, these moments of vital and immediate delight pass, but that is the very reason for building up at the conscious level a framework of human affection within which such moments may have meaning. Do turn away from the intellectual and moral self-conceit, that is the source of death in your heart. Build up your love, instead, and, when death comes, feel that life has not been wasted.'

This whole section of this essay may seem, again, a very long treatment of a very short poem. Mr. Wain in his brilliant pioneer essay on Empson could afford to be more summary because he was being more dogmatic. I wanted to take the reader along with me, point by point; and I can only claim that the poem seems to me powerful, wise, and beautiful enough to be worth the effort I have spent on it; and it also seems to me that, in spite of the necessary wordiness of the method, it does help the reader new to this kind of analysis to be shown step by step —and to have the chance to disagree about the steps—how the critic arrived at his paraphrase. Moreover, the Empson example, like the Denham example, is a step towards a more general argument. It is a step towards an argument, roughly, against the possibility of isolating the poem as an object in itself. If I have interpreted, with the aid of Mr. Wain's fine original essay, this poem of Mr. Empson's in a fashion at all plausible or helpful (and if a Japanese professor, say, more learned in English literature than myself, might be stumped by it) the reason is not that I have a kind of specialized interest, or acuteness, such as enables people to solve mathematical problems or cross-word puzzles. It is simply that, unlike a Japanese scholar, I am able to set Mr. Empson without much trouble in his cultural context.

Contextualism, in this Batesonian sense, can, at times, of course, seem both fussy and flippant. A literary historian of the future would be extremely vapid if he said that this poem was 'about' the impact of fashionable literary generalizations from Freud ('Repression is a bad thing'), plus real Freud '(Repression is an inevitable mechanism'), plus Freudian-Schopenhauerian-Buddhistic pessimism ('I have felt the death-wish, too'), plus ordinary Bertrand Russell-Havelock Ellis hedonistic humanism ('Have a good time, but be decent about it') on a traditional rather stern, simple, and puritanical or stoical English public-school morality ('Cold baths, straight bats, long walks . . .'); but it helps one to understand Mr. Empson's very condensed small poem that one knows these are the kind of influences a writer of his class and generation will have come under; and not to know this not only makes the poem very puzzling to a contemporary Japanese reader but may very well make it almost impenetrable to English critics a hundred years from now. In other words, I am against the purism of these 'New Critics' who want to extrude background information from their examination of a poem, or who claim that the necessary background information is always, for a sufficiently sensitive reader, implicit in the poem itself. You could claim that, taken in complete isolation, 'The Teasers' makes a kind of elliptical logical sense; it only makes social, or full aesthetic, sense as a statement by a man like Empson, in his time and place.

III

Mr. Alvarez, in a conversation with me about this paper, described both the lines from Denham and the short poem by

Mr. Empson as being what he called examples of *grammatical* (rather than even *rhetorical*) poetry; everything, I think he meant, depends on a kind of precision and balance, combined also with a certain puzzlingness, in the poet's use of words, and the process of explication has to have a kind of patient attentiveness to how the words interlock; it is not unlike parsing of nouns and analysis of complex sentences. You have to go point by point, and not miss anything out. Not all poems are like this, and probably none of the greatest. Even 'grammatical' poetry can depend for some of its force on the associative power of images. The associations of a river help Denham; it helps Mr. Empson's poem very much, I think, that we read into his first two stanzas not only contemporarily fashionable ideas about sexual desire and the mechanism of repression but the powerful traditional images of Styx and Hades. This was part of what I meant when I said, earlier on, that we might be brought farther round than we would like towards Sir Herbert Read's idea that 'imagery' is 'the primary instrument of the poetic consciousness'.

There are a number of types of poem, it seems to me, in relation to which the kind of expository method I have been illustrating so far in this essay is almost worse than useless. There would be no point, for instance, in a line by line analysis of 'The Ancient Mariner'. The meanings as story, as statement, and the intended emotive effect in detail, are always quite clear. Yet there is a sense in which 'The Ancient Mariner' is a more profoundly difficult poem than, say, any poem by Mr. Empson. The difficulty is about its meaning in depth. One reaches a stage at which one sees that the whole poem turns on the moment when the Ancient Mariner, having loathed the slimy things that crawled with legs upon the slimy sea, suddenly sees them as beautiful—the lovely shiny colours and coiling movements of the water snakes—and a spring of love gushes into his heart and he unconsciously blesses them. It is the same pattern of spiritual death and rebirth that we are presented with subjectively, as autobiography, in 'Dejection; An Ode'. If we have got this central thing, we have got the poem. We can still criticize it, say that it is too long and full of tushery, that after the watersnakes Coleridge takes an unconscionable time steering the Ancient Mariner home, and that the Hermit of the Wood and the Pilot's Boy (like the Wedding Guest himself) might be straight out of 'Monk' Lewis or *The Castle of Otranto*. Yet these minor points, though they no doubt display our discrimination, do not on the whole matter. Nor does any ingenuity about the symbolic significance of the Albatross. It is enough that it was strange and white and harmless, a bird of good omen, and that in the Ancient Mariner's killing of it there was something of the awful arbitrariness (rather than obvious malice) which seems to be the special note of all sinful acts. He did not need to do it. Again, it hangs round his neck 'instead of the Cross' (a Christian burden, but the wrong sort); and it finally, like Bunyan's Christian's burden when he reached the wicket-gate, drops off his neck into the sea. We either, in a poem like 'The Ancient Mariner', recognize this deep layer of meaning under a phantasmagoric surface, or we dismiss the poem as mere phantasmagoria. And I would say that considerations of a rather similar sort apply to a modern poem which has always seemed to me to have deep affinities with 'The Ancient Mariner', Mr. Eliot's 'The Waste Land'.

'The Waste Land' is also a phantasmagoria, of an equally vivid but more complex sort. The critic needs to be able to spot allusions and borrowings, but he needs no grammatical subtlety: scenes, personalities, voices succeed each other, each as dramatically 'there' as the various elements of a good radio feature. The deep problem is that of relating the various episodes, seeing how they hold together, and unifying one's emotional response to them. Nobody can perhaps really grasp the deep meaning of 'The Ancient Mariner' who has not experienced something at least resembling, even if on a less dramatic level, the hero's experience of complete dereliction and merciful unexpected recovery; nobody can perhaps grasp the deep meaning of 'The Waste Land' who has not, like Mr. Eliot, watched crowds flowing over London Bridge with a sense of their apparently hopeless drift, and the apparently hopeless drift of our time. The reader gets from a great poem what he can bring to it; and though there are many kinds of poem in which it is important that the reader should bring an adroit responsiveness to verbal play, a dexterity in seizing nuances, it is always more important that he should bring what one can only call experience of life and openness to life, depth and humility. I hope that this book of examples of close criticism will enable many readers to look at poetry in a more flexible and alert way. I hope, however, also, that it will not set an intellectual fashion of the wrong sort; and that readers will not come to value poems less for what they are than for the ingenuity of the remarks that may be made about them. There are great moments in all poetry that will not, in the last resort, 'bear analysis'; their springs are too deep, and what they touch off in us is too deep; we should explain what we can explain, for a false mysteriousness, a cult of mystery for its own sake, is detestable; but we should also be ready at all times to say, 'This is splendid and moving, this line concentrates the poem, the poem turns on this line; I can see that, and you should be able to see it; but I cannot tell you why.'